5.99

CW01668098

EMDEN

THE LAST CRUISE OF THE CHIVALROUS RAIDER · 1914

FRANZ JOSEPH, PRINZ VON HOHENZOLLERN-EMDEN

Introduction by Fregattenkapitän d.R. Meinrad, Prinz von Hohenzollern-Emden, lic.jur.

Foreword by Admiral Sir John Woodward, KCB ADC RN

LYON

First published in Great Britain in 1989 by
LYON PUBLISHING INTERNATIONAL
The Lyon Press Limited
23A Crescent Road, Brighton, East Sussex BN2 3RP

UK Trace Sales
GREENHILL BOOKS/LIONEL LEVENTHAL LIMITED
Park House, 1 Russell Gardens, London NW11 9NN

© Meinrad, Prinz von Hohenzollern-Emden, 1989
'The Ship' and appendices excluding the bibliography,
© The Lyon Press Limited, 1989
This edition © The Lyon Press Limited, 1989

All rights reserved. No part of this book may be reproduced or transmitted in any form or by any means electronic or mechanical (including photocopying, recording or storage in any information retrieval system) without the written permission of the Publisher.

Publisher's note

The memoirs appear substantially in their original form. Though they have been modernized where appropriate, it is hoped that they remain true to the spirit of the original . . . if not in every letter. Virtually all material dealing with imprisonment in Malta has been omitted: the story is, after all, about the final cruise. A few minor errors of fact, chronology and spelling have been corrected unobtrusively, and explanatory notes added where appropriate. However, these are comparatively minor changes. New information has been deliberately separated, excepting captions and merchant-ship details — the latter 'boxed' in the text.

The modernization of the book has created problems with geographical names, owing to the comparatively recent independence granted to the Netherlands East Indies — now Indonesia — and the partial abandonment of the traditional Wade-Giles system of transliterating Chinese ideographs. To be true to the spirit of the original text, therefore, place-names have been given the form current at the beginning of August 1914: thus the German protectorate is 'Tsingtau', rather than Qingdao; the Indian port now known as Nagapattingam is 'Negabatam'; and Simelue island is given its Dutch form of 'Simaloer'. Where appropriate, the maps show both the preferred style and the modern name.

German navy ranks are left in their original form; in some cases, there are no precise equivalents in the Royal Navy hierarchy. *Emden*'s officers ranked from Fähnrich z.S., or midshipman, through Leutnant z.S. (sub-lieutenant in Royal Navy terms) and Oberleutnant z.S. (lieutenant). Then came Kapitänleutnant (lieutenant-commander), Korvettenkapitän (commander) and Fregattenkapitän or senior commander.

Among the men, 'Matrose' was an ordinary seaman; 'Heizer' was a stoker. The suffix '-gast', usually applied to technicians, may be encountered in preference to 'matrose' (e.g., 'Signalgast'). The prefix 'Ober-' simply meant 'Senior' or 'leading' — 'Obermatrose', leading seaman. A 'Maat' was a petty officer, while 'Bootsmannsmaat' (a warrant officer) was a bosun's mate.

British Library Cataloguing in Publication Data
Franz Joseph, Prinz von Hohenzollern-Emden, 1891-1964
Emden: the last cruise of the chivalrous raider, 1914. — (War at Sea).
1. World War 1. The Indian Ocean campaign. Naval operations by Germany
I. Title II. Series III. Emden. *English*
940.4'54

ISBN 0-904256-45-6

Designed by John Walter
Origination by Service Twenty Four Limited, Brighton, East Sussex
Printed and bound by The Bath Press Limited, Bath, Avon, England

Contents

Acknowledgements

Fregattenkapitän d.R. Meinrad, Prinz von Hohenzollern-Emden, and The Lyon Press Ltd wish to thank Admiral Sir John Woodward KCB ADC RN, formerly Commander-in-Chief, Naval Home Command, Portsmouth, for generously providing the Foreword; Admiral Sir John Fieldhouse GCB GBE RN, formerly Chief of the Defence Staff; Captain A.G.Y. Thorpe RN, Portsmouth; Captain P.F. McGuire RAN, Australian Defence Staff, London; Fregattenkapitän Walter Reichenmiller FGN, commanding officer, Fregatte *Emden*; Commander Adrian Munns RN and Major Hugh Minchinton RA of the Ministry of Defence, London; Mr Anthony Evans, London, for supplying an original book and for cheerful assistance thereafter; Mrs Barbara Jones of Lloyd's Registry, London; Mr Paul Kemp of the Department of Photographs, Imperial War Museum, London; Mr David Lyon MA, Head of Enquiry Services, National Maritime Museum, Greenwich; Mr Andrew Jack, Assistant Curator, Information Services, Australian War Memorial, Canberra; Mr K.C. Adams JP, Honorary State Secretary, Naval Association of Australia, Sydney; Mr R.H. Pelvin, Naval Historical Officer, Department of Defence, Canberra; Herr Joachim Görtz, München; Dr. Hofmann of the Bundesarchiv, Koblenz; Mr Derek Brennan of the Philatelic Bureau, Cocos (Keeling) Islands; Mr Paul Gilbert of philatelists Harry Allen; and Fregattenkapitän a.D. Alfred Nitzschke of the Deutsches Marinebund e.V., Laboe

Efforts to locate photographs of *Emden*'s victims have been hindered by the primitiveness of the cameras of the day, and so illustrations of identical sisters have often been used — an enterprise in which the assistance of the National Maritime Museum, Mr Norman Middlemiss and, particularly, Mr Laurence Dunn is gratefully acknowledged.

Foreword

Admiral Sir John Woodward KCB ADC RN

Formerly Commander in Chief, Naval Home Command

To me, as any submariner, the 'Raider Concept' is bound to have special appeal, relevance and associations. The raider is out there on his own and assumes that every man's hand is turned against him. In lesser commanders than von Müller, persecution mania — mild or severe — can set in from the start, greatly inhibiting operations; but not in this extraordinary man, who took his ship and her 'people' into history.

While there is a sense of doom, simply because the end is known to the reader before the story begins, the author and his shipmates were hopeful and enthusiastic until the final, almost inevitable act. Confidence, competence and camaraderie ring through this remarkable first-hand account of *Emden*'s three-month rampage among Britain's Far East trade routes at the beginning of the First World War.

That the last cruise of *Emden* was both brilliantly successful and fatally doomed is the first and main mark of its historical import. That it was also conducted with impeccable gallantry and humanity is the second — this probably being the aspect that made *Emden* a name renowned in a great many more navies than the German alone. That such a cruise is unlikely ever to recur in this ever-contracting modern world is the final mark of this unique story.

So, while I may not agree with the political sentiments of the author, the professional lessons and qualities are there for all of us to see, learn, and apply to the future. The author's own words — 'The unforgettable exploits of *Emden* were at an end. I hoped that they would inspire our descendants, and that the example of *Emden* would once again awake in our people the spirit of loyal co-operation in times of joy or sorrow' — say it all for any professional naval man, regardless of nationality or persuasion.

Nevertheless, the *Emden* story has also to be seen in the context of the rest of the Kreuzergeschwader (the German Far East cruiser squadron), which was to prove so troublesome under von Spee at Coronel before meeting its equally inevitable end off the Falklands as 1914 drew to a close. Nor can I leave the matter without a final reference to the *Admiral Graf Spee* incident — the Battle of the River Plate, which provided the Royal Navy with its first major success of the Second World War. These three stories are interconnected, with their classic underlying themes of tragedy far from home.

I can only conclude by saying this account of the last cruise of *Emden* begins the trilogy with pride and honour.

Admiral Sir John Woodward KCB ADC RN. By courtesy of the Photographic Section, Royal Naval Home Command, Portsmouth.

Kapitän z.S. Karl von Müller after his return to Germany, *c.*1921. From Karl Bartz, *Der Kommandant der Emden*, Berlin 1939.

Prinz Franz Joseph and the Emden Tradition

Fregattenkapitän d.R. Meinrad, Prinz von Hohenzollern-Emden, lic.jur.
Secretary-General, Confédération Interalliée des Officiers de Réserve (CIOR)

I have often been asked about my father's early career but, frankly, he never said much about his exploits in the First World War. Only occasionally did we children learn snippets at table, or from old-and-trusted servants.

Father, the second of twin brothers, was born on 30th August 1891 — almost a century ago — in the Baltic seacoast spa of Heiligendamm, between Lübeck and Rostock but some five hundred miles north-east of our family home in Sigmaringen. My paternal grandmother, Fürstin Maria-Theresia, a princess of the royal house of Bourbon-Parma, was a renowned beauty whose melancholic face, captured in oils by the famous portraitist Lászlo, now looks down from the walls of a Schloss Sigmaringen salon. Sadly, this "fleur d'autrefois" died in Cannes in 1907, at the early age of 42.

My father was raised with his elder sister Auguste-Victoria (b.1890) — later the consort of Manuel II of Portugal — and his 'senior twin' Friedrich Victor, my godfather. The name Franz Joseph was rare in our family, but, as Sigmaringen had once been a Habsburg fief, Emperor Franz Joseph of Austria asked my grandfather Fürst Wilhelm to give the name to one of the twins. A gold pocket-watch with the initials 'FJ' lies on my desk.

I can still picture my grandfather puffing enormous cigars, though I could rarely see through his smoke veil from my small boy's viewpoint! Fürst Wilhelm died in 1929, when I was only four years old; consequently, my memories of him are few and far between. Alone since the death of his first wife, he had married Prinzessin Adelgunde von Bayern, daughter of King Ludwig III, in 1916; 'Grossmama' was a true lady, and we loved her dearly.

Father's childhood included holidays at a family country seat, six miles south of Sigmaringen, where our family gathered after the traumas of the Second World War before scattering once again. Transport in such country retreats was usually provided by porte-chaise prior to 1914, and I am sure that my father and the other Hohenzollern children would have teased the servant-porters unmercifully.

In 1906, Prinz Franz Joseph joined the Rheinische Ritterakademie, a semi-military college for the sons of noblemen in Bedburg, near Bonn. When the time came to join the colours in March 1911, Father was persuaded to join the navy by Prinz Adalbert von Preussen, the son of Kaiser Wilhelm II — instead of serving 1.Garde-Regiment zu Fuss, in

Fregattenkapitän d.R. Meinrad, Prinz von Hohenzollern-Emden, lic jur. This portrait taken specially for this book in 1989.

Prinz Adalbert von Preussen, son of Kaiser Wilhelm, was responsible for Prinz Franz Joseph's entry into the Kaiserliche Marine. He is shown in this 1909-vintage photo-postcard (published by Photochemie, Berlin, from an original portrait by Sandau) in the uniform of a Kapitänleutnant. By courtesy of The Lyon Press archives.

Prinz Franz Joseph's naval education included a spell aboard the training ship *Hertha* — sister of *Vineta*, seen here in tropical colours. This postcard was sent by Paul Sandross in Rüstringen (Oldenburg) to his family in Braunschweig on 20th March 1912. The text of the card (a good-quality mezzotint-screen product of M. Dieterle, Kiel) reveals that lucky cadet Sandross had just returned from a training cruise to the West Indies. By courtesy of The Lyon Press archives.

which Fürst Friedrich Victor alone upheld our family tradition. Franz Joseph was the first Swabian Hohenzollern to go to sea.

As 'Crew 11', he went first to the naval college in Flensburg-Mürwik and then to the training-ship *Hertha*. In 1913, he was finally posted to *Emden* at Tsingtau. On 3rd August 1914 he was promoted Leutnant zur See, but the news took some time to get through. On 9th November 1914, however, after *Emden*'s last battle, he was captured by the Royal Australian Navy and imprisoned on Malta until February 1920. During his confinement, on 20th April 1917, he was promoted Oberleutnant zur See but left the navy on 28th February 1920 — immediately after his return to Germany.

In addition to serving the Kaiserliche Marine, my father had another maritime connexion. Grandfather Wilhelm's younger brother Ferdinand became King of Romania in 1914; thus Franz Joseph became an honorary rear-admiral in the Romanian navy, whose largest warships between the wars were the British-designed Italian-built destroyers *Regele Ferdinand* and *Regina Maria*.

Neither my grandfather (b.1864) nor my great-uncle (b.1865) can be considered as stars among European royalty, but they must both have had charm: what else could explain their outstandingly beautiful wives? I have already mentioned grandmother Maria-Theresia, whom I never knew, but great-aunt 'Missy' — Queen Maria of Romania, mother of King Carol II and grandmother of King Mihai* — was still a striking lady when I met her in München in 1938. Born in 1875 to Queen Victoria's son Alfred, Duke of Edinburgh,† and Grand-duchess Maria Alexandrovna of Russia, she was a princess of Sachsen-Coburg-Gotha as well as a royal princess of Great Britain and Ireland. She was also George V's cousin.

My maternal grandfather Friedrich August III, King of Saxony, was head of the House of Sachsen-Coburg-Gotha. He was apparently most surprised when his cousin George V changed the name of his cadet branch to 'Windsor' in July 1917!

Early memories

It takes a child some years to become properly aware of its parents — how they look, what they do, their actions and reactions.

My father rarely spoke of his association with *Emden*, five years imprisonment in the Maltese Fort Verdala (Valletta) having been enough for him. My mother told me that Dad was often very melancholic in the early days of their marriage, even though there were no material or financial difficulties.

In the late 1920s and early 1930s, our family portraits were habitually taken by a renowned photographer; each photo took him ages, hidden behind a monster of a wooden camera. Looking at the these photographs now, after more than half a century, you can see the *paterfamilias* with his eldest sons already in sailor suits. It was on one of these occasions that I realized the importance of such a dress: white for special occasions, navy blue — very scratchy! — in winter, and all from the famous one-time Hoflieferant‡ Busch in Kiel. My father generally wore his beribboned Kaiserliche Marine Gala Uniform with the distinctive reserve officer's silver flashes beneath shoulder straps of an Oberleutnant zur See.

After the great Wall Street crash in 1929, my parents decided to move from München to Zürich. There I can still remember the four of us children — my sister included — in our white sailor suits, with white caps displaying S.M.S. EMDEN on their black ribands. But my father never wore a uniform while we were in Switzerland; at home, even on formal occasions, he appeared without decorations as a gesture of respect for our host country's neutrality.

My mother, Princess Maria Alix, Duchess of Saxony and daughter of Friedrich August III, had wide interests. While we were in Switzerland, for example, she studied with the famous psychoanalyst Professor Carl-Gustav Jung — once a pupil of Sigmund Freud.

I liked Zürich, where I was schooled in Swiss-German (still useful when I visit former haunts), but this milk-chocolate life did not last long. The advent of the Third Reich in 1933 and the

* Usually known in English as 'King Michael'.

† Alfred Ernest Augustus, Duke of Edinburgh (1844-1900), had a notable career in the Royal Navy and rose to flag rank. He married the Grand-duchess in 1874.

‡ 'Supplier to the Royal Household'.

Franz Joseph Maria Ludwig Karl Anton Thassilo, Prinz von Hohenzollern-Emden (1891-1964), and his bride, Prinzessin Maria Alix (b.1901), Herzogin von Sachsen, pictured at Sibyllenort on their wedding day: 25th May 1921. By courtesy of Meinrad, Prinz von Hohenzollern-Emden.

This family photograph, dating from 1931, includes (from top to bottom) Prinz Franz Joseph, Prinzessin Maria Margarete (b.1928), Prinz Emanuel Joseph (b.1929), Prinzessin Maria Alix, Prinz Karl Anton (b.1922) and, in the foreground, Prinz Meinrad (b.1925). By courtesy of Meinrad, Prinz von Hohenzollern-Emden.

immediate prohibition of currency transfer forced us back to Germany. There we settled in a beautiful München villa owned by US Consul Semler. Still US Government property, it is currently occupied by a special branch of the US Navy.

Recently, my wife and I were invited to revisit my former home; we were welcomed in what had been my mother's bedroom, now fulfilling an entirely different function. The whole place seemed much smaller than I had remembered, but then the scale of things is so different to an eight-year-old.

At table in the villa, my parents had reminisced with friends and relatives. Toys and railways were popular topics, I recall; ships were definitely never mentioned in 1933. München was then a strange mixture of 'White and Blue' Bavarian conservatives; former First World War soldiers; Communists; and the Wespen ('Wasps') – what we children called the members of the NSDAP, owing to their brown uniforms.

My father joined Stahlhelm, an old comrades association of former Imperial soldiers; thereafter, the black, white and red pennant always flew on his Röhr sedan. He organized the Bavarian motorized section of Stahlhelm in an era when motoring associations were none too well developed. My elder brother Bobby and I joined the Scharnhorst youth group. I still remember 1935-vintage scuffles with Communist youth groups in Giesing, a leftist suburb of München.

When Stahlhelm was dissolved by the NSDAP, Father was engaged by the Colonial Office in München on the strength of his pre-1914 posting to Tsingtau. The Colonial Office was controlled by Bavarian General a.D. Ritter von Epp, who had served in East Africa prior to the First World War; its purpose was to maintain contact with residents in what had once been German colonies, offering advice and, where necessary, charity and Christian ministrations.

Prinz Franz-Joseph was called up by the Kriegsmarine in 1935. This is the earliest I can remember him in his dark-blue navy Ergänzungs-Offizier* uniform. As anti-aircraft defence had become important, Father was posted to a training camp on the East Frisian island of Wangerooge; there, we children enjoyed our summer holidays, forever splashing about the unpolluted waters. Most of the officers and their wives stayed at the Koopmann boarding house, where, as a result, there was a particularly convivial atmosphere.

From the mid 1930s onward, my father regularly spent a couple of evenings a month in the München navy officers' mess, bowling and exchanging gossip. Even today we have such institutions in many German cities, where friendly monthly gatherings may include wives, children and guests. Here in Stuttgart, we are privileged to number among our guests several US Navy officers on exercises or stationed at USEUCOM HQ. We are members of the Marine-Offizier-Vereinigung (MOV), which encompasses every crew and all ages within its on-going tradition.

* 'Reserve Officer' – comparable in status with an officer in the Royal Naval Reserve ('RNR') in Britain.

The Second World War

I still remember 1939 and the outbreak of war. We had just returned from our summer holidays in Sigmaringen; school started on 1st September. My father was sitting in the chair of his favourite München hairdresser when the news came through. No sooner had he returned in his navy-blue BMW, with his driver Anton Schwarz, than the telephone rang and München military regional office (now the Wehr-Bereichs-Kommando or WBK) asked him to contact his North Sea unit immediately. He left by train for Hamburg the very next day; from there he was sent as Batteriechef (commander) of Marine Flak-Abteilung 214, a naval anti-aircraft battery at Brunsbüttelkoog in Schleswig-Holstein that protected the strategically important western exit of the Nordsee-Ostsee Kanal.

Telephone communications between Brunsbüttelkoog and München were complicated and, as there was then no automatic service, connexions took ages. An additional complication was that our cook, a virtuous woman from Mondsee in Austria, had severe problems understanding the sharp North German accents. German dialects can lead to misunderstandings even today!

Our Swabian driver Schwarz was conscripted into a Bavarian regiment; as he was a skilled mechanic, the unit — as it would do today — guarded him jealously, together with its other specialists. On 1st September 1940, however, my father was promoted Korvettenkapitän and became commandant of Cuxhaven in May 1941. This allowed him to have driver Schwarz transferred to the navy as his orderly. It is easy to imagine the happy faces on both sides of this deal.

Dad became very popular in Cuxhaven, which caused much jealousy among the local Party officials and a good deal of special investigation. But Father's staff officers were true gentlemen of the old school; as a matter of interest, Korvettenkapitän Fritz Brune — my father's successor — and his family have been friends of ours now for half a century. Senator Brune has a beautiful home in Baden-Baden, and you would not guess from his sprightliness that he was 94 in the Spring of 1989. We are members of the same international racing club and meet regularly. Of course, his sons also served in the navy; Carl-Horst, his eldest, was my Best Man when I married Baroness Edina von Kap-herr in 1971.

I still remember 30th August 1941, and Father's fiftieth birthday celebrations in Schloss Sigmaringen with his twin Fürst Friedrich Victor. A detachment of Dad's unit arrived unannounced under Korvettenkapitän Brune's command — in full dress, notwithstanding not only that it was wartime but also five hundred miles back to base!

Kapitänleutnant Dr.jur. Hans Nebelsieck, another of my father's staff and a former supreme judge, still lives in Celle. Now 88, it seems that the navy has given him eternal life.

Korvettenkapitän d.R. Franz Joseph, Prinz von Hohenzollern-Emden, pictured on the occasion of his fiftieth birthday: 30th August 1941. By courtesy of Meinrad, Prinz von Hohenzollern-Emden.

My navy career

I had wanted to join the mountain troops (Gebirgsjäger) in Mittenwald, but Father smelled a rat; and so, instead of taking a train to the Bavarian Alps in July 1943, I had papers for a very different destination — the island of Dänholm, near Stralsund on the Baltic, where most aspiring naval officers received their basic, very brief training. Then I went eastward to Swinemünde, where my 'boss', Kapitän z.S. Axel Löwe, a veteran of the battle-cruiser *Seydlitz*'s heroics at Jutland, had been primed to keep an eye on me. Father's influence was everywhere! From Swinemünde I travelled to Bornholm and thence to Peenemünde, home of the research station from which the V1 and V2 'Vergeltungswaffen' emanated. My call-up class — VII/43 — had meanwhile been scattered to the four winds.

The summer of 1944 brought Count Stauffenberg's ill-fated attempt on Hitler's life. These were worrying times, as the NSDAP seized the chance to be rid of those who did their duty for their country rather than the régime. With my cousin King Mihai of Romania about to declare war on Germany — he did so on 25th August 1944, after Antonescu's fall — Father's days of service were numbered. On 30th June 1944, Berlin simply discharged him from military service without honours. The Gestapo then interned the entire family, children included, in a 'silence camp'. There my parents first met the popular German television reporter Peter von Zahn and his British wife.

My mother and I had arranged to insert a secret password in our correspondence in cases of extreme emergency. When I received such a letter in the eastern Baltic, in mid-September 1944, I immediately reported to Axel Löwe and was granted a short leave. After crossing war-torn Germany by day and night, under the most chaotic transport conditions imaginable, I found my family behind barred windows and under permanent Gestapo questioning.

Luckily, I was in the uniform of a Fähnrich zur See and could refer the authorities to Axel Löwe, my far-off commandant; with gnashing of teeth, the Gestapo let me return eastward. It was to be more than a year before I heard anything more from my parents, yet it is said to be an ill wind that blows nobody good: the remoteness of my eastern unit probably saved me from the grip of the Gestapo. The detachment's last position was in Liepaja in Lithuania, now part of the Soviet Union.

9th May 1945: war was over. I had survived. I had even survived an encounter with a sea-mine. When you are a twenty-year-old Leutnant zur See, being alive is everything. I had learned English prior to my call-up, not from the München Gymnasium but while drinking tea and playing cards with Miss Marple-lookalike Nora McElligott, once a native of Dublin. Now time spent in such pleasant pastimes helped me to get along with the Allied forces.

Prinz Franz Joseph in uniform, a photograph taken in 1944. By courtesy of Meinrad, Prinz von Hohenzollern-Emden.

Leutnant (M.A.) Meinrad, Prinz von Hohenzollern-Emden, pictured in the early summer of 1945.

Schloss Sigmaringen, as restored after 1978 – though no external changes have been made since 1893. By courtesy of Meinrad, Prinz von Hohenzollern-Emden.

When I finally found my family, a couple of miles away from Sigmaringen, our castle was occupied by French Moroccan troops. The disgraced French Marshal Pétain and one-time Premier Pierre Laval played a guest role there for some months, after which French troops occupied the whole of south-west Germany. Father was unsportingly placed under 'automatic arrest' in a camp in Niederbayern, his activities for the Colonial Office being considered subversive endeavours to return the territories to German rule.

In 1949, after his release, my father finally rejoined us in a nice little villa in Hechingen, cradled in the foothills below Burg Hohenzollern. Here he would spend the remaining fifteen years of his life quietly. Until his death on 3rd April 1964, he steadily renewed contacts with old navy friends and was even able to attend the launch of the frigate *Emden* IV in Hamburg in 1959.

Emden renaissant

Late in the Spring of 1964, an Australian film-crew came to Germany to interview the survivors of the original *Emden*. The same had been done with survivors of the victor, HMAS *Sydney*, as the Tingira Old Boys Association wished to commemorate the fiftieth anniversary of the final battle off the Cocos Islands on 9th November 1914 by telling both sides of the story. Unfortunately, my father had died only a few weeks earlier and I had to explain his part in the fight. I took Claus Bergen's famous painting to Augsburg, where we met in the house of Kapitän z.S. d.R. Fikentscher-Emden. There I first met Heyo Aden-Emden, the sole remaining survivor, who celebrated his 99th birthday in March 1989. In 1985, I congratulated him on his 95th birthday and, in remarkably steady handwriting, he had answered:

"I want to thank you especially for your very kind letter and your thoughts for my birthday. It was celebrated at the Park-Hotel in Osnabrück, where about eighty friends came by air, rail and car to shake my hand... Over 100 friends and comrades were congratulating me by letter or telephone-call. It was an unforgettable event for me and my guests. Looking back, I thought of your father who — when I was badly wounded — stuck loyally by my side to save me dying from thirst. I was just looking at his picture, when he was visiting the 'Emden' comrades in Essen. You, dear Prince, have continued the traditional links with your House, for which the 'Emden-Family' is grateful."

The Autumn of 1974 brought a great surprise. I had not even thought of re-enlisting when, at the age of nearly fifty, I received a letter from Bonn informing me that I should rejoin the navy as a reserve officer for a special exercise. My wife was in the ninth month of her pregnancy; days passed, nothing happened. Fortunately, the navy understood the situation. Finally, on St Nicholas Day, our daughter Stephanie-Antoinette was born in Stuttgart under the watchful eye of another former navy officer, Prof.Dr. May, director of the Landesfrauenklinik. A happy father then donned his uniform after almost thirty years, to leave wife and daughter alone for the delights of a frigate on the North Sea.

There have since been many exercises and many highlights. Particularly notable was 27th November 1976, when I set first foot on *Emden* IV (F221) during STANAVFORLANT. So I am one of the few bearers of the byname 'Emden' to serve as an officer aboard a ship with that same famous name, following my father's footsteps in a great tradition.

I do not believe that one should live in the past, of course, but rather that the great traditions of the past can be beneficially adapted to today's needs. Five ships have borne the Emden name; but my father could not know that his son would serve on the ship whose launch he had attended in 1959, any more than Heyo Aden-Emden could know that it would be me — together with Kapitän z.S. von der Planitz — who would assist him aboard *Emden* V when the new frigate was commissioned at Wilhelmshaven by Vizeadmiral Fromm on 7th October 1983.

And is it fate that the second captain of *Emden* V should have been Kapitän z.S. Thomas Kempf from Calw (thirty miles from my home in Hechingen), and that the present commander is Fregattenkapitän Walter Reichenmiller from Tübingen... a mere fifteen miles distant?

The Emden Tradition

To celebrate a glorious event in German naval history, the 1916-vintage *Emden* II was granted the Eisernen Kreuz (Iron Cross), with the imperial crown and 'W II' cypher of the last German Emperor. Only the submarine *U9*, a contemporary of *Emden* I, has been similarly honoured in the entire history of an order founded by the King of Prussia, Friedrich Wilhelm III, in 1813.

The tradition of the first *Emden* was perpetuated by the Reichsmarine's *Emden* III, laid down in December 1921 and launched in 1925; by the 1959-vintage *Emden* IV, now serving the Turkish navy; and by *Emden* V, launched in December 1980. The older vessels carried the Eisernen Kreuz proudly on their bows; the two postwar vessels have displayed it on the bridge.

During the First World War, there had been a move to bestow a particular honour on the members of the ship's company — the right to add the suffix 'Emden' to their surnames. This request was briefly considered by the Prussian authorities in 1920-1, but was not resurrected until 1931. It was then agreed that interested parties should register in the 'Bürgerlichen Gesetzbuch' (Emden statute book) prior to the last day of 1933. And then, on 16th March 1934, the Reichspräsident formally granted the honour.

Some time previously, however, the former Kaiser Wilhelm II was approached to grant my father — a member of the

Commissioning the frigate *Emden* V: Wilhelmshaven, 7th October 1983. In the foreground, from the left, are the Bürgermeister of Emden and his wife; Fregattenkapitän d.R. Meinrad, Prinz von Hohenzollern-Emden; Heyo Aden-Emden, the last surviving member of the original crew; and Fregattenkapitän von der Planitz, the ship's first captain. By courtesy of Meinrad, Prinz von Hohenzollern-Emden.

The frigate *Emden* IV, F221, launched in 1959 and commissioned on 24th October 1961, was sold to the Turkish navy in 1983. By courtesy of the Bundesmarine, Bildstelle Wilhelmshaven.

exiled royal family — the special permission necessary to add the byname 'Emden' to 'Hohenzollern'. Once this had been forthcoming, the grant was approved by the Prussian Minister des Innern on 18th November 1933.

The byname was originally to descend only to male children and would have been extinguished after an additional generation, but Federal Law now permits its perpetuation. Each year, the 'Emden-Family' meets somewhere in Germany under the watchful eye of Kapitän z.S. a.D. Hans-Henning Bess, Class X/39, who once commanded *Emden* IV. The Family currently numbers about sixty men, women and children.

I take such great pleasure in introducing this new version of my father's memoirs not merely because it is still such a rattling good sea-story, but because of the high regard in which I hold the tradition of *Emden* I, her conqueror *Sydney* and, indeed, all navies worthy of the name. Speaking as Secretary-General of the CIOR during our visit to HMS *Nelson*, Portsmouth, on 28th July 1988, I stated that the Royal Navy's traditions of:

'chivalry, bravery and gallantry give me the feeling that my father, Prinz Franz Joseph, is standing behind me — supporting his son in the continuation of these values, which have lost nothing among civilized countries even today.'

It is a feeling that I hope will stay with the descendants of my father and his *Emden* colleagues for the years to come.

Fregkpt.d.R. Meinrad, Prinz von Hohenzollern-Emden, lic.jur.
Stuttgart, 5th July 1989

1 'S.M. Unterseeboot 9. Kommandant Kapitänleutnant Weddigen. vernichtete die 4 englischen Panzerkreuzer Aboukir, Hogue, Cressy u. Hawke. Die Besatzung wurde mit dem Eisernen Kreuz ausgezeichnet.' The only other German warship to be awarded the Eisernen Kreuz (Iron Cross) was the submarine pictured here in a sepia-tone postcard published by M.L. Carstens, Hamburg (no.3058) from an original photograph by K. Koch, Kiel.

---

2 A view of *Emden* II alongside a pier, probably taken in 1918. The view shows the bow-mounted Iron Cross to advantage. Just visible is the stern of another cruiser — possibly *Graudenz* or *Regensburg*. By courtesy of WZ-Bilddienst, Wilhelmshaven.

'Unterseeboot "U 9" bei einer Tauschübung'. This postcard, published by M. Dieterle & Sohn of Kiel ('Reihe Heimat Nr.5256') from an original photograph by Ferd. Urbahns, shows the 1935-vintage *U9* on a practice dive, accompanied by the tender T156 — built as a torpedo-boat in 1908 and finally sunk in Kiel harbour on 3rd May 1945. Note the large Eisernen Kreuz on the submarine's conning tower. Built by Germaniawerft of Kiel, and commissioned on 21st August 1935, *U9* was sunk by Russian bombers off Constanţa, on the Romanian Black Sea coast, on 20th August 1944. 3

Both submarine photographs by courtesy of The Lyon Press archives.

Launching *Emden* V from the Nordsee-Thyssen-Werft, Emden, on 17th December 1980. By courtesy of Meinrad, Prinz von Hohenzollern-Emden.

Emden V, F210, at sea; 1988. By courtesy of Fregattenkapitän Walter Reichenmiller, whose portrait is inset.

THE SHIP

Note: tonnage figures for German warships are given in the contemporary standard 'tonnes dwl' (i.e., displacement at designed waterline), a system adopted in 1882. Full load tonnages could be appreciably greater, which means that a variety of differing — yet still defensible — figures will be encountered elsewhere.

German cruiser design before *Emden*

As the twentieth century dawned, German cruiser design — like that of Britain, with which parallels could be drawn — had evolved into 'protected cruisers', intended to fight alongside the battle fleet, and lighter ships destined primarily for commerce-raiding. The first group had evolved from sail-and-steam corvettes and light cruisers such as the Schwalbe and Bussard classes, displacing 1,111 and 1,559-1,612 tonnes respectively; the commerce raiders had grown out of specialized torpedo boats dating back, in the Kaiserliche Marine at least, to the 1875-vintage 1,101-tonne *Zieten*.

The introduction of much larger vessels late in the 1880s — the 4,271-tonne sister-ships *Irene* and *Prinzess Wilhelm*, then the 6,056-tonne *Kaiserin Augusta* — reduced the value of the old sail-and-steam ships appreciably. It also presaged a move towards much larger armoured cruisers; *Scharnhorst* and *Gneisenau*, authorized in fiscal year 1903/4, displaced 11,616 tonnes and approached the size of the largest Kaiserliche Marine pre-dreadnoughts.*

Armoured cruisers were ineffectual guardians of the meagre, but far-flung overseas territories Germany's late entrance into colonialism had provided. To protect large tracts of Africa, a scattering of South Sea islands, and a toehold on the Chinese mainland at Kiautschou, smaller and more economical ships were required.

* *Scharnhorst*, laid down in 1904, displaced 11,616 tonnes and measured 143.8m on the waterline; the battleships of the Deutschland class (laid down in 1903-5), displaced 13,191 tonnes on a waterline length of 125.9m. Even the first German dreadnoughts, the 18,873-tonne Nassau class, measured only 145.6m on the waterline.

The solution was soon found. Torpedo-cruisers (or Avisos) had descended from *Zieten* to the 2,050-tonne *Grief* by way of the sister-ships *Blitz* and *Pfeil*, but had then returned to the smaller single-funnel *Jagd* and *Wacht* (1,246 tonnes) before blurring back into torpedo-boat destroyer design in the early 1890s. The three-funnel *Greif* was the most promising. Though comparatively unsuccessful in service, her rakish silhouette and complete reliance on twin-shaft simple-expansion marine engines pointed to the future.

The German designers then produced the 'cruiser corvette' *Gefion*, displacing 3,746 tonnes on a waterline of about 109 metres. With her iron hull sheathed in wood, and protective deck armour, *Gefion* was the first German warship to mount 10.5cm Schiffskanone C/88 ('SK C/88') in what was to become the classical kleine Kreuzer manner — paired fore-and-aft, with three additional midship guns each side. Schichau-built *Gefion*, commissioned on 27th June 1894, could squeeze nearly twenty knots from triple-expansion engines rated at 9,000hp. After serving the Kreuzergeschwader faithfully, being rebuilt early in the twentieth century, she served as an accommodation ship throughout the First World War and was then oddly (and unsuccessfully) transformed into a merchantman.

Excepting her armament, *Gefion* was a precursor of the Viktoria Luise-class armoured cruisers rather than an early *Emden*: the Aviso *Hela*, a contemporary of *Gefion* built by AG 'Weser' and commissioned in May 1896, was closer to a light cruiser. With a single funnel, an armoured deck, a ram bow and a comparatively light armament of four 8.8cm guns, the slender *Hela* — displacing 2,027 tonnes on a waterline measuring nearly 105 metres — was hardly a flyer: twenty knots was all that could be attained from triple-expansion engines generating

Blitz, an 'Aviso I.Klasse' shown here off Molde *c.* 1910, was built by the Norddeutsche shipyard. Laid down in 1881, launched on 26th August 1882 and commissioned on 28th March 1883, she was discarded in March 1921. Displacing 1,381 tonnes, with a service speed of 15½ knots, *Blitz* originally carried one 12.5cm and four 8.7cm guns, plus a torpedo-tube. By courtesy of The Lyon Press archives.

An 'Aviso I.Klasse', eventually rebuilt and reclassified as a light cruiser, *Hela* was laid down in the AG 'Weser' yard in 1893, launched on 28th March 1895 and commissioned on 3rd May 1896. The 2,027-tonne ship was originally armed with four 8.8cm and six 5cm guns, plus three torpedo tubes, and could make twenty knots. After being reboilered in the early 1900s, when the original single funnel seen in picture taken about 1898 was replaced by two, the ship was torpedoed by the British submarine *E9* in the North Sea on 13th September 1914. By courtesy of the Trustees of the Imperial War Museum, London; negative Q 41273.

6,000hp. However, colonial service soon proved her to be a very good seaboat. Extensively rebuilt in 1903-6, acquiring a second funnel and the general appearance of the later Gazelle class, *Hela* was torpedoed and sunk by the British submarine *E9* on 13th September 1914.

The great shipbuilding programmes of the late 1890s called for Kleine Kreuzer of what would be known as the Gazelle class. The first vessel — *Gazelle* herself — was laid down in Krupp's Germaniawerft shipyard, Kiel, in 1897. Launched on 31st March 1898, she was commissioned in October 1900.†

The ten Gazelles differed in detail, but were all about 105m long and offered similar performance. The oldest, *Gazelle* and *Niobe*, each displaced 2,643 tonnes; the second batch — *Nymphe, Thetis, Ariadne, Amazone* and *Medusa* — displaced 2,659 tonnes; while *Frauenlob, Arcona* and *Undine* (2,706 tonnes) carried ten more crewmen. Eight of them could make about 21 knots, the exceptions being the semi-experimental

† Two of her sisters were commissioned earlier — *Niobe* on 25th June 1900 and *Nymphe* on 20th September 1900.

'S.M.Kl. Kreuzer Ariadne am 28. Aug. 1914 im Seegefecht bei Helgoland gesunken' — the small cruiser *Ariadne*, seen here from the port bow, was sunk at the Battle of Heligoland Bight. Built by AG 'Weser' of Bremen, displacing 2,659 tonnes and capable of 21½ knots, she was commissioned in May 1901. This mezzotint Feldpostkarte, published by M. Dieterle of Kiel (no.726), was sent by Richard Krug of II.Torpedo-Division to his brother in München. Dated 10th March 1915, it also bears the censor's mark of XIV.Halbflotille. By courtesy of The Lyon Press archives.

twenty-knot *Gazelle*, with her charthouse between the two slender widely-spaced funnels; and *Niobe*, the greyhound of the group, which attained 22 knots under full power. Armament duplicated *Gefion*'s, ten 10.5cm SK C/88 being reinforced by six machine cannon and two torpedo tubes.

Gazelle and her sisters were very successful, all excepting the war-losses *Undine* and *Frauenlob* being particularly long-lived. The Kaiserliche Marine was sufficiently impressed to order essentially similar vessels under the 1902 programme, merely enlarging the basic design to displace 3,278 tonnes‡ on a waterline of 111 metres. The increase permitted better armour protection, more boilers and power necessary to attain 23 knots. The new three-funnel vessels were named after German towns, the first ship, AG 'Vulcan'-built *Hamburg*, being commissioned on 8th March 1904. All seven were in service by the Spring of 1907. Two were lost during the First World War: *Leipzig*, sunk on 8th December 1914 during the Battle of the Falkland Islands, and *Bremen*, mined in the North Sea on 17th February 1915. Three were broken up in the immediate postwar period, but *Hamburg* and *Berlin* were not hulked until well into the Reichsmarine period.*

One ship of the *Bremen* class, *Lübeck*, laid-down in the AG 'Vulcan' shipyard in Stettin in 1903 and completed in April 1905, received two-shaft Parsons turbines instead of triple-expansion engines.† Though she developed no greater speed than her conventionally powered sisters, *Lübeck* convinced the German naval constructors that turbines had an exciting future; *Emden*, laid down in 1907, would be the last kleine Kreuzer to receive reciprocating machinery.

The Bremen class led to *Königsberg*, ordered in fiscal year 1903/4. After *Emden*, the 3,390-tonne 115-metre *Königsberg* was the most famous kleiner Kreuzer of the First World War. At the end of July 1914, shortly before hostilities commenced, she had left Dar-es-Salaam in German East Africa to cruise off Aden under the command of Korvettenkapitän Max Looff. After capturing the British steamship *City of Winchester*, shortage of coal forced *Königsberg* to seek refuge in the Rufiji Delta – sallying to surprise and sink the British protected cruiser *Pegasus* off Zanzibar Island on 20th September 1914. Eventually, forced ever farther up the Rufiji, *Königsberg* was blown apart by the British river monitors *Severn* and *Mersey* in an episode only marginally less fascinating than *Emden*'s last cruise.

The three ships of the Stuttgart class – *Stuttgart*, *Stettin* and *Nürnberg* – were authorized in the fiscal year 1904/5. Similar to their solitary predecessor *Königsberg*, excepting that they were a little larger (3,469-3,480 tonnes) and about two metres longer, they had a characteristic gap between the second and third funnels. *Stettin* had twin Parsons turbines driving four propellor shafts, attaining 25.2 knots on the measured mile, while her slower twin-screw sisters all had vertical triple-expansion machinery. Main armament remained ten SK C/88, though the secondary battery was increased to eight 5.2cm Schnellade-Kanone L/55 (ten in *Nürnberg*). Each crew mustered 322 men.

Then came the two famous ships of the Dresden class (Fiscal Year 1905/6), the name-ship herself – built by Blohm & Voss of Hamburg – and *Emden*. With a design displacement of 3,664 tonnes, the two ships were all but indistinguishable externally. However, *Dresden* had two Parsons turbines driving four propellor shafts, while *Emden* had conventional twin-shaft vertical triple-expansion machinery. Not only was *Dresden* appreciably faster – more than a knot on the measured

‡ The turbine-engined *Lübeck*, marginally lighter than her sisters, displaced 3,265 tonnes.

* *Berlin* was not reduced to a hulk until 1935, being sunk in the Skagerrak in May 1947 with a cargo of poison-gas shells; *Hamburg*, hulked as a U-boat accommodation ship in 1936, was sunk by Allied bombing in the Autumn of 1944.

† The first cruiser to receive turbines was HMS *Amethyst*, laid down in Armstrong's Elswick shipyard in January 1903 and completed in March 1905; *Lübeck* was the world's second turbine-driven cruiser.

SMS *Leipzig*, built by AG 'Weser' of Bremen, was commissioned in April 1906. Typical of the second batch of the earliest three-funnelled light cruisers – still with the foremast ahead of the bridge – she displaced 3,278 tonnes, carried ten 10.5cm guns and could make 22 knots. This good-quality postcard was published *c.*1910 by 'NPG', probably from an original by Gebr. Lempe, Kiel. Falling victim to the guns of HM Ships *Cornwall* and *Glasgow*, luckless *Leipzig* sank in the evening of 8th December 1914 during the Battle of the Falkland Islands; 315 men were lost with her. By courtesy of The Lyon Press archives.

mile – but the knowledgeable could detect differences in the funnel casings and steampipe arrangements.

According to Erich Gröner, in his authoritative *Die deutschen Kriegsschiffe 1815-1945*, the upper section of *Dresden*'s forecastle breakwater folded whereas *Emden*'s was fixed. *Emden* had no external steampipe on her middle funnel, and the pipe on the side of the forefunnel was distinctively cranked rather than vertical. In addition, the searchlight platform on the mainmast was two metres lower in *Emden* than *Dresden* – though the difference was difficult to detect from a distance. For the first year of her commission, *Dresden* had only a single searchlight on the mast platforms: her sister had always had two. By the beginning of 1910, however, *Dresden* also carried two lights on each platform.

SMS *Emden*

Authorized on 23rd December 1905 as the 'Kriegsschiff der IV.Rangklasse, des Kleinen geschützten Kreuzer 'Ersatz Pfeil'...', *Emden* was laid down in the Kaiserliche Werft, Danzig, on 1st November 1906. Building was protracted – *Dresden* was launched and commissioned first – even though the Danzig fitting-out basin was supposed to be cleared as quickly as possible to allow rebuilding of the armoured cruiser *Hansa* to begin. Finally, at noon on 26th May 1908, the mayor of Emden, Bürgermeister Fürbringer, christened the new warship.

The ship displaced 3,664 tonnes and measured 118.3 metres from the aftermost part of the stern to the tip of the bow-ram. Beam was 13.5 metres, while the designed draught was 5.13 metres forward and 4.53 aft. The two steel masts towered to 41.3 metres, while the caps of the three slender wire-stayed funnels were more than eighteen metres above the design waterline. The lightly armoured deck had a flat central section and sides sloped at about 37°.

The principal armament comprised ten 10.5cm C/88 Schnellade-Kanonen in Marine-Pivot-Lafette C/04, which gave a maximum elevation of 30° and a depression of 10°. Only the bow, stern and midships guns were shielded, the other upper deck guns being in sponsons. A total of 1,500 10.5cm shells was provided, all but thirty being high-explosive. The remainder was loaded with shrapnel.

Emden originally also carried eight 5.2cm Schnellade-Kanonen L/55, paired on deck above the sponson guns with additional guns at bow and stern. The authoritative Lochner book makes no mention of these guns, even though photographs of *Emden* on trial and departing for the Far East show them clearly. However, no 5.2cm weapons are visible in pictures of the wreck; either they were unshipped during the last cruise or, more probably, had been left behind in Tsingtau. The bow and stern guns could not be used in heavy seas, while utility of those above the 10.5cm sponsons would have been greatly reduced in combat by blast and smoke.

Four 1900-pattern 8mm Maxim machine-guns – stowed beneath the armoured deck forward – were provided with ten thousand rounds apiece, while a solitary 6cm short-barrelled Schnellade-Kanone L/21 on Bootslafette C/00 was supposedly carried for use on ship's boats.‡ A Landungslafette C/00 was provided for the 6cm gun, plus two tripod mounts (MG-Dreifuss-Lafette C/00) to allow machine-guns to be taken ashore.

S.M.S. EMDEN

This elevation of *Emden* is based on general-arrangement drawings of the 'Dresden class' in the Bundesarchiv collection (SZ/185 and SZ/186). These, which are not original, represent the ships as designed rather than built; consequently, there are a serious discrepancies in constructional details, deck fittings and rig. Though many changes have been embodied in the drawing reproduced here, which is thus more accurate than the Bundesarchiv version, no single drawing of *Emden* yet published is truly authoritative.

Illustration by John Walter.

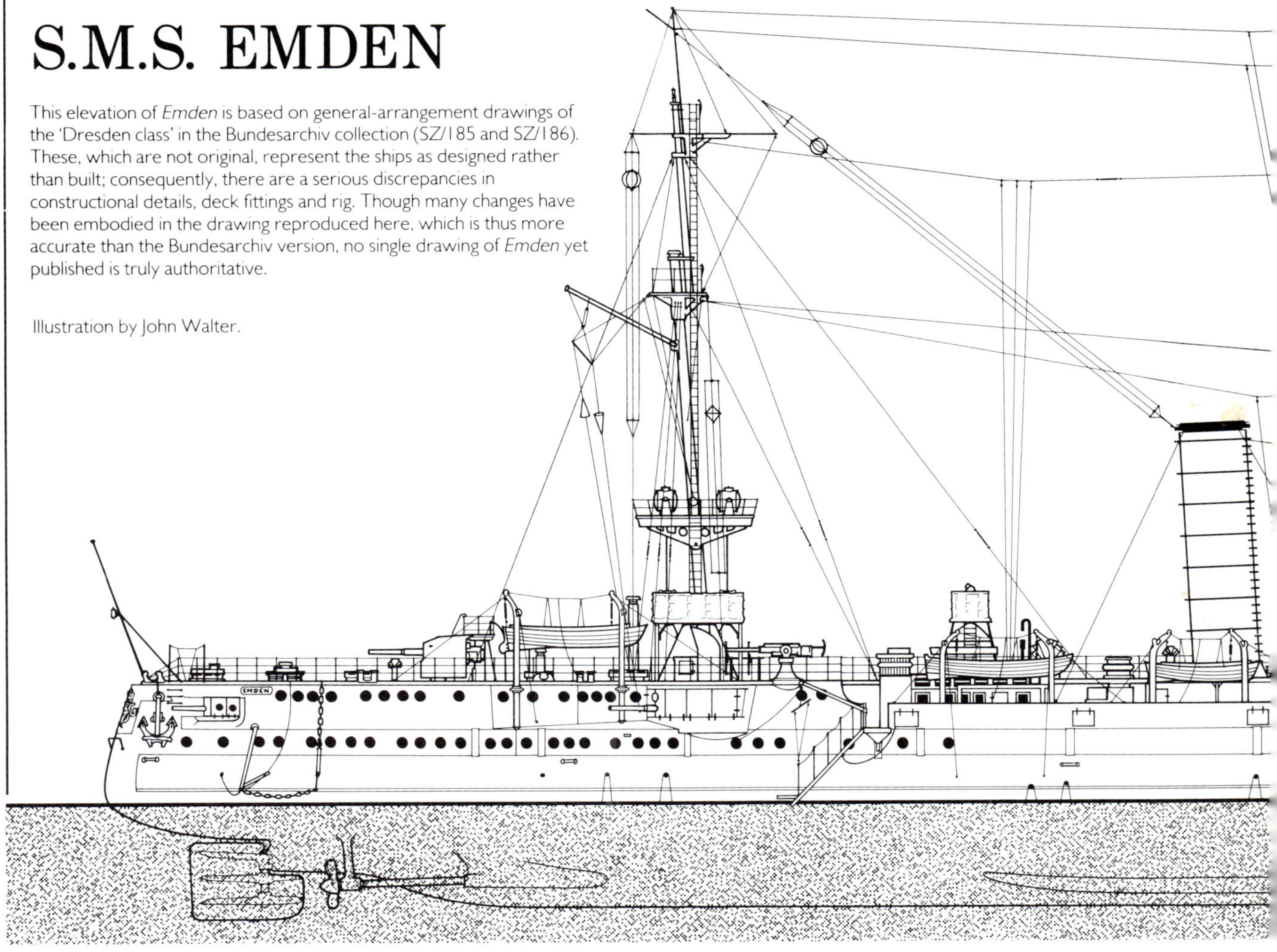

The torpedo tubes, one to port and the other to starboard, were angled 20° ahead of the beam. Five 45cm C/03 torpedoes were carried.

Emden and her turbine sister-ship *Dresden* began their acceptance trials on 10th July 1909. In a six-hour forced draught run on 10th August, under the watchful eye of Fregattenkapitän Engels, *Emden*'s two three-cylinder vertical triple-expansion engines — fed from twelve smallbore water-tube navy boilers — generated 15,683shp to propel the ship at more than 23 knots. A top speed of 24.014 knots was reached on the Neukrug Mile on 20th August.

Emden's most economical speed was eight knots, though her optimal cruising speed was reckoned to be twelve; the highest maintainable speed was authorized as twenty knots, with a forced short-duration performance of 23.85. However, 24 knots could be exceeded in times of great need, in a tailwind, or even on a favourable tide.

Dresden was generally reckoned to be capable of two knots more than her maximum measured-mile speed (25.2 knots), working up to an estimated 27 knots while escaping the carnage of the Battle of the Falkland Islands. Both ships were good seaboats, except in swells coming from abeam or astern, but shipped water when pitching. They were handy and manouverable, with a tactical radius of about 450 metres at eleven knots or 550 metres at twenty knots.

Trials were successfully completed by 21st August, a few days after which the brand-new *Emden* was selected to escort the imperial yacht *Hohenzollern* to Swinemünde. After the 'Kaisermanöver', *Emden* continued final fitting-out and had been completed by the end of the year.

As work had taken longer than expected, *Nürnberg* had to be sent to the Kreuzergeschwader to replace *Niobe*. *Emden* was to proceed to the China Sea in the Spring of 1910 by way of Buenos Aires, where she would help celebrate the centenary of the founding of the Argentine Republic.

The Kaiser initialled the sailing orders on 26th March 1910; on 1st April, *Emden* mustered the crew of *Arcona*, which had returned for lengthy repairs, and readied for sailing. In the morning of 12th April 1910, freshly painted in tropical white with buff superstructure, the cruiser entered the Holtenauer Schleuse under the command of Korvettenkapitän Waldemar Vollerthun; an epic journey around Cape Horn had begun. Never again would she see home waters. And never, indeed, would the people of Emden see the ship they had sponsored.

Emden anchored in the harbour of Porto Grande on 22nd April; crossing the Atlantic had been a fine way of acclimatizing the crew to their new ship. By 10th May 1910, the cruiser had moved to Montevideo roadstead and thence — on 18th May — to Buenos Aires in company with SMS *Bremen*.

At the end of May, *Emden* left Buenos Aires to sail round Cape Horn, reaching Punta Arenas in the Straits of Magellan on 3rd June and Valparaiso, the principal port of Chile, eight days later. 23rd June found *Emden* coaling in Talcahuano harbour, ready for a voyage that, after passing within sighting distance of Easter Island and Pitcairn was to end in Papeete (Tahiti) on 12th July 1910.

From Papeete, Vollerthun and his crew sailed to Apia and a rendezvous with SMS *Scharnhorst*, flying the flag of the officer commanding the Kreuzergeschwader, Konteradmiral Gühler. Not until 17th September did *Emden* make a grand entrance

‡ There is no evidence that the 6cm gun was being carried on *Emden*'s last cruise.

1

2

3

into her new home port of Tsingtau. There, pristine appearance and elegant lines proved a great attraction and she soon gained the nickname 'Swan of the East'.

Emden's career on the Far East Station was eventful: courtesy visits to China and Japan, forays to exotic islands, manoeuvres of short duration that allowed the crew much enjoyment in the equable climate and pleasant surroundings of Tsingtau. Not surprisingly, the posting was greatly sought by younger officers.

On 28th December 1910, *Emden* and *Nürnberg*, accompanied by two gunboats, set off to quell a rebellion on the island of Ponape in the Caroline group, where the German district commissioner had been murdered. After shelling the principal rebel-held hilltop positions on Jokaj island, the landing party successfully fought its way up through daunting terrain. Though fighting rumbled on for several weeks on Ponape and neighbouring islands before the last rebels surrendered, order was eventually restored at minimal cost to the German force.

Emden returned to Tsingtau on 14th March 1911. Little else was to happen during the year, though the ship was damaged in a typhoon that struck Yokohama in July.*

1 This model of *Emden*, from a glass negative in the Bundesarchiv collection (Bild 134-B1364), seems to be 'as projected' rather than as built. Many minor discrepancies may be noted in comparison with photographs of the ship running trials. By courtesy of the Bundesarchiv, Koblenz.

2 A photograph of *Emden*, probably running trials in 1909. By courtesy of the Bundesarchiv, Koblenz; Bild 134-B243.

3 This interesting photograph shows *Emden*, from slightly abaft the starboard beam, dressed ship with the quarterdeck awning in place. Owing to the presence of an Argentine ensign ahead of *Emden*'s bow, the harbour must be Montevideo; the celebration, therefore, is the centenary of the Argentine Republic — 25th May 1910. By courtesy of WZ-Bilddienst, Wilhelmshaven; photograph KM 11826.

Prelude to war

Konteradmiral Gühler died of typhoid in Hongkong in March 1911, and was succeeded by Konteradmiral von Krosigk. During a wholesale rotation of officers in November 1912, *Emden* gained two men who were to stay for the final fateful cruise — the then-Fähnriche z.S. von Guérard and Fikentscher — and a third who would achieve greater fame: Oberleutnant z.S. Lothar von Arnauld de la Perière, who would become the highest-scoring U-boat ace of all time.

Korvettenkapitän von Restorff had replaced Waldemar Vollerthun as captain of *Emden* on 23rd November 1911, and was himself replaced at the end of May 1913 by Korvettenkapitän Karl von Müller. Accompanying the new skipper, who arrived on the Norddeutscher Lloyd steamship *Königin Luise*, were others whose names will become familiar in the Hohenzollern memoirs: Oberleutnant z.S. Robert Witthoeft, torpedo officer and later to captain *Emden* III in 1930-1; Oberleutnant z.S. Ernst Gaede, the gunnery officer; and the chief surgeon, Stabsarzt Johannes Luther.

No sooner had von Müller taken over command than news of serious unrest in northern China reached the Kreuzergeschwader, on a courtesy visit to Rabaul in Kaiser-Wilhelm-Land.

Emden returned briefly to Tsingtau to re-equip, whereupon Kapitänleutnant Hellmuth von Mücke — the navigating officer — became first officer, and skipper von Müller was promoted to Fregattenkapitän. Their ship reached Nanking on 12th August, to join HMS *Hampshire* and ships from the Japanese and US navies. On 27th August, *Emden* came under fire from a fort near Tongling and replied with five salvoes from her port 10.5cm guns: at a range of less than 1,500 metres, the holder of the Kaiser's Kreuzergeschwader shooting prize for 1913 could hardly miss.

For his dashing leadership, which had included a foray upstream to Hankow, the outwardly taciturn von Müller was suitably rewarded.†

Leutnant z.S. Prinz Franz Joseph von Hohenzollern had joined the crew on 31st August 1913, but had not gone on the Chinese excursion.

On 20th June 1914, Vizeadmiral Maximilian, Graf von Spee, who had succeed von Krosigk in March 1913, took the Kreuzergeschwader on a cruise into the Pacific — excepting the ageing gunboats and *Emden*, left in port for minor attention. Von Müller, as senior officer, was charged not only with protecting the port but also implementing the contingency plans if war should begin. The captain was an adroit tactician, taking as his basis the probability of conflict with the 'Triple Entente' of Britain, France and Russia from 1st August 1914. He would not be far wrong.

In the absence of the remaining ships of the Kreuzergeschwader — the armoured cruisers *Scharnhorst* (flag) and *Gneisenau*, plus the light cruisers *Nürnberg* and *Leipzig*‡ — von Müller had little at his disposal other than the gunboat *Cormoran*, docked for extensive repair, and two large gunboats of the Iltis class. He told the river gunboats in China to scuttle, and their crews to return to Tsingtau; two additional 'Iltis' vessels were ordered back, as was the obsolescent torpedoboat *S90*. The old Austro-Hungarian cruiser *Kaiserin Elisabeth* subsequently arrived in Tsingtau roads, but could offer little offensive power.

Ordering two of the gunboats and *S90* to remain in Tsingtau at the disposal of the governor, Kapitän z.S. Meyer-Waldeck, von Müller slipped *Emden*'s moorings on the evening of 31st July. On the day Britain proclaimed war, 4th August 1914, the cruiser took the first prize to be gained by the Kaiserliche Marine in the First World War — the Russian mail steamer *Ryazan*.* It is at this point that Prinz Franz Joseph's story really begins.

* During the squall, *Emden* was struck by the Japanese merchantman *Kenkon Maru* and slightly damaged aft.

† Receiving the Königlichen Kronenorder, third class with swords.

‡ Detached on a visit to the Pacific Seaboard of the USA.

* Receiving the guns of the disarmed gunboat *Cormoran* and renamed *Cormoran* II. *Ryazan* subsequently served as an armed raider.

The *Emden* wardroom

Emden's captain, Karl Friedrich Max von Müller, son of Oberst Hugo von Müller and his wife Charlotte, had been born in Hannover on 16th July 1873. Hugo von Müller wished his son to follow him into the army and, after elementary education in the Gymnasia in Hannover and Kiel, young Karl entered the Kadettenanstalt at Plön in 1888.

In April 1891, however, Hugo von Müller permitted his son to take an unusual step from the army into the navy. After a sojourn on the schoolship *Stosch*, Fähnrich Karl von Müller embarked on the 'cruiser-frigate' *Gneisenau* for a lengthy cruise to the Americas. In October 1894, he was promoted Leutnant zur See and became the signals officer of the battleship *Baden* before transferring to her sister *Sachsen*. After serving as an officer of the watch on a selection of ships — the cadet-ship *Moltke*, the cruiser *Gefion*, the torpedo-schoolship *Blücher*, the Aviso *Blitz* and the coastal battleship *Aegir* — Karl von Müller was promoted Oberleutnant z.S. in April 1897 and posted to the small cruiser (Kleiner ungeschützeter Kreuzer) *Schwalbe*, which left Kiel on 20th April 1898 for Zanzibar and German East Africa.

Here von Müller caught the malaria that would trouble him for the rest of his life. He returned to Germany in 1900, becoming adjutant of I.Matrosen-Division (Kiel) before returning to sea as the second gunnery officer on the battleship *Kaiser Wilhelm II*. He was promoted Kapitänleutnant on 28th March 1903. After serving on the battleships *Kaiser Friedrich III* and *Kaiser Wilhelm der Grosse*, and after receiving the Roten Adlerorden (Order of the Red Eagle), fourth class, Karl von Müller was appointed to the staff of the fleet commander – Admiral Prinz Heinrich von Preussen, younger brother of Kaiser Wilhelm II – aboard the flagship *Deutschland*.

There is no doubt that von Müller, promoted Korvettenkapitän in December 1908, was rated highly by his immediate superiors – as a proliferation of testimonials proves. From 1909 to 1912 he was seconded to the Reichs-Marine-Amt in Berlin, where his abilities were noticed by no less a person than the redoubtable Admiral von Tirpitz. But what he appears to have really wanted was a sea-going command. Finally, he got his wish: the light cruiser *Emden*, berthed in Tsingtau.

After successfully shelling the Nanking forts during the rebellion of 1913, von Müller received the Königlichen Kronenorden (Royal Order of the Crown), third class with swords, in recognition of his ship's performance. During the last cruise of *Emden*, on 31st October 1914, he was awarded the first and second classes of the Eisernen Kreuz (Iron Cross). And finally, after returning home after incarceration in Malta and the Netherlands, von Müller was awarded the Pour le Mérite. Interestingly, the grant of Germany's highest gallantry award was hotly contested by superiors who regarded the attempt to cut the transoceanic cable at Direction Island as a risky mistake, and believed that *Emden* should have sunk with colours flying instead of being run aground. Eventually, however, the pro-Müller camp successfully refuted the charges jealously laid against him.

In the final analysis, the destruction of *Emden* owed much to luck and the presence of powerful warships escorting an undetected convoy a mere sixty miles from Direction Island. It was unfortunate that *Emden*'s most experienced gunlayers had gone ashore with the landing party, and that the funnel stays had been removed in anticipation of coaling. But neither occurrence had been crucial; the reserve gunlayers shot well enough in the early phases of the battle, until range-finding and fire-control equipment had been shot away, and the collapse of the funnels came only when the outcome was assured. *Sydney* was bigger, faster, better armoured and had more powerful guns. But for a miracle, *Emden* would always have been vanquished.

Karl von Müller was promoted Kapitän z.S. on 1st October 1918, but resigned his commission in January 1919 and retired to Blankenburg im Harz to court general's daughter Jutta von Hanstein.

In poor health, his malarial afflictions sharpened by his enforced captivity, Karl von Müller spent his last few years working for the good of not only his crew but also the local people. He died in Braunschweig on 11th March 1923, a few months short of his fiftieth birthday.

Excepting in his reconstructing the lost *Emden* log, and his official reports, von Müller never wrote a word about his experiences – repeatedly declining to make money from the blood of his dead crewmen.

This great concern may hold the key to the failure of a highly-rated officer, idolized by his men, to climb rapidly through the ranks even before the outbreak of the First World War. He was clearly a shrewd tactician, but virtually no clues to his true character survive. These Hohenzollern memoirs confirm the popular view that von Müller was withdrawn and probably very shy; he was rarely seen on deck, preferring the solitude of the captain's cabin or the businesslike atmosphere of the bridge. Socializing and daily dealings with the ship's company were left to the extrovert first officer, von Mücke.

'Fregattenkapitän v. Müller'. Müller, the gallant and courteous commander of *Emden*, was born in 1873 and died of pneumonia in Braunschweig in March 1923. This excellent three-quarter length sepia portrait, published by Friedr. O. Wolter ('FOW') of Berlin W35, was based on a Fechner original believed to date immediately prior to von Müller's departure to take command of *Emden* at Tsingtau. He wears the uniform of a Korvettenkapitän, a rank from which he was promoted in August 1913. By courtesy of The Lyon Press archives.

In an era where promotion could still depend on patrimony, favouritism and an aptitude for social graces, von Müller's quiet professionalism may simply have passed unnoticed. Yet it is ironic that, with some of the admirals and a submariner or two, he is now among the best-remembered Kaiserliche Marine officers.

Emden's first officer, Kurt Hellmuth von Mücke, was born into the minor nobility in Zwickau (Saxony), the son of Hauptmann Kurth von Mücke. He entered the navy in April 1900, accompanying the schoolship *Charlotte* to the Mediterranean, and had been promoted Fähnrich in April 1901. After serving on the battleship *Kaiser Friedrich III*, von Mücke became Leutnant z.S. in September 1903 and was posted as officer of the watch to the light cruiser *Nymphe*. Thereafter, his rise to prominence was rapid: Oberleutnant z.S. in 1904, first officer of 3.Torpedoboots-Reserve-Halbflottille in 1907, then flag-lieutenant to the admiral commanding the Aufklärungsstreitkräfte in 1908. After receiving the Königlichen Kronenorden (Royal Order of the Crown), fourth class, Hellmuth von Mücke took command of the torpedoboat *S149* in 1910. Then came a staff appointment, and a posting to *Emden* as navigating officer (Autumn 1913) and ultimately first officer in the Spring of 1914.

'Kapitänleutnant von Mücke': first officer of *Emden*, commander of the landing party abandoned on Direction Island as the warship sailed out to do battle with HMAS *Sydney* on 9th November 1914. This excellent half-length sepia portrait – arms folded, Mücke sits in an armchair – was published *c.*1915 by 'NPG' (no.5902), from an original photograph by Ferdinand Urbahns. By courtesy of The Lyon Press archives.

Prinz Franz Joseph, pictured in 1925 in the Gala Uniform of a Oberleutnant zur See. This portrait accompanied the original *Emden* book; the original is now lost, however, the version here seemingly being a reproduction from the book-plate!

By courtesy of Meinrad, Prinz von Hohenzollern-Emden.

Von Mücke served his captain loyally through the cruiser's last campaign; when the time came for the last fight, however, he was ashore on Direction Island with the landing party. While *Emden* was being battered by HMAS *Sydney*, von Mücke coolly organized his defences; but the Australians did not appear, so he seized the 97-ton trading barquentine *Ayesha* to embark upon an epic journey – across the Indian Ocean and up the Arabian Peninsula, eventually reaching Constantinople on 23rd May 1915. The story of the *Ayesha* and the trek back to Germany is told graphically in many of von Mücke's postwar books; it is no less absorbing than that of the *Emden*, but less dramatic. However, as von Mücke returned to Germany well before the survivors of the last battle, he reaped the lion's share of rewards and the benefit of publicity.

Awarded the Eisernen Kreuz (Iron Cross) first class, together with the Saxon Militär-St.-Heinrich-Orden, the Bavarian Militärverdienstorden fourth class and a gold medal from the Hamburg-Seefahrt-Verein, Hellmuth von Mücke seemed assured of a glittering career. But his extrovert personality, so perfect a foil for von Müller's courtly reserve aboard *Emden*, was to prove his undoing; too many diplomats had been antagonized by what they saw as meddlesome assessments of the Turkish situation, while naval circles disliked von Mücke's flair for self-promotion.

Von Mücke had been posted to command 15.Torpedoboots-Halbflotille in June 1915, and then packed off to command the Euphrates gunboat flotilla in January 1916. Returning to an inconsequential staff appointment in Germany in the autumn, he was dispatched again in March 1917 to command the Donau-Halbflotille. After a spell as navigating officer aboard *Derfflinger*, he commanded I.Abteilung der II.Torpedoboots-Division from May 1918 until the end of the war. Shortly after the Armistice, he was finally promoted Korvettenkapitän.

Von Mücke, never short of opinions, then ventured into extreme right-wing politics to form the 'Mücke-Bund' in Saxony (1919) before flirting with national socialism. However, he objected to the personality cult that built up around Adolf Hitler – a nice irony – and soon broke with the movement to fund his political trilogy *Linie* with colourful 'Emden' lecture tours. Only the first part of the magnum opus, *Revolution, Nationalsozialismus und Bürgertum* (1931), was ever published. Its author soon drifted farther into the realms of unreality, a situation the death of a son in Russia in February 1943 did nothing to inhibit. Hellmuth von Mücke died in Ahrensburg/Holstein in 1957, unnoticed and largely unmourned excepting by his American-born wife and four surviving children.

On the eve of war, *Emden* carried nineteen officers. Von Müller and von Mücke presided over Kapitänleutnants Hans Gropius (navigating officer) and Ernst Gaede (gunnery); Oberleutnants z.S. Robert Witthoeft (torpedos), Ernst von

The 4,362-tonne 130m-long small cruiser *Cöln*, commissioned in June 1911, is seen here in the Kaiser-Wilhelm-Kanal. Built by Germaniawerft of Kiel, she carried twelve 10.5cm guns and could make 26 knots. The good-quality photo-card, published by Postkarten-Vereinigung of Rendsburg (no.96), was sent to Kiel in August 1934 but clearly comes from a pre-1914 negative. The cruiser was sunk at the Battle of Heligoland Bight. By courtesy of The Lyon Press archives.

Levetzow and August Geerdes; Oberleutnant z.S. d.R. Julius Lauterbach; Leutnants z.S. Albert von Guérard, Erich Fikentscher, Fritz Zimmermann, Prinz Franz Joseph von Hohenzollern and Robin Schall; the four engineers under Marineoberingenieur Ellerbroeck; surgeon Johannes Luther; and Marineoberzahlmeister Arthur Woytschekowsky. The total complement stood at 369 German sailors, plus three Chinese laundrymen.

Many adjustments were made to the complement between July and November 1914, with the attachment of reservists and the detachment of prize crews; at one time, indeed, the crew mustered over 400. After the detachment of prize crews and the Direction Island landing party, however, only 313 German sailors, the officers' cook (a civilian volunteer) and three Chinese washermen faced HMAS *Sydney* in the final skirmish.

The later cruisers

The loss of *Emden*, comprehensively outgunned by HMAS *Sydney*, was no surprise. Even before the war, some German experts had argued that a typical kleiner Kreuzer was far better armed with six 15cm guns than the classical ten or twelve 10.5cm SK C/88. It was not that the 10.5cm gun was poor — sixteen rounds a minute could be fired to 12,200 metres, outranging older British 6-inch guns — but simply that a 10.5cm shell was not heavy enough to deal with the armoured cruisers *Emden* would encounter in a colonial campaign against the Royal Navy.

The debate had not prevented the four ships of the Kolberg class, authorized in Fiscal Year 1906/7, from carrying anything more than an additional pair of 10.5cm guns amidships. *Kolberg, Mainz, Cöln* and *Augsburg* displaced 4,362 tonnes on a waterline length of 130 metres but, though substantially bigger than *Dresden* and *Emden*, they offered no real increase in offensive power. The additional displacement was used to increase power, *Mainz*, the fastest, touching 27.2 knots on trial. *Cöln* and *Mainz* were blown apart in the Battle of Heligoland Bight (28th August 1914), bravely facing British battle-cruisers against which their light armour and puny guns were no protection, but their sisters survived the war.

The Magdeburg class superficially offered little but additional size — 4,535-4,570 tonnes, 136 metres on the waterline — but the incorporation of far better armour protection into the structure of the ship was a considerable technical achievement, even though it delayed completion of the ships until 1912. *Magdeburg* was destroyed after running aground on the Baltic island of Odensholm on 26th August 1914; *Breslau*, having been sold to the Turkish navy, was mined off Imbros on 20th January 1918. *Strassburg* and *Stralsund* survived the First World War, the former being ceded to the Italian Regia Marina. Scuttled at La Spezia in September 1943, she was raised only to be sunk again a year later.

The two ships of the Karlsruhe class, authorized under the 1910 programme, were essentially similar to the Magdeburgs. Displacing 4,900 tonnes on a waterline length of 139 metres, they still mounted twelve SK C/88 10.5cm guns. *Karlsruhe*, under the command of Fregattenkapitän Otto Köhler, had a most successful raiding career — but an inglorious end in an accidental magazine explosion on 4th November 1914.† *Rostock* had to be scuttled on 1st June 1916, disabled by a torpedo-hit amidships during the Battle of Jutland.

Graudenz and *Regensburg* were three-funnel ships built under the 1911 programme. Driven by turbines, these 4,912-tonne cruisers were fast — achieving more than 29 knots in shallow-water acceptance trials and undoubtedly capable of exceeding thirty in favourable conditions. They initially carried twelve 10.5cm and two 5cm guns, plus two torpedo-tubes, but were subsequently re-armed with seven 15cm SK L/45 and two 8.8cm anti-aircraft guns.

Excepting two sequestered cruisers building for Russia in the Schichau shipyard when war was declared,‡ and the two fast minelayer-cruisers of the Bremse class commissioned in 1918, the remaining kleine Kreuzer followed the pattern set by *Graudenz*. However, all received 15cm guns at the outset.

The two ships of the 5,180-tonne Wiesbaden class — *Wiesbaden*, sunk at Jutland in 1916, and *Frankfurt*, destroyed in US bombing tests in July 1921 — were followed by four ships, authorized under the 1913 programme. These were eventually named after famous raiders sunk earlier in the war: *Königsberg, Karlsruhe, Nürnberg*... and *Emden*.

† At a position 11°07'N, 55°25'W.

‡ These were the first to receive 15cm guns, which were substituted for the original 13cm Russian pattern.

Emden II, built by AG 'Weser' of Bremen, was laid down in 1914, launched on 1st February 1916 and commissioned on 16th December 1916. She was much larger than her illustrious predecessor, displacing 5,440 tonnes on a waterline measuring nearly 146 metres, and carried eight 15cm guns. Her twin-shaft navy turbines could drive her at about 29 knots. Owing to the exigencies of war, however, no deep-water speed trials were ever run.

Among the most distinctive features of *Emden* II was the Eisernen Kreuz (Iron Cross) carried proudly on the bow in memory of Karl von Müller and his gallant crew. In contrast with the heroics of the original *Emden*, the new cruiser's war was to pass without incident. After serving the Scouting Forces, *Emden* II was surrendered with the High Seas Fleet and was interned in Scapa Flow.

On 25th March 1919, she became the flagship of Konteradmiral Ludwig von Reuter after a near-mutiny on the fleet flagship *Friedrich der Grosse*. Consequently, the famous order to scuttle came from *Emden* II in June 1919. The ship herself was successfully beached in a sinking condition. Given to the French as war reparation, *Emden* II had suffered too greatly to resume active service and was instead expended in trials of explosives and armour-plate. The hulk was broken up at Caen in 1926, less than a year after *Emden* III had been commissioned into the Reichsmarine.

The Königsberg II class was the penultimate pattern of the Imperial Kleine Kreuzer, being succeeded only by the 5,620-tonne Cöln II ships. Only two of these were completed, though all but three of the ten vessels planned had been launched before the Armistice. 'Ersatz Emden',* had been laid-down in the AG 'Weser' shipyard in 1915, but was never launched; what remained of the hull was broken up on the slipway in 1921.

* Before names had been allocated, German warships were known by the name of the vessel they were to replace. Thus 'Ersatz Emden' simply signified 'replacement (or substitute) for *Emden*'.

Emden's achievements

The immolation of the ship was no more than her crew had expected since the opening day of war; a detached cruiser, alone in the Pacific Ocean, would not survive for long when Tsingtau was so obviously indefensible. Quite apart from seizure of so many prizes, however, the shipping lanes had been threatened seriously enough to discourage trade; convoy duty had drawn many ships away from more valuable tasks elsewhere; and a veritable fleet of British, French, Australian and Japanese warships had been set against one small German cruiser.

The last cruise of *Emden* excited such great interest that von Müller and his crew were almost as well known in Britain as they were in Germany; indeed, during the early weeks of the cruise — certainly up to the shelling of Madras and the incursion into Penang harbour — the *Emden* was probably better known in the British Empire than in her native land. With characteristic regard for the underdog, many Britons were sorry that the final battle exacted such a terrible toll among von Müller's crew. In London, *The Times* recorded:

'... that the *Emden* finally found her inevitable end was received in this country with great relief ... Since the first September days when the *Emden* appeared in the Gulf of Bengal, her daring and enterprising actions have shown her to possess attributes which people with England's naval tradition must admire. Cut off from all logistical support

Built by AG 'Weser' of Bremen, displacing 4,535 tonnes and capable of more than 27 knots, SMS *Magdeburg* was commissioned in August 1912. On 26th August 1914, she ran aground on Odensholm Island in the Baltic and was partially destroyed by firing the magazines. However, the Russians managed to salvage the code-books and German security was compromised for some time. This interesting sepia/black duotone mezzotint — 'S.M. geschützter Kreuzer Magdeburg' — was published by 'G&M' (Gravuryt 64544) in 1913. By courtesy of The Lyon Press archives.

Emden II was built by AG 'Weser', Bremen (yard no.211), and commissioned in December 1916. Displacing 5,440 tonnes and capable of about 27½ knots, she is seen here steaming to surrender on 26th November 1918. She was partially scuttled in Scapa Flow on 21st June 1919, while acting as the flagship of Admiral Ludwig von Reuter, but was soon salvaged. Ceded to France as war reparations and expended as a target, the remnants of the once-proud ship went to the breakers at Caen in 1926. By courtesy of the Trustees of the Imperial War Museum, London; negative Q 19307.

and with poor prospects of gathering supplies, the *Emden* travelled alone on the wide oceans of the world. Her destiny was an honourable fight for existence. She lead it with a daring which friend and foe alike had to acknowledge. If she ran out of coal, she caught a coal ship; if she required provisions, she fetched them from merchant ships on the high seas. Nevertheless, there is no charge of violence that can be held against her. As reported, Commander von Müller treated the crews of his captured ships nobly and even-handedly. At no time did he destroy human life unnecessarily. As far as is known, he strictly obeyed and observed the code of international law. At Madras, he let his crew fire only on oil tanks and the fort... We are pleased that the cruiser *Emden* was finally destroyed, but we acknowledge Commander von Müller as a valiant and chivalrous adversary. We hope that his life was spared, for should he come to London, we would prepare for him a rousing welcome. Our sea-faring nation knows how to admire a daring and resourceful seaman, and there are few events in the new history of sea warfare which are more remarkable than the bright career of the little *Emden*.'

Even the notoriously jingoist and xenophobic weekly, *The War Illustrated* (21st November 1914), grudgingly admitted that:

'The captain of the Emden was a foeman whose daring excited the admiration of the entire world, and his reputation is untarnished by any act of barbarity... He acted the part of a sportsman and a gentleman in his conduct of war, and the British attitude towards him shows that, while we object to barbarism in warfare, we pay tribute to gallantry.'

The singularly unpleasant task of burying the German dead was left to crewmen of HMS *Cadmus*, whereafter mementoes from the wreck were conveyed to London. In January 1915, after a visit to the wreck by HMS *Pioneer* and advice from the Admiralty, *Cadmus* was ordered back to North Keeling Island to salvage two safes and at a least one gun. On 9th February 1915, Admiral Jerram reported to London that *Cadmus* had recovered £500-worth of Mexican dollars, two guns and their mountings, a searchlight and a torpedo from the wreck.

At least one of the guns was subsequently displayed in London, but was apparently returned to Australia after 1918. One gun is now owned by the Australian War Memorial in Canberra, while the other stands in Hyde Park, Sydney, to commemorate not only the German dead but also the five sailors who died on HMAS *Sydney*. One of the *Emden* builder's plates, taken from the wreck by *Cadmus*, was presented to President Hindenburg by the Australian High Commissioner in London in 1932; this survived the Second World War to grace the wardrooms of *Emden*s IV and V. Indeed, the Officers' Mess of *Emden* IV was nicknamed 'Die Kaiserliche Werft' owing to the positioning of the original builder's plate near the doorway.

Emden achieved what no surface warship was ever to achieve again. Once wireless telegraphy grew out of its infancy, as it was so soon to do, no longer would endless ocean guarantee immunity from pursuers equipped as primitively as the quarry.

In his last cruise of merely fourteen weeks, von Müller achieved infinitely more than Korvettenkapitän Lüdecke, the timid commander of *Emden*'s sister-ship *Dresden*, remembered more for running than fighting; more than Max Looff of *Königsberg*, with his curious demise in an African backwater; and more even than the captain of *Karlsruhe*, Otto Köhler, who — despite costing the Allies nearly eighty thousand tons of shipping — remains in ill-merited anonymity by the nature of his destruction.

By 1915, however, it had been realized that light cruisers made poor commerce raiders; though they had speed and adequate offensive power, they lacked the endurance needed to tramp many thousands of miles in search of prey. Prinz Franz Joseph's recollections constantly underscore the great debt owed to colliers such as *Markomannia* and *Buresk*, and to the efforts of German agents to organize coal supplies worldwide. Good coal was essential, otherwise efficiency was severely compromised, tell-tale smoke was emitted by the funnels and furnace-hearths clogged.

The initial desire to convert passenger liners also proved to be a mistake. Though many were very fast — *Kaiser Wilhelm der Grosse* and *Kronprinz Wilhelm* had each once held the Blue Riband — they consumed fuel profligately, presented huge targets and mustered large crews.

Colonial gunboats were too old, too slow and too weakly armed to achieve much, so merchantmen were converted for commerce raiding. By selecting modern cargo vessels, the navy gained strength, comparatively small size, extraordinarily economical engines and thoroughly anonymous appearance. The ships were fast enough to overhaul many British merchantmen and sufficiently powerful to take on small warships on an equal footing.† Thus the exploits of *Möwe* and *Wolf* — commanded by Nikolaus von Dohna-Schlodien and Karl-August Nerger respectively — owed much to the 'Emden Tradition', though never reaching such spectacular heights. Possibly the most glamorous of the later raiders was *Seeadler*, formerly the Clyde built full-rigger *Pass of Balmaha*, which enjoyed a successful cruise under the enthusiastic command of Graf Felix von Luckner before coming to grief in a gale.

† *Wolf* carried no less than seven 15cm guns, four 50cm torpedo tubes, 465 mines, and three 5.2cm guns to arm auxiliaries. *Leopard* was armed with five 15cm and four 8.8cm guns, plus two 50cm torpedo tubes. However, not all the ships were fast: though *Kaiser Wilhelm der Grosse* and *Kronprinz Wilhelm* were both capable of 22-23 knots in their prime, *Wolf* could only attain a little over ten!

1 Commander of the raider *Möwe*, Korvettenkapitän (later Kapitän z.S.) Nikolaus, Burggraf und Graf zu Dohna-Schlodien was one of the more famous German mariners of the First World War. Born in 1879, he died in 1956. This excellent half-length portrait was published by 'N.N.' (no.70/125) from an original photograph by Kloppmann.

2 'Führer des Hilfskreuzers "Seeadler"...' Felix, Graf von Luckner was born in Dresden on 9th June 1891. A turret commander aboard SMS *Kronprinz* at the Battle of Jutland, Luckner went on to command the raider *Seeadler*. Remaining in the service of the Reichsmarine in postwar years, when he commanded the sail-training ship *Niobe*, von Luckner died in Malmö on 13th April 1966. This good-quality oval sepia half-length photo-card was published by 'NPG' (no.6214) from an original by 'Ferd. Urbahns Hofphot.', Kiel.

3 Kapitänleutnant Lothar von Arnauld de la Perière, 'Erfolgreicher Kommandant des Tauchbootes "U 35" versenkte 126 Schiffe, Wert 450 Millionen Mark'. Of French Huguenot ancestry, von Arnauld de la Perière was born in Posen on 18th March 1886 and retired from the Reichsmarine in 1931 having, amongst other duties, commanded the cruiser *Emden* III. He was recalled at the beginning of the Second World War, becoming senior naval officer in occupied western France, but died in an air crash at Le Bourget (Paris) on 24th February 1941. He remains the most successful submarine ace of all time; this half- length portrait photo-card was published by 'NPG' (no.6007) from an original by Hänse Herrmann, Berlin. By courtesy of The Lyon Press archives.

Postscript

The first cruiser to be built for the Reichsmarine under the provisions of the Treaty of Versailles‡ was named *Emden* as a mark of respect for the tradition of the original ship. Of all the exploits of the Kaiserliche Marine in the First World War, none excited public imagination outside the Reich in quite the same way. The Eisernen Kreuz (Iron Cross) had been granted to the crew of submarine *U9* after the sinking of four British armoured cruisers, but most Anglo-Americans saw the exploits of the German submariners as cowardly rather than chivalrous.

The design of *Emden* III reflected pre-1918 origins; but for two funnels rather than three, she bore a considerable resemblance to the 1916-vintage *Emden* II. Laid down in the Wilhelmshaven dockyard on 8th December 1921, *Emden* III was launched early in January 1925 and commissioned on 15th October under the command of Kapitän z.S. Lothar von Arnauld de la Perière — the famous First World War submarine ace, and a one-time member of the original *Emden* crew on the Chinese Station. She displaced 6,056 tonnes on a waterline measuring 150.5 metres, and carried eight 15cm L/45 guns in single shielded mountings permitting a maximum elevation of 40°.

Introduced during a time of peace, and under the watchful eye of the Allies, *Emden* III was a compromise within the displacement limits of the Treaty of Versailles. In a naval sense she was not particularly successful, being under-gunned and unable to bring more than six of her eight 15cm guns to bear abeam. With a maximum speed of about 29 knots, she was appreciably slower than the contemporary British and French designs. But as a symbol of the best German naval tradition she had no peer.

Emden III spent most of the period before 1939 on training duties, undertaking nine protracted cruises during one of which, it is said, a crewman was eaten by a lion. Typical of her wanderings had been a trip to the Far East... and North Keeling

‡ The few ships permitted the Reichswehr could only be replaced after completing 25 years' service. Thus *Emden* III was originally known as 'Ersatz Niobe', *Niobe* — commissioned in June 1900 — being the oldest of the Reichsmarine cruisers and thus replaceable after June 1925.

1

2

3

1

2

3

Island, where, on 16th March 1927, Kapitän z.S. von Arnauld de la Perière sent a message to the city of Emden: 'Over the grave of the first *Emden* we stand in silence in honour of you, the sponsor'. Soundings were also taken in the Pacific Ocean, 'Emden Deep' (10,497 metres) remaining on the charts until replaced in post-1945 days by 'Johnson Deep' marking a marginally deeper sounding by an American submarine.

At the outbreak of war in 1939, *Emden* II was considered for the role of a commerce raider. Her distinctive profile and comparatively weak main armament did not suit her to the role, however, and the task eventually fell to converted merchantmen just as it had done in the First World War.

There was a particularly poignant twist to the story. The first HMAS *Sydney*, conqueror of *Emden* I had gone to the breakers in 1929, eventually to be replaced by another cruiser of the same name: *Sydney* II, a member of the three-ship Perth class, was completed in September 1935. Displacing 6,830 tons when built, about 563 feet overall and capable of 32½ knots, she carried eight 6-inch and four 4-inch guns, plus eight torpedo tubes. On 19th November 1941 *Sydney* encountered a suspicious merchantman that proved to be 'Raider G', formerly the Hamburg-Amerika-Linie motorship *Steiermark* and otherwise known as HSK 8 or *Kormoran* – the name adopted by the first prize *Emden* I had taken in the First World War.

Kormoran caught the Australian cruiser by surprise, torpedoing her abreast of 'A' and 'B' turrets. As the outwardly peaceable vessel also had six 15cm guns, *Sydney* was all but overwhelmed before she could retaliate. Eventually, the cruiser drifted away, exploded and sank with all hands; *Kormoran*, fatally damaged, foundered shortly afterwards with the loss of eighty of her company. And another chapter had been written in the saga begun in 1914.

Equally ironically, *Emden* III sustained the first Kriegsmarine fatalities of the Second World War. In an air attack on Wilhelmshaven shortly after the declaration of war in September 1939, a Blenheim bomber crashed onto the ship's deck while she was anchored in the Jade. Eleven men were killed.

After participating in the invasion of Norway and the opening stages of Operation 'Barbarossa', when more than six hundred shells were fired at shore targets, *Emden* III was seconded to the training flotilla in the Baltic and remained comparatively inactive until the winter of 1944-5. But she was to have a curious demise.

---

1 'Emden. Neuer Hafen mit Kreuzer "Emden"...', a souvenir photo-card celebrating a courtesy visit to the cruiser's home town. Published by Verlag Paul Andreas, Bremen (no.481), it is postmarked 'Emden (Ostfriesland). 4.4.30'. The design of *Emden*'s masts shows that the original photograph was taken after 1926.

2
3 Two views of *Emden* III. The upper photograph was taken on 11th November 1934, showing the rebuilt cruiser leaving port for an overseas cruise. Note the reduction of the mainmast, and that wireless aerials have been added to the after funnel. The second view – a blue/black duotone card 'Kreuzer "Emden". Geschwindigkeit 29 Seemeilen, Länge 150,5 m, Breite 14,3 m, Tiefgang 5,3 m, Wasserverdrängung 5400 t' – was published in *c.*1936 by Hans Andres of Hamburg, no.K9551.

Firmly in the 'Emden Tradition', Panzerschiff *Admiral Graf Spee* began her commerce-raiding exploits almost as soon as the Second World War had begun. However, after the Battle of the River Plate (13th December 1939) *Graf Spee* was sufficiently damaged by her British opponents – the cruisers *Exeter*, *Achilles* and *Ajax* – to put into Montevideo for repairs, succour for her wounded and burial for sixty dead. Built by the Reichswerft, Wilhelmshaven and armed with six 28cm guns in two triple turrets she had been commissioned on 6th January 1936. Though the three 'pocket battleships' nominally displaced 10,000 US long tons in accord with the restrictions of the Treaty of Versailles, all were overweight: *Graf Spee*, the heaviest as built, displaced about 14,890 tonnes dwl. Showing the arms of the Spee family to good advantage, this photograph was taken during the fleet review of 1938. By courtesy of The Lyon Press archives. **4**

1

These four stamps issued by the Cocos (Keeling) Islands, with the First Day Cover, commemorate the 75th anniversary of the final battle. By courtesy of the Cocos (Keeling) Islands Philatelic Bureau and PCS, Toorak, Victoria. 1

In September 1944, *Emden* III was ordered back to the Skagerrak from the Baltic, but ran aground while navigating Oslofjord on 9th December and was diverted to the Schichau yard in Königsberg. Arriving on Christmas Day, she immediately docked. By 21st January, with repairs incomplete and the Russians less than thirty miles from Königsberg, a desperate plan to tow the ship to Pillau was mooted. On 23rd January, thanks to superhuman efforts but weighed down with a thousand refugees and the stone coffin of Paul von Hindenburg, *Emden* III was towed slowly away from Königsberg under the command of Kapitän z.S. Wolfgang Kähler. The engines were reassembled in Pillau, Gotenhafen was gained on 30th January and the main guns were speedily re-mounted.

On 2nd February, able to steam at no more than ten knots even though offensive capacity had been restored, *Emden* III escorted a flotilla of smaller boats westward to Kiel – a short journey that, in the unfavourable circumstances, took four days. *Emden* III was so severely damaged in an air-raid in April that she had to be beached in Heikendorfer Bay. The wreck was blown up on 3rd May 1945, and broken up soon after the end of hostilities.

This picture, allegedly showing *Emden* (far right) at Nanking in August 1913, appeared in Karl Bartz's book *Der Kommandant der Emden* in 1939. However, few of the ships visible tally with information given by Lochner and a precise date of the photograph may be questioned. Close examination suggests that the two vessels visible to the left may be the Japanese cruisers *Tsushima* and *Niitaka*; then an Iltis-class gunboat – possibly *Luchs* – outboard of a British cruiser of the Pelorus class; what appears to be a small three-funnel ship (but is actually at least two small craft moored together); and then *Emden* 2

THE FIRST PRIZE

Wednesday 29th July – Wednesday 5th August 1914

On 29th June 1914, we received the fateful telegram telling us that Archduke Franz Ferdinand of Austria, heir to the throne, and his consort, the Duchess of Hohenberg, had been murdered in Sarajevo.

None of us in Tsingtau immediately thought of a European conflict, even though few of us believed that Austria-Hungary would let such a Serbian outrage pass unnoticed. We naturally spent the succeeding days in constant suspense, descending eagerly upon the dispatches from home as they arrived. But we still lived peaceably, with little thought of war.

Aboard *Emden*, we exercised our guns and torpedoes continually; new hands had to be thoroughly familiarized with their duties. For us officers, those weeks were filled with variety. Bathing was popular in off-duty moments, and we practised swimming wholeheartedly. The time was also enlivened by entertainment; we were much in demand ashore, and threw many cheerful parties aboard in return. The ship made a perfect setting in the summer weather.

Our original intention had been to proceed to Shanghai during July, and thence to guardship duties in the Yangtsekiang. Those of us who did not yet know the Yangtse – most of us, indeed – looked forward to new places to see and new tricks to learn. On 7th July 1914, however, everything changed and we received orders to remain in Tsingtau. At first we were aghast at this news, unexpected and unwanted as it was, but it was obvious that higher authorities did not regard our situation as free from danger.

Service duties increased perceptibly, 'Action stations' and 'Clear ship for action' frequently being on the orders of the day. The whole ship's company had to be honed until it was fit for action at any time – day or night. Though this had always been the case aboard a warship, new hands needed extra work to gain the experience of practised crewmen. Only by seemingly endless repetition could this be achieved with certainty.

In the middle of our work, a surprise appeared in the form of the Austro-Hungarian cruiser *Kaiserin Elisabeth*. This was clearly no mere act of courtesy. Our ally was seeking shelter and support in the company of a friendly ship. She was particularly wary of the offensive power of the Russian fleet, as Russia had always played patron to the Slav states and regularly influenced the

Tsingtau, prior to 1914. From Karl Bartz, *Der Kommandant der Emden*, Berlin 1939.

This picture of *Emden* in her pre-1914 tropical colours – white hull, buff uppers — shows the elegant lines that earned her the sobriquet 'Swan of the East'. By courtesy of the Australian War Memorial, Canberra; negative A3683.

foreign policy of the countries concerned. Austria-Hungary had been a brake on the expansion of Greater Russia from time immemorial; now it seemed likely that Russia would delight in the removal of such an obstacle. The political situation in the Balkans would give Russia the opportunity to interfere.

The arrival of our ally in Tsingtau roadstead gave us a new excuse for hearty festivities. There were many friendly exchanges between ships, and cordial relations were soon established among the officers. We motored to the Laushan mountains and Mecklenburg House together, or out into the beautiful countryside surrounding Tsingtau. In addition, we were all guests at galas organized by the Tsingtau garrison.

But the gaiety could not blind us to the burgeoning political uncertainty. Our commanding officer, Korvettenkapitän von Müller, and his faithful adjutant, Leutnant z.S. von Guérard, were constantly in touch with both the high command in Berlin and the Kreuzergeschwader, cruising the South Seas. This was vitally important, as *Emden* acted as a 'home news' relay station for the remainder of the squadron.

As the European political situation continued to change, Serbia – supported by Russia – maintained a stand against Austria-Hungary, who fell back on an ultimatum. Germany stood by to assist Emperor Franz Joseph should Russia attack.

We received the news that Austria-Hungary had declared war on Serbia on 29th July. If there was still no 'pressing danger of war' for Germany, it remained the duty of our commanding officer (senior officer of the Kreuzergeschwader in the absence of Admiral von Spee) to prepare for the possibility of war by mobilizing all our resources to equip and maintain the squadron.

Late in the evening of 29th July, our captain received a telegram from Berlin telling him of the escalating conflict. A council-of-war was held aboard *Emden* on 30th July, involving all the officers commanding ships in Tsingtau roadstead. Among the decisions were that the specially chartered collier *Elsbeth* should be prepared as soon as possible for the impending Kreuzergeschwader cruise into the South Seas, and then proceed to Yap. The gunboat *Cormoran*, docked for repair, was to be overhauled with greatest possible speed.

Korvettenkapitän Sachse, commanding the gunboat *Iltis*, was ordered to place the Tsingtau dockyard on war footing immediately. Owing to the imminent danger of war, the navigating officer of *Tiger*, Oberleutnant z.S. Baumaken, was to be despatched to Batavia as base officer. Gunboats *Jaguar* and *Luchs*, plus the torpedo-boat *S.90*,* were to be placed at the disposal of the governor of Tsingtau to maintain the security of the roadstead and the harbour. The commanding officer of *Jaguar*, Korvettenkapitän Luring, on secondment in Shanghai, was to reorganize our naval base there; and a roster of gunboats was devised to protect the auxiliary cruisers.

We did not remain idle during this period, as we had to unship all articles defined by Paragraph 'A' – principally things that would be a handicap to fighting the ship efficiently: light flammable goods such as clothes and linen, for example, or toiletries and personal effects.

On 30th July, our officers were all called into the captain's cabin to enable Kapitän von Müller to explain the political situation. Soon a shore party had been told-off to the telegraph office to facilitate the dispatch of telegrams.

On 31st July came a telegram announcing political tension between the Central European Powers and the 'Triple Entente' – Britain, France and Russia. At the same time, the Admiralty ordered Tsingtau depot to ship ten thousand tons of coal to the Kreuzergeschwader. It was up to us to organize transport, so we landed all items listed under Paragraph 'B'. As this meant carpets, curtains and wooden furniture, our creature-comforts reduced dramatically. Cruisers on foreign stations invariably carry more equipment than home-station sisters, and anything that might splinter or burn dangerously now had to be stowed below the armoured deck or sent ashore.

Considerable additional effort on our part was needed to comply with our orders, especially as gunnery officer Gaede claimed part of the ship's company to take in ammunition while those of us in the torpedo department strove to secure our warheads. Provisions and coal were loaded from the dockside, where our first officer, Kapitänleutnant von Mücke, had work and worry to spare.

The work was completed almost as though it were play. *Kaiserin Elisabeth* had made fast alongside No.1 Mole to land her superfluous fittings, while *Elsbeth* filled her holds with the coal for the Kreuzergeschwader. Ashore, Tsingtau garrison parties could be seen guarding our possessions until they could be moved under cover in the dockyard.

We were now clear; steam was raised in the boilers, ready-use ammunition was brought up to the guns and the torpedo warheads were attached. These tasks all required the utmost precision.

Finally, we retrieved several members of the ship's company from their convalescence in the base hospital. We were ready for action at last.

Our commanding officer had decided to sail on 31st July, to avoid any blockade hostile warships should mount. We received his order to be clear for sea by 1900hrs. Punctually, we cast off from the coaling wharf of the Kaiserliche Werft, Tsingtau, and steamed southward in company with *Elsbeth*. We had hardly left harbour when the call 'Clear ship for action' was given by drum and bugle. Great was our suspense; we had been conditioned to expect that hostile ships would accost us as soon as we left Tsingtau. Were we now threatened with a premature demise?

As nothing untoward happened, we assumed the alarm was a precaution. Only later did we learn that Admiral Jerram, commanding the Royal Navy's East

* This vessel had been officially become 'T.90' prior to the First World War, but there is no evidence that the Kreuzergeschwader ever bothered with the new designation.

The gunboat SMS *Tiger*, seen here in white, was built by the Kaiserliche Werft, Danzig, and commissioned in April 1900. Displacing 894 tonnes and capable of about fourteen knots, she was scuttled off Tsingtau on 29th October 1914. By courtesy of WZ-Bilddienst, Wilhelmshaven; photograph KM 10248.

Asiatic Squadron, had indeed intended to cruise in open formation outside Tsingtau and seize any of our ships he encountered. This had always been a possibility, as his ships were then lying off Weihaiwei, the British protectorate north-eastward of Tsingtau. What a rich prize the Royal Navy would have gained, as the greater part of the Kreuzergeschwader's colliers and supply-ships lay in Tsingtau. Happily, we had an involuntary ally in Winston Churchill, the First Lord of the Admiralty. Churchill ordered the British squadron to assemble in Hong Kong, whence it was to proceed southward against us. This bought us time we could not otherwise enjoy.

In addition to the dispositions of the Royal Navy, we had also to consider that the French squadron – the armoured cruisers *Montcalm* and *Dupleix*, plus some torpedo-boats – may be steaming from Vladivostok to Weihaiwei. There were more than enough hostile ships to make things unpleasant for us!

We were not seen, however, and steamed away southward. Nightfall brought 'war watches', set at the guns, searchlights and torpedo-tubes. The other watches turned into their hammocks fully clad and were, moreover, so placed that they could reach their 'Clear ship' stations quickly. Special lookouts were distributed between the positions on the masts, captain's bridge and after superstructure, to give notice of anything suspicious. Some posts were supervised by officers to ensure that a specially sharp watch would be kept. We subsequently called these 'full war watches' to distinguish them from 'light war watches' introduced during our cruise. It was hard work for everybody, for there were but two watches rather than the normal four.

At about 2100 we parted with *Elsbeth*, laying our course for the Quelpart island.† Here we intended to cruise until the political situation gelled, though we remained in regular contact with Tsingtau's wireless station and constantly agitated for information.

Our first night at sea was undisturbed and the ensuing day – 1st August – was similarly uneventful. Lively wireless conversation was monitored, however, from which we gathered that British warships must be nearby. A sharp lookout had to be kept, and so officers were ordered up to the mast-top positions. I was stationed in the maintop, which was no sinecure at speed: streams of soot-flakes, or 'stokers' as we called them, were drawn from the funnels with the smoke and continually interfered with vision. We scanned the horizon in vain, seeking tell-tale smoke or the masts of hostile ships.

We wished to get well away from the shipping lanes from Weihaiwei to Shanghai, steaming all the farther eastward. Little of note occurred, as most of the ship's company was employed in the conversion of our ammunition from its practice state to battleworthiness. But early in the evening of 1st August we received a wireless message telling us that Germany had ordered mobilization.

Uncertainty was at an end; this news was synonymous with the declaration of war. Excitement aboard *Emden* reached fever pitch. There could be no doubt that France and Russia were our enemies, but whether Britain would also participate remained an open question.

2nd August was a Sunday. Once the conversion of the ammunition had been completed, Divine Service was held. Then the command 'All hands aft' presaged a speech from Kapitän von Müller, telling us of the mobilization and emphasizing that he expected from the ship's company the performance of its duty to the bitter end – so that, after the war, each of us would be able to hold our heads 'proudly before the War Lord'. We then gave three enthusiastic cheers for the Kaiser. The ship's company was allowed a pause to recover from the strain of the opening phases of our cruise, but it was back to full war watches in the evening and throughout the night.

The morning of 3rd August brought news of the outbreak of war with Russia, and imminence of conflict with France. Our wait was over.

Our captain ordered a northerly course. *Emden* was to cut the Nagasaki-Vladivostok shipping lane, while avoiding the enemy's ships of war. Our primary objective was to cripple trade, as most of the ships on the chosen route were Russian. We immediately made for the Straits of Korea.‡

At about 0200 on Tuesday 4th August 1914, amid a strong white squall, we fell in with a ship but could see nothing but her stern light. We did not press farther forward, in case we had found a French cruiser. We still believed that French warships were on their way to Weihaiwei, so Kapitän von Müller set sail for the Straits of Korea in very bad weather and heavy seas.

I was lying peacefully in my bunk when 'Clear ship for action' wakened all aboard. I hurried to my action station, which was then in the conning tower, to find *Emden* racing towards a cloud of smoke at full speed. First the masts and then the stern of the ship came into view.

She flew masthead flags, but we could not make them out. Was she a hostile warship or not? When the distance had closed sufficiently, we saw she was a Russian passenger ship – but one speedy enough to make a break for neutral waters. We fired a warning blank, which our quarry disregarded, and then put a few live shells across her bow. The last shot fell so close that the steamer turned about and hove-to. She tried to send an SOS by wireless, giving her name and position, but we successfully jammed the transmission.

We had finally taken *Ryazan* of the Russian Volunteer Fleet in 35°5′N 19°39′E. Built by the Schichau yard in Danzig and still fairly new, she carried very little cargo – but eighty passengers whose anger at their captain's attempt to run had apparently caused the turnabout.

The dispatch of the prize crew under Oberleutnant z.S. d.R. Julius Lauterbach proved hazardous. As the cutter went alongside under *Ryazan*'s boarding ladder, it was nearly stove-in by the heavy seas. A second boat was piped away to offer assistance but, luckily, an accident was avoided.

† Now known as Cheju-do.
‡ Also known as the Straits of Tsushima.

Ryazan
FIRST SHIP INTERCEPTED

From an August 1914-vintage photograph published in Karl Bartz, *Der Kommandant der Emden*. Note the guns.

Displacing about 5,200 tonnes (3,522grt) and mesuring 99m on the waterline, this mail steamer was delivered by Schichau of Elbing (yard no.831) to the Russian Volunteer Fleet Association in November 1909. Capable of about seventeen knots, *Ryazan* – call sign PABJ – was captured on 4th August 1914 while travelling from Nagasaki to Vladivostok. The first prize taken by the Kaiserliche Marine in the First World War, she entered Tsingtau on 6th August. Fitted with eight 10.5cm guns and two searchlights taken from the colonial gunboat *Cormoran*, she was renamed *Cormoran* and commissioned as an auxiliary cruiser with the Kreuzergeschwader. Commanded by Kapitänleutnant Adalbert Zuckschwerdt, she was interned at Guam on 14th December 1914 and scuttled on 7th April 1917 to prevent impressment into the US Navy. There has been confusion about her original Russian name, but she was christened after the city of Ryazan', rather than bearing the Russian word for 'mummer' – Ryazhen'i.

Once *Ryazan* had been secured, she was ordered to follow in our wake. Our captain intended to bring the prize into Tsingtau where, as she had sufficient speed, *Ryazan* could be converted into a useful auxiliary cruiser. So we wheeled about and set course for home.

The morning passed quietly. Aboard *Ryazan*, however, something seemed amiss. Perhaps some unforeseen difficulty had been encountered, or was the Russian crew proving awkward? Our captain sent a message to his Russian opposite number pointedly reminding him that *Ryazan* was now our prize and, therefore, subject to German martial law. The Russian then followed obediently.

On board *Ryazan*, Oberleutnant Lauterbach, conscious of his duty as captain of the prize, inspected the wireless log. He deduced that the Russian vessel had been in continual contact with the French squadron up to the very moment she had been taken. The news was passed to us, whereupon von Müller ordered Lauterbach to detach and proceed separately to Tsingtau if we chanced to meet enemy warships. Should escape be impossible, *Ryazan* was to scuttle.

In *Emden* we were to redouble our watches, and a signalman was sent aloft to the fore-top. This became a feature of our later voyages, as visibility from the crow's nest was far greater than from the bridge.

About 1500hrs we met with a Japanese trawler, which we left undisturbed. It may have been 1700 or 1730 when the lookout reported the smoke of five ships on the starboard bow. Then the smoke could be seen from the bridge; the crow's nest already had masts in sight. Now we knew where the French squadron could be found.

We were then south of the Island of Tsushima; the Frenchmen were, in all probability, cruisers *Montcalm* and *Dupleix* plus their escorting destroyers. We assumed the Frenchmen had passed through the western channel of the Straits of Korea and were making for Shanghai.

We had no wish to fall onto the guns of the French, so our captain ordered an easterly course. Only when darkness had fallen did we slowly return through north-northwest to our original westward heading. *Ryazan*, cleared for scuttling, dutifully followed.

It was 'war watches as usual' that night. We met no other ships, but saw that the black-out aboard our Russian prize was far from perfect. Several times we had to use our signal-lamp to tell Lauterbach and his men to extinguish the offending lights.

Emden laid her course for Tsingtau, passing between the Island of Quelpart and the Korean peninsula. About noon on 5th August, we came upon two large Japanese ships which dipped their flags by way of greeting and were answered with equal courtesy. We sighted more smoke clouds in the afternoon, ducking away prudently lest we encountered the Frenchmen again.

As evening drew in, the wireless informed us that Britain had also declared war on Germany; now *Emden* could act with perfect freedom. We had enemies enough, but everyone in *Emden* knew that much could be endured amid such cheerful companionship. It could only be to our advantage if thought no longer need be spared for Britain, whose merchantmen, most plentiful in the East, promised rich booty.

We now had to be doubly alert; it was possible, indeed probable, that British warships would be lurking off Tsingtau to seize any of our ships that presented themselves. But it was imperative that we try to reach home in company with our valuable prize, *Ryazan*, whatever the risks involved. We badly needed coal and had to collect our reserves of men.

Our captain was determined to succeed. He contacted Tsingtau by wireless, being encouraged by the news that no enemy ships had been seen in the roadstead. *Ryazan* had been steaming ahead of us, which made it easier to keep her under constant observation, but now she was sent astern so that we could protect her long enough to escape (or scuttle) if we encountered an enemy.

As we approached Tsingtau, the order 'Clear ship' was given and a full head of steam was raised in the boilers. Lively wireless transmissions could be monitored aboard *Emden*, their strength allowing us to deduce that our enemies were very near.

We set our course first for Chalientao lighthouse, which stood on an island protecting the bay of Tsingtau, and then for Cape Yatau. Shortly before 0300 we sighted a ship with a very bright stern light. Suspense on our bridge grew: had we an enemy vessel in sight? Many eyes strove to pierce the night, but could discern nothing.

As we plotted a course along the towering rocky coast, an alarm cry suddenly rang out. Another followed almost immediately: suspense became unbearable. But then we saw not enemy destroyers, as we had supposed, but peaceable Chinese junks.

In the grey of the early morning we reached the mine barrier, near which the steamer *C. Ferd. Laeisz* was waiting to enter. Tsingtau was already on a war footing. Not a light could be seen, and the town that had once glittered so brightly was now cloaked in impenetrable blackness.

Near the Island of Maitau, we gave a signal and were promptly answered by the so-called Entry Gun. As we had announced our arrival by wireless, everything was prepared. *Jaguar*, lying outside the mine barrier, immediately sent a steam pinnace across to us. The Captain of the Boom, Kapitänleutnant von Saldern, and our old friend Mathiessen the pilot came aboard to guide *Emden* safely through the entrance. *Ryazan*, having followed us faithfully, was ordered to wait outside the barrier.

Emden entered harbour at about 0530 and made fast to the coaling mole, protected by a boom of chains and timber. The mole-head was already guarded by guns and men of the Matrosen-Artillerie-Abteilung. Soon we were welcomed by many of the senior officers – including the captain of old *Cormoran*, who inquired anxiously about *Ryazan*'s speed. As the obsolescent gunboat had been docked for an extensive refit requiring months to complete, her captain now hoped to transfer his guns and men to *Ryazan*. His wish was soon to be realized.

The armoured cruisers *Fürst Bismarck* (left) and *Hansa* (right) alongside the coaling mole in Tsingtau. 10,690-tonne *Fürst Bismarck* was a product of the Kaiserliche Werft, Kiel, while 5,885-tonne *Hansa* came from the yard of AG 'Vulcan' of Stettin. They were commissioned in April 1900 and April 1899 respectively. The photograph must have been taken prior to 1906, when *Hansa* returned to Germany. The nearest merchantman at the quayside is probably *Loongmoon*, as she appears to be flying the diagonally-quartered Hamburg-Amerika house flag at the mainmast. By courtesy of WZ-Bilddienst, Wilhelmshaven.

A RENDEZVOUS AT PAGAN

Thursday 6th August–Friday 14th August 1914

Seen here off Port Said prior to 1914, in Norddeutscher Lloyd colours, *Prinz Eitel Friedrich* was converted into an auxiliary cruiser shortly after the First World War began. Under the command of Korvettenkapitän Thierichens, she had a successful career before entering internment in Newport News, Virginia, on 9th April 1915. By courtesy of Laurence Dunn.

We were to coal as quickly as possible, taking on up to 950 tonnes, leave harbour again in the evening of 6th August, and steam for Pagan Island in the Marianas to rejoin the Kreuzergeschwader. To complete coaling and unship unnecessary items, while taking on new equipment, required haste if we were to sail for Pagan on time. To bring the ship's company up to war strength, we welcomed three more officers, a Deckoffizier,* thirteen technicians and seventeen seamen. We also gained a Catholic priest, so that those of us who followed the Roman Church could receive the sacraments and general absolution.

While the work was being cheerfully undertaken, we had many visitors. All Tsingtau wished to see the ship after her first wartime cruise and hear our accounts at first hand. The most amazing blood-and-thunder stories were being circulated – not least being that we had sunk the Russian cruiser *Askold* in a fair fight. But some of our friends and acquaintances merely wished to take leave, not knowing if we should ever meet again.

Tsingtau was a changed place. Guns had been emplaced on the coaling mole; the big floating dock was cleared for sinking. Most of the ships at the mole were fully laden and waiting only on the order to leave, among them *Prinz Eitel Friedrich* of Norddeutscher Lloyd. She had been refitted as an auxiliary cruiser. *Markomannia* of the Hamburg-Amerika line had also been ordered to accompany us, under the command of her peacetime skipper Faass, and was already lying clear.

Our captain reported *Emden* clear at about 1800hrs, and soon we had left port to the cheers of our friends staying in Tsingtau. Torpedo-boat *S90* accompanied us out to Cape Yatau. We anchored in the outer roads for a short period, allowing Kapitän von Müller to go over to *Markomannia* for a conference. When he returned, we were piloted through the mine barrier and set to sea along the shipping lanes from Yokohama to Shanghai. The night of 6th August passed undisturbed.

Work was made as light as possible throughout the following day to allow us to recover from our exertions in Tsingtau. That night *Markomannia* and *Eitel Friedrich* took the first steps in a colossal masquerade. The

* A commissioned petty officer, ranking below midshipman (Fahnrich z.S.).

former was given the appearance of a Blue Funnel steamer, while the latter, conscious of her rank, took the colours of the distinguished P&O line. Repainting large ships at sea was by no means easy, but the results were rewarding – even if *Markomannia* lacked the large funnel so characteristic of Blue Funnel vessels.

Late in the morning of 8th August, a smoke cloud was sighted. We immediately approached at full speed while our companions maintained their original stations. We were curious to see what would be revealed. Our expectations were dashed, however, for the anticipated prize proved to be a Japanese ship of the Nippon Yusen Kaisha – a neutral. Nothing was left for us but to put on a brave face on misfortune and return to our convoy.

As *Markomannia* was the slowest, she was sent on ahead to bypass the Japanese Ryuku islands and meet *Emden* south-eastward of them. We then cruised along the shipping lane betwen Nagasaki and Shanghai with *Eitel Friedrich*, in the hope of meeting some fatted morsel. Nothing came our way and so, as time was running short, we concentrated on getting to Pagan. We chased a steamship in the afternoon of 8th August, but she also proved to be Japanese. As luck was not in our favour, we left the hunting ground in twilight to enter the Colnett Straits between the Ryuku islands.

That evening, for the first time since leaving Tsingtau, we received wireless messages telling us of developments in the European theatre. It was good news: of successful battles in Belgium, and stout resistance presented to the Russians in Ostpreussen.† The greatest interest to us, of course, lay in news of the navy. The well-known pleasure steamer *Königin Luise* had sewn mines effectually in the Thames Estuary, but had been overwhelmed by hostile warships. The price did not seem too high, however, as the little British cruiser *Amphion* had sunk on the mines.‡ In addition, our *Goeben* and *Breslau*, despite being surrounded by their enemies, had succeeded in escaping eastward through the Straits of Messina.

The heartening news of our comrades at home made us proud, and we saw in it the results of the energetic and comprehensive training given to the Kaiserliche Marine.

As Saturday 8th August drew to its close, we intercepted a message stating that *Emden* was to be found in the East China Sea with two captured steamships. It was easy to guess whom we should thank for disclosing our position: it could only have been one of the Japanese merchantmen. Our enemies must have been well pleased.

One other piece of news was that the British liner *Empress of Japan*, of the Canadian Pacific line, was bound for Hong Kong and would be passing the southern Japanese coast. As we had been cruising since dusk in the Colnett Straits, though which the liner must pass, we were bound to meet her. Punctually at 2100hrs, in accordance with our expectations, a lookout announced a steamship. We were after her like a fox. As the range narrowed, our searchlight stabbed out – but all we had run down was another confounded Japanese. How we cursed! But strong words could not repair our actions. The searchlight was extinguished and we continued on our way in the darkness. Our lucky hour was still to come.

9th August, a Sunday, was kept as a day of rest. The ship's company scattered over the deck after Divine Service, talking or playing cards. Kapitän von Müller even joined us in the wardroom. In balmy weather, with the sea like a mirror and the sky a splendid blue, there could be no finer thing on earth than to laze on the quarterdeck. However, Kapitänleutnant von Mücke, our first lieutenant, wished to use this time to explain the events of the European war to the ship's company with the assistance of a large map. This was repeated every Sunday in August and later, whenever events permitted, every Sunday after Divine Service. The more intelligent men appreciated these lectures greatly, however sparing the news may have been.

Monday 10th August was a *dies irae* in the truest sense of the phrase. The last vestiges of our amenities had to be sacrificed to the needs of war – the small amount of surviving upholstery went overboard, followed by the wood panelling from the wardroom. Away with all comforts! A sailor's heart is not beguiled by tinsel, but I have to admit that some of us regretted that the wardroom, hitherto well-appointed and attractive, should be turned into nothing but a cold dank flat; it was all so very depressing.

Consolation was to be found in necessity. War made such sacrifices essential, so overboard had gone the curtains, the screen that divided the wardroom from the after battery, and even the remaining lockers in our cabins. This had to be. But the wardroom still needed to be habitable, so its walls were covered with green paint of a particularly objectionable shade. In time, we hoped, the human race will adapt itself to anything.

News received that evening was far from cheering. We learned, more or less clearly, that Britain's ally Japan was abandoning her neutral stance, promising active measures against German shipping should British interests in China – or Japanese merchantmen – be threatened by our warships.

Most unpleasant, from our viewpoint, was the news that the cruiser *Tone* and four destroyers had left Japan in a southerly direction. If Japan did indeed intend to take measures against our ships, our present course was ill advised. Though there was no immediate danger, the greatest caution was necessary.

We met *Eitel Friedrich* at the appointed spot. However, the absence of *Markomannia* caused us great anxiety. We attempted to contact her by wireless, but could raise no answer.

11th August saw us acting as a target-tug for *Eitel Friedrich*, whose inexperienced gunners required practice with their charges. We tried to call *Markomannia*

† In English, 'East Prussia'.

‡ *Amphion* sank with the loss not only of substantial numbers of her own ship's company, but also of eighteen men rescued from *Königin Luise*.

again, only to receive the enigmatic 'Am at the rendezvous. Give your position!' What did this message mean? Surely our collier had no need to know where we were? *Emden* became a council chamber in which pessimists argued that *Markomannia* had been taken by the enemy, and that the message was intended to dupe us into revealing our whereabouts.

We decided to contact the Kreuzergeschwader. The reply – 'Do not wireless!' – was even more remarkable. Our telegraphist reported that both answers had been given with the same strength, whereupon we decided that the message ascribed to *Markomannia* had actually come from *Scharnhorst*. But we knew nothing for certain; suspense grew as we sought an answer to the riddle, concerned for the safety of the missing ship.

The concern made no difference to our duties. Gunnery officer Gaede held a much-needed practice for his men with the help of a short-range target. Our steam pinnace

---

1 Maximilian, Graf von Spee, 'Der Sieger der Seeschlacht in den chilenischen Gewässern': a good screened head-and-shoulders pencil portrait on cream board, published by Stengel & Co. GmbH of Dresden ('no.49180'). By courtesy of The Lyon Press archives.

2 With her sister-ship *Gneisenau*, SMS *Scharnhorst*, seen here at speed — probably running trials — was the last and largest of the classical German armoured cruisers. Displacing 11,616 tonnes dwl and capable when new of 23½ knots, she was commissioned on 24th October 1907 and sunk at the Battle of the Falkland Islands on 8th December 1914. This postcard by M.L. Carstens of Hamburg — 'S.M.S. "Scharnhorst" Grosser geschützter Kreuzer' — was clearly a Dieterle, Kiel, original ('M.D.K.3304'). By courtesy of The Lyon Press archives.

1

2

towed a target float adorned with a 20cm-square metal plate hung in gimbals. A specially constructed rifle was inserted into the guns, allowing ordinary 8mm ammunition to be used. This was particularly useful to the gunlayers and the 'Numbers One', the latter specially trained to take the place of the layers when necessary.

The guns' crew were kept in good practice by this method; though unsteadiness rendered it useless in any sea, it was an excellent aid in calm conditions.

We were scheduled to arrive in Pagan on 12th August. The Marianas Islands hove into sight at midday and soon we had passed the outliers. As the afternoon drew on, the Island of Pagan, crowned by a volcano of considerable height, could be seen at last. The Marianas are really mountains sunk in prehistoric times to leave nothing but their peaks as a memorial. Few of the islands were ever inhabited, despite the exceptionally rich and fertile lava soil. However, many had been sought out by the Japanese whose cocoa and banana plantations were tended by the remaining natives.

As we approached Pagan Bay, we encountered the Kreuzergeschwader auxiliary *Titania* and replied to her identification signal. *Emden* then turned to starboard into the bay, entering to find feverish activity. In addition to the armoured cruisers *Scharnhorst* and *Gneisenau*, and the little cruiser *Nürnberg*, a great convoy of merchantmen had assembled – *Prinz Waldemar*, *Holsatia*, *Mark*, *Yorck*, *Staatssekretär Kraetke*, *Gouverneur Jaeschke* and *Loongmoon*. We anchored well into the shelter of the bay; all around us, the other warships were busily coaling.

Scarcely had we anchored than Kapitän von Müller was ordered aboard the flagship of Admiral Graf von Spee, while we received visitors of our own. A cutter from *Gneisenau* came alongside to inquire whether we had any mail, but was sent away disappointed.

In the Bay of Pagan we heard that officers of my year had been promoted to Leutnant z.S., which was good news for all of us who had joined the service in 1911. Our life aboard *Emden* hardly altered, as we kept our allotted duties. But how we celebrated that evening, even though light war-watches for men and full war-watches for the officers were ordered that night.

The next morning – 13th August – was remarkable for a particularly strenuous day's coaling. Lauterbach, whose peacetime command had been *Staatssekretär Kraetke*, brought up his charge with her stern alongside us to port. *Gouverneur Jaeschke* then came up to starboard. Coaling began at once, and the work was by no means light.

My division was charged with coaling from *Staatssekretär Kraetke* and mightily we sweated over it in the tropical heat. Neither merchantman was properly equipped as a collier; in peacetime, after all, both had plied passengers between Shanghai, Tsingtau and Port Arthur. Their holds were particularly poorly placed to handle coal effectually. So the work proceeded slowly, and only about 450 tonnes had been taken aboard *Emden* by nightfall.

An unpleasant discovery was made during the day. Like most ships in the East, we had Chinese washermen. These Chinamen were indispensable, for nobody could

The Norddeutscher Lloyd liner *Yorck* was impressed to serve the Kreuzergeschwader as a transport. Interned in Chilean port of Valparaiso in October 1914, she was returned to her owners after the First World War had ended. By courtesy of Laurence Dunn.

wash as well as they could. Our three had learned from countrymen in the other ships that *Staatssekretär Kraetke* was to return to Tsingtau; during the coaling, much to our surprise, we discovered our three Chinamen hidden in Lauterbach's ship. They were immediately brought back to *Emden*, where a demand that they continue their duties elicited an uncompromising 'No!' However, their faces fell when they heard that no ship was to return to Tsingtau and resistance finally crumbled.

During the arduous work of coaling, we had no time to muse on the fate of the vanished *Markomannia*. Our surprise was all the greater when she ran safely into Pagan harbour at about 0900 the next morning. It was to be some time before we learned about her experiences as, after coaling had been completed, we were required to provision. When provisioning had also finished, we exchanged elderly Kapitänleutnant d.R. Metzenthin for Leutnants z.S. Gyssling and Schmidt, who subsequently rendered *Emden* yeoman service as prize officers.

The morning of 13th August was also distinguished by a conference, aboard the flagship, where the officers commanding the cruisers were joined by the officer commanding the convoy of merchantmen, Korvettenkapitän Thierichens of the auxiliary cruiser *Prinz Eitel Friedrich*.

Kapitän von Müller reported to us that the commander-in-chief of the Kreuzergeschwader, Graf von Spee, had given his views of the situation and the utility of his squadron. He had emphasized the threatening posture adopted by Japan, and the advantages of keeping the cruiser squadron in reserve as long as possible. The uncertainty about its position and aims would, he believed, occupy the attention of many enemy warships. Graf von Spee also spoke of the difficulties of coaling, especially as *Scharnhorst* and *Gneisenau* consumed prodigious quantities. Consequently, he had decided to proceed to the western coast of South America.

The commanding officers were then each asked to give their opinions. Our captain opposed his admiral's views, believing that the Kreuzergeschwader would be practically ineffectual for several months it took to traverse the Pacific Ocean; that it could do little harm to the enemy; and that great importance should be attached to the 'fleet in being' theory, especially with regard to the future of the navy and the consolidation of German sea power that depended upon it. If the coaling difficulties were too great to permit the entire Kreuzergeschwader to operate in East Asiatic, Australian or Indian waters, Kapitän von Müller had boldly continued, would it not be advisable to send at least one of the smaller cruisers to the Indian Ocean? There, conditions would be especially favourable for cruiser warfare and the appearance of German warships off the Indian coast would dent the morale of the Indian people.

The chief-of-staff, Kapitän z.S. Fielitz, and apparently some of the other commanding officers, supported our captain's view. The admiral then stated that he had thoroughly investigated whether the entire squadron should proceed to the Indian Ocean, but had concluded that coaling difficulties would be insuperable. He agreed to consider Kapitän von Müller's proposal.

The use of auxiliary cruisers was also discussed, but Graf von Spee placed little reliance on *Prinz Eitel Friedrich* and *Cormoran* (formerly *Ryazan*). They were too slow, he said, and their coal consumption was high enough to threaten the limited supplies for the warships.

The Kreuzergeschwader was to leave Pagan that evening, all ships ordered to be clear for sea by 1730hrs. A decision to send us into the Indian Ocean was taken sometime that afternoon. However, only Kapitän von Müller knew about it outside the flagship. But it was an important decision, for we were now to be independent.

Punctually at 1730 we weighed anchor and, in line ahead, the Kreuzergeschwader headed a long train of supply ships out of the stillness of Pagan Bay. *Scharnhorst* led, followed by *Gneisenau*, *Nürnberg* and *Emden*. At the end of the first line steamed *Titania*. A second line formed on the starboard quarter, where *Eitel Friedrich* led the remaining merchantmen in descending order of size. Good order was kept even by the commercial vessels, which had no practice in collective manoeuvring. Our course was eastward; speed, ten knots. Full warwatches were set at nightfall.

Dawn light revealed a shambles. The warships were still in line ahead, but no vestige of organization could be seen in the second line. It took all the patience of the leaders to bring the merchantmen back onto station – not that their captains could be blamed, of course, as they were more used to steaming alone. We slowed in the hope that our companions would regain their positions, but the smallest ships were nowhere to be seen. We had to turn about to look for them until, slowly, all had been shepherded back to the convoy.

As our course remained easterly, pundits in the wardroom believed our destination to be the western coast of America. This was the most likely possibility, as enemy trade was particularly plentiful between South America and Australia. Understandably, we all hoped to round Cape Horn and return home with the squadron intact.

At 0800hrs on 14th August 1914, therefore, we received a surprise when the flagship ran up the signal '*Emden* detached. Good luck!' Great rejoicing and excitement spread throughout the whole ship. We were on our own at last, to act independently as we – more accurately, our captain – pleased.

Our orders, we learned, were to proceed independently and harrass the enemy as often as possible. Kapitän von Müller was just the man for such a task.

He immediately signalled the flagship 'My dutiful thanks for the confidence placed in me. Success to the squadron, and bon voyage'. *Markomannia*, ordered to 'Follow *Emden*!', immediately sent over one of her signalmen to facilitate understanding between us.

Steaming south-southwest at twelve knots, we were able to guess our destination. The course led directly to the East Indian archipelago. But it was also the way to the Indian Ocean.

GOING SOLO

Friday 14th August–Tuesday 25th August 1914

The British-built collier *Markomannia*, owned by Hamburg-Amerika-Linie and commanded by HAL-Kapitän Faass, was *Emden*'s most faithful companion. After leaving the cruiser on 30th September, intent on reaching a neutral port in the Netherlands Indies, she was intercepted by HMS *Yarmouth* and scuttled on 12th October 1914. Painting by courtesy of Laurence Dunn.

The Kreuzergeschwader was soon out of sight, and we were alone at last. Alone! The word had a particular significance for us. In the squadron we had always been little more than a cog in the wheel; now, however, *Emden* was a fighting unit in her own right. Anyone who knows naval life knows what this means. Every opportunity could be taken and the credit, with luck, would go to us. With good luck would come the laurels, whereas they would inevitably go to the central command in squadron warfare.

Our course was initially southerly, running discreetly parallel to the Marianas Islands. Our immediate goal was Angaur Island, in the Palau Group, where we hoped to meet a collier. Once clear of the Marianas, our course was changed to south-westerly.

The voyage to Angaur lasted until 19th August, the intervening period being used to bring the ship to full fighting trim. Half our ship's company lacked experience, and training was needed in the gunnery and engineering branches in particular. For example, gunners, magazine details and range-takers all received special instruction. *Markomannia*, our companion, gave priceless service as a target; without her, range-finding and gunlaying would have been impossible. As each day passed, so the men became more familiar with their weapons.

Gunnery was not the only task, however. Under the direction of Kapitänleutnant von Mücke, the protection of *Emden* was improved. Splinter screens of interwoven hempen hanks masked the guns in the forecastle and under the quarterdeck, the after gun control – the action station of my friend Oberleutnant z.S. von Levetzow – and the wireless room, which stood between the second and third funnels. Unfortunately, these precautions proved all but useless in the final fight against *Sydney*. They simply made rich fuel for the exploding shells!

Our work in the torpedo section was limited to ensuring our charges were battle-ready, as no time could be spared for shooting practice. The engineers had plenty to do. Our boilers' tubes had not improved with hard use and, though easy to change, needed constant renewal. Fortunately, the engines needed to kept in nothing more than good running trim.

Care was taken to ensure that sleeping quarters should be as close as possible to action stations. The men enjoyed nothing worse than light war watches in this period, as they needed sufficient sleep to recover from their strenuous daytime efforts. The principal difference between light and full war-watches was that the former lasted only a couple of hours. Torpedo personnel, however, were on duty continuously. Men in the night watches were granted extra rest by day and more food. Stokers' watches could not be similarly modified, however, and compensation by way of extra nourishment was accepted.

There was no respite for the officers. This was simply impossible; the posts we commanded could not be reduced without endangering the ship.

The wireless-room staff was also maintained through the night, as this was the most favourable time for transmission. Each evening Tsingtau sent us details of events in differing theatres. I still remember how, one evening, Leutnant z.S. von Guérard (who was wireless officer as well as adjutant) ran into the wardroom with the news that four British warships had been sunk and others crippled during a night attack by our torpedo flotillas in the Humber. How we rejoiced, and, as our stock of wine was still plentiful, the news was appropriately celebrated. It was a shame the story was contradicted. Where it came from we never knew.

We received other less heartening news – news which left no doubt that Japan would shortly join our enemies. The cause, of course, was Tsingtau. Cherished by Germany with the greatest care, this protectorate had awakened Japanese jealousy. Indeed, after Tsingtau fell, the Japanese tried to make the base into a Gibraltar on Chinese soil. As none of the northern Chinese harbours was as modern or well equipped as Tsingtau, we had no doubt that Japan would seize our base at the earliest opportunity. Britain, Japan's ally, was also naturally seeking relief in the East to concentrate on the European theatre.

In the evening of 19th August, a Wednesday, *Emden* was so near the Palau Group that we would have arrived at Angaur before dawn. This was unwise, so 'Slow ahead!' was rung down to allow us to pass the islands with sufficient dawn-light to spot the collier awaiting us. We did not know whether she would be anchored off Angaur or another island in the chain.

We sighted the first of the Palaus in the grey of the morning, running past at slow speed, but could see nothing of our collier. At 1100hrs we reached Angaur, the southernmost island of the archipelago, and dropped anchor in the northern roads. The island is not large, but its valuable phosphate deposits were fortuitously leased to a German company. Our arrival was reassuringly greeted by a German flag floating on the breeze. Then *Markomannia* ran in and made fast to the buoy. We weighed anchor, went alongside her and prepared for coaling – an operation which, in the tropics, can never truthfully be described as enjoyable.

Shortly after our arrival, the manager of the phosphate company (doubling as government representative) came aboard in company with the island's doctor to visit Kapitän von Müller. Several other German employees also came out to *Emden* to be entertained in the wardroom. In spite of the choking coal dust and other disadvantages, our guests evidently felt at home. The government representative asked whether we could spare provisions but, with the best will in the world, there was little we could give. However, limited exchanges were possible.

We learned to our chagrin that a British ship laden with 7,000 tons of phosphates had left Angaur only three days previously. Our hearts sank at the escape of such a valuable prize. Our captain then told the reservists on the island that we already had our full complement and

Shown here passing unreasonably closely to the Statue of Liberty on this pre-1914 postcard, the artist having ignored the breadth of Liberty Island, Norddeutscher Lloyd's *Prinzess Alice* was interned in Cebu on 20th August 1914. That she had achieved nothing of note during the opening weeks of the First World War came as no surprise to the crew of *Emden*. By courtesy of Laurence Dunn.

could not accommodate them. Suddenly there was gloom on both sides.

The afternoon of 20th August promised the arrival of the mail steamer *Prinzess Alice*, owned by Norddeutscher Lloyd, which had wirelessed the Kreuzergeschwader some days earlier without receiving a reply. Kapitän von Müller had decided to order *Prinzess Alice* to Angaur. At 1400hrs the signalman in the crow's nest reported smoke clouds in the northerly direction. Soon he reported that a large black steamship with buff funnels was approaching the island.

Prinzess Alice registered nearly eleven thousand tons and was much too large to anchor. To remain stationary required constant manoeuvring of her screws. Our captain wished to board the steamer, taking Leutnant z.S. von Guérard, the Schiffszahlmeister, Marine-Oberzahlmeister Woytschekowsky and me with him, once von Guérard returned from inspecting the wireless station ashore.

I was glad of the opportunity to board *Prinzess Alice*, the ship in which, in 1913, I had taken the four-week voyage from Genova to Shanghai. The memory of that happy time made me glad to see her again. Once aboard, we were heartily greeted; our name had already become famous thanks to the capture of *Ryazan*. Kapitän von Müller dealt with the question of reserves, and then naturally asked for news. We learned that *Prinzess Alice* had loaded over £850,000 Sterling in gold for the Indian government, to be landed in Hong Kong. Between Singapore and Hong Kong, however, the captain learned of the outbreak of war, steamed full speed for the neutral harbour in Manila in the Philippines, and delivered the gold into 'safe keeping'. How the British government must have wept over its loss!

Our consul in Manila instructed the captain of *Prinzess Alice* to take on as much coal, provisions and fresh water as she could hold, and then join the Kreuzergeschwader. But the attempt had not succeeded, and the moment had been lost.

We learned from the liner's captain that a Royal Navy squadron comprising the armoured cruisers *Minotaur* and *Hampshire*, plus the light cruiser *Yarmouth*, had appeared off the German island of Yap on 7th August. The officer commanding the squadron told the wireless station that it would be shot to pieces after three hours, the warning being sensibly heeded. After destroying the station, the British ships had sailed away without attempting a landing.

The most important news, as far as we were concerned, was that Japan had sent Germany an ultimatum requesting that all military forces evacuate Tsingtau by 5th September. An answer had been demanded by 23rd August. It was crystal clear to us aboard *Emden* that our government would not concur, the consequences being all too obvious.

This was doubly unpleasant, as we had now to reckon Japan among our enemies. Our hearts were heavy; at the expiration of the ultimatum, Tsingtau would undoubtedly be attacked by Japan. That our home port would not be able to hold out, we already knew. Its fate was sealed.

Prinzess Alice also supplied some American newspapers, whose contents were so unreasonably sensational that we could hardly believe them. While we received news, the Zahlmeister was negotiating for provisions. Kapitänleutnant von Mücke then came aboard, mindful of the same goal, but little progress was made as time was wasted completing requisition forms and receipts. The celebration of St Bureaucratius aboard the liner bordered on orgiastic. The mail steamer's pursers lacked common sense, insisting that peacetime procedures should be maintained in a war! Our objective of satisfactorily provisioning a man-of-war was not to be completed.

My task had been easier. I had to obtain beer, cigars and cigarettes for the wardroom: that I was personally acquainted with many of the people in *Prinzess Alice* was a great help, and my raid was a great success. I freely admit that I used the spare time to quaff good German beer in the steamer's mess – a rare enough treat for any of us in those days, though my pleasure was somewhat diminished by the thought that it would not happen again for a very long time.

When all arrangements had been made, the reserve seamen were brought aboard *Emden*. Thus we gained Kapitänleutnant a.D. Klöpper and Vizesteuermann d.R. Meyer, two petty officers, two reservists and six volunteers. Many others would have come over, but we had to limit our intake owing to lack of space.

About 1900hrs we returned to *Emden*. Our island guests took a hearty leave and went ashore in their boat. The collier we had expected never appeared. She remained lost, and we never discovered where she had gone.

At about 1930 we cast off from *Markomannia* and put to sea on a south-westerly course with light war-watches set. *Prinzess Alice* had been ordered to accompany us and now followed astern of *Markomannia*. This arrangement had one major drawback: our faithful companion now hid the mail steamer, hindering communication by signal lamps. Despite the slow speed, *Prinzess Alice* once lost touch with us completely – unseen by our lookouts, as all lights had been dowsed. We soon gained the impression that *Prinzess Alice* wished to operate independently and was not co-operating. We could not pass instructions by wireless however great our annoyance, as it was imperative to withhold our position from the enemy.

In the night of 20th August, by which time we were in serious need of provisions, we were finally forced to wireless *Prinzess Alice* to convene a meeting the next day. The answer was disappointing. The captain of the steamer announced that he was short of coal and had troublesome boilers, adding that both voyage and rendezvous would have to be abandoned. Kapitän von Müller ordered him to proceed into the neutral waters of the Philippines to avoid capture. We heard later that he obeyed this order and reached his goal successfully. But

Members of a ship's company queue to receive a midday meal. Given to one of *Sydney*'s crew, it was clearly taken aboard one of the Hilfschiffe – probably *Markomannia*. By courtesy of the Australian War Memorial, Canberra; negative EN0233.

his behaviour was peculiar and our disappointment – perhaps even anger – was understandable.

Both *Emden* and *Markomannia* needed provisions. We were soon to learn the consequences: two months on a maddeningly monotonous diet of corned beef, rice and a few dried vegetables. Though officers' cook Schultz became a master at dressing the stuff in differing ways, corned beef and rice remained what they were: boring.

Among the most important considerations was the quality of the men's food, every opportunity being taken to obtain fresh meat for them from the ships we captured. It was natural that the men should be given preference, as they did more manual work than we did and had greater need of good nourishment. This principle was richly rewarded by the absence of serious shipboard illness during the cruise. That a man could be afflicted by overly strenuous work could hardly be marked down to illness.

After taking leave of *Prinzess Alice*, we endeavoured to get news of the Japanese attitude through to the Kreuzergeschwader. However, our cautious attempts went unanswered until – much to our astonishment – we received an acknowledgement from the old colonial cruiser *Geier*, formerly stationed in the South Seas. *Geier* gave a position that enabled us to lay a course to meet her on 21st August. Kapitän von Müller wished to talk to her capitan, Korvettenkapitän Grasshof.

In mid-afternoon, the lookout in the crow's nest spotted *Geier*. Our first, almost comical sighting was a large steamship, high out of the water; only then came the cruiser, dwarfed by her collier *Bochum*. Soon we were near enough to stop engines, and *Geier* put out a boat to bring Korvettenkapitän Grasshof and his adjutant, Oberleutnant z.S. Sauerbeck, over to *Emden*. As officer of the watch, I had to ensure all was clear to receive our visitors. Our captain received Grasshof and Sauerbeck at the Jacob's Ladder, as the boom had been stowed beneath the armoured deck for safety. The three men then went forward to the captain's cabin, where orders were issued.

Not much could be done with *Geier*. Her guns were light, her torpedo equipment obsolete, and she could never hope to exceed twelve knots again. She was so hopelessly out-of-date that she would have fallen prey to any modern enemy cruiser and, moreover, had she wished to participate in the war against commerce, many merchantmen could have out-run her! It was difficult for Korvettenkapitän Grasshof to achieve anything significant.

Had *Prinzess Alice*'s boilers been in better condition, the fast mail steamer could have been equipped as an auxiliary cruiser with *Geier*'s guns. But the steamer had already left for internment in the Philippines. We later received reports suggesting that *Geier* had met with some success* but, as her boilers and engines had become untrustworthy, she eventually put into Honolulu.

Less than an hour after climbing aboard, *Geier*'s officers left us. Three hearty cheers were given on both sides, and the old ship disappeared on a north-easterly

* *Geier* attempted to attack the British steamer *Southport* (3,588grt) in September 1914, but succeeded only in seriously damaging her.

course as we laid ours for the Straits of Molucca. We then held several concerted battle exercises so that all the branches of the ship could become accustomed to working together.

On the evening of 22nd August – Saturday – we crossed the Equator, the first time I had done so. As we were at war, however, none of the usual baptismal ceremonies were possible. But magnificent scenery and a mirror-sea made the day more than simply memorable.

On 23rd August we met a Japanese passenger ship and an unpleasant situation, for although we knew that an ultimatum had been despatched to Germany we did not know whether Japan had actually declared war. Our captain could not afford to sink the steamer, so we suffered considerable chagrin at the loss of a choice prize. The Japanese was very polite, hoisting and dipping her flag to us. We assumed she had taken us for a British ship, as she could hardly have expected a German cruiser in these waters.

As midday approached, we saw the marvellous spectacle of a school of porpoises leaping out of the water and then, despite numbers reckoned almost in thousands, cleaving the sea in ordered ranks as if on parade. We delighted in the march-past for more than a quarter of an hour.

By the time twilight gave way to dusk we had reached the entrance of the Straits of Molucca, giving a wide berth to the two lights we sighted for fear of revealing our position. We assumed they belonged to the Dutch coastal steamers we had no wish to see. The southern end of the Straits of Molucca is formed by Amboina Channel and the islands of Boero and Ceram. There are, in addition, several smaller islands of importance no greater than to assist navigation. We traversed the channel in darkness, hoping that we were invisible from land.

We then laid our course for the Nusaberei Straits, which lie between the north-east point of the island of Timor and the little island of Leti, bounded to the east by a screen of islets known as the Leti Archipelago. A merchantman – *Tannenfels*, if I am not mistaken – had been ordered there to provide us with coal. Reserves in *Markomannia* were to be kept for emergencies.

24th August found us making for the eastern point of Timor, a day before the appointed meeting with the collier. The steamy climate and the arduous nature of the work meant that coaling was to take place before daybreak. Preparations had to made the previous night. We hoped to finish the work before the sun (and the temperature) was at its highest. It was also cool in the evening, of course, but then the men were tired and the effort would prove even more debilitating. We can look back with the greatest pride in the conduct of our splendid crew during early-morning coaling.

Emden and *Markomannia* ran into the rendezvous in the pre-sunrise grey of Tuesday 25th August. But there was no collier. Our ship was running low on fuel and had to be coaled under any circumstances, so we had to relieve *Markomannia* of some of hers. So pressing was our need that this was unavoidable.

Hard work enabled us to take 470 tonnes aboard, raising our total stocks to 950. The Divisionsleutnants, Leutnant z.S. Schall and I, joined in coaling by way of encouragement and example. We were soon joined by Leutnants z.S. Gyssling and Schmidt. As the divisions were divided into port and starboard watches, each saw it as a point of honour to load more than its rival. Should we be first, I told my men of the port watch, I would present them with some cigars. The bribe did the trick; it was a joy to see them work, and a pleasure to fulfil my promise.

While most of us were coaling, a few men were sent ashore to find fresh food for *Markomannia*'s cow. I no longer remember whether the hunt was successful, but I do remember our envy of a run ashore when we had been condemned to coal dust...

PIRATES' PROGRESS

Wednesday 26th August – Sunday 13th September 1914

'S.M.S. "Emden" am 9.11.14 im Indischen Ozean vernichtet.': a good-quality photo-card published by 'NPG' and Gebr. Lempe, Kiel ('Dess 109'). Taken from abaft the starboard beam, it shows the complex rigging to good advantage. The reverse is stamped 'Offizielle Feldpostkarte. Spende für das Denkmal der Gefallenen des Kreuzers "Emden". Emden 1922'. By courtesy of The Lyon Press archives.

Our missing collier failed to appear, even after coaling, so we put to sea on a westerly course along the coast of Timor while the ship was cleaned of the worst grime.

Our next goal was the island of Tanajampea, where a ship had already been ordered to meet us. Previous experience suggested that we should all be pessimistic about finding her.

The voyage was beautiful, favoured by magnificent weather and in continual view of the small volcanic islands. Off the port side towered the island of Timor, to a height of three thousand metres. Wireless communications became much more lively after nightfall and, by intercepting messages, we learned that Brussels and Namur had fallen before the German attack. Naturally, we rejoiced greatly.

On the morning of 27th August we sighted Tanajampea, steering round until we could enter the bay from the south. Nothing was to be seen of our collier, which came as no great surprise. Instead we saw a warship approaching us, flying her mast-head flags; for a moment we could not tell whether she was neutral Dutch or an enemy. The order was given to clear *Emden* for action and our mast-head flags were set. The range was about two kilometres; our gunners were ready. At the last moment, Kapitän von Müller saw that the stranger was flying the Dutch flag. However, as she had come directly toward us, nothing could be seen in her build to reveal her nationality.

We lowered our flags immediately and ran into the bay, as the Dutch battleship *Tromp* crossed our bows and turned to follow. We now saw that a collier lay in the bay, but our joy was short-lived: *Batavia* was Dutch, not German, and our spirits fell accordingly.

So that protocol should not be lacking, our steam pinnace was called away to take an officer to *Tromp* with *Emden*'s compliments. The Dutchman was ahead of us, however; an officer was already on his way across and soon came aboard. Kapitän von Müller announced his intention to visit *Tromp* immediately, boarding our pinnace – which had come back alongside in the intervening moments.

Everyone in *Emden* knew that this was merely politeness to the neutral, but we still felt some suspense. It was as if our affairs were to take a new turn.

True enough, the captain returned with the news that our collier had been sent away by *Tromp*. The establishment of a German coaling point in Dutch waters would not be permitted, as the Dutch captain had received instructions from his government to preserve the strictest neutrality. Warships of the warring states could remain in Dutch waters for merely 24 hours every three months.

Though *Tromp*'s captain had acted quite correctly, his actions scarcely allayed our anxiety as coal was running low. The Dutchman had pro-German sympathies and had even invited our officers aboard for a glass of beer, but we had been forced to decline his hospitality. For all the officers to leave the ship in wartime would have been disgraceful.

Emden and *Markomannia* weighed anchor and proceeded northward, with *Tromp* politely accompanying us as far as the so-called three mile limit. When we left neutral waters, the Dutchman took leave with a friendly exchange of signals. Scarcely was *Tromp* over the horizon than we reversed course for our true objective – the Lombok Straits – which lay to the south.

Our fourth funnel now made its first appearance. It was less beautiful than its sisters, but good enough to deceive from a distance. Our first officer, Kapitänleutnant von Mücke, devised the ruse.* Made of deck awnings and broad strips of sailcloth, with wooden frames top and bottom, the funnel was initially cylindrical. Then it became oval and acquired additional internal stiffeners. We hoisted it forward of our foremost funnel so that, from a distance at least, I believe we looked sufficiently like the British cruiser *Yarmouth* (then on the China station) to deceive spies. We wished to pass the Lombok Straits on 28th August, heading for the Indian Ocean, and expected the narrow channel to be guarded by enemy warships. The liveliness of wireless communications confirmed our belief, and one Dutch message even announced that a 'torpedoboat with four funnels' had been sighted in the neighbourhood of Batavia. As an aid to our safety, the dummy funnel must be acknowledged as a brilliant success.

We had to be ready for anything and to take all care to avoid being sighted by the enemy. We believed the Indian Ocean to be our best hunting ground, but did not wish to draw attention to our plans.

Towards midday, we sighted the mountains of the islands of Lombok to the east and Bali to westward, guarding the flanks of the Lombok Straits. Sunset was magnificent: the dark rim of the mountains against a red-gold sky, reflected in the sea, was truly worthy of a Master's brush.

Night fell quickly, as it always does in the tropics. Our false fourth funnel was hoisted, sharp war-watches were set, and special lookouts were posted. Soon we sighted some sailing ships and began the passage of the straits at about 2200. Many eyes strained into the night. We met a steamship; then some sailing vessels. But no hostile warship was to be seen, and nothing could be missed in the bright moonlight. Shortly after midnight we were safely through.

Our captain must have offered a prayer for reaching our objective unseen.

For several days we steamed westward, standing some seventy miles off the coasts of Sumatra and Java. So beautiful was the weather that the voyage became a pleasure as well as a much-needed rest. Sunday 30th August was my birthday, so I was awakened by a cheerful serenade from the ship's band. Since the declaration of war, to relieve overworked adjutant von Guérard, I had taken over the work of band officer. My duties, and those of the band, were not heavy – war presents little opportunity for music – but tuneful encouragement was always offered on coaling days. In Wecke, the Oberhoboistenmaat, I had an assistant to whom everything could invariably be left.

Our next objective was Simaloer, north-westward of Sumatra and the last of the island chain protecting it. Our captain had selected Simaloer for coaling, as nothing could be seen of its sheltered bay from seaward. The voyage to this charming island took several days, filled with shooting practice, cleaning ship and, as far as possible, repairing *Emden*'s flanks. By this time our once-elegant cruiser bore little resemblance to her pre-war nickname, 'Swan of the East'. Continual coaling had dented and ripped our flanks, while the paint was too scratched and blackened to remain swan-white. Slowly but surely, seawater rusted the exposed metalwork; though the hull was repainted wherever possible, in patches and stripes, there was no time to be thorough.

Dust exuded continually from the sacks of coal carried on deck. Fuel was usually carried in the bunkers below deck, but we needed extra supplies for the long voyages necessary in wartime. The sacks were stored on the deck, the quarterdeck and the after part of the forecastle. Carrying larger coal-stores spared the men, but not the linoleum deck-covering. We strove as faithfully as possible to keep this clean and in the good order prescribed by regulations. But frequent coaling scratched and tore the deck covering until, towards the end of the cruise, it had been completely destroyed. War was war, and *Emden*, a warship, was not on a pleasure cruise. The main considerations were our fighting trim and a good state of health aboard.

The men had to be kept healthy and cheerful. This was achieved more often than not, though some things – particularly lack of nourishment – occasionally warranted anxiety. Everything was sacrificed so that the crew could eat fresh food for as long as possible. Officers willingly stood aside in favour of their men, which meant that the wardroom had long since foregone fresh provisions while the men still received them.

The peacetime stock of tinned food sufficed when fresh food for the wardroom was finished. However, when constantly offered as a main meal, even pâté de foie gras quickly awakens a most remarkable yearning for ordinary fresh meat.

Our captain busied himself in a fatherly way, procuring as much fresh food as possible for his crew and then personally supervising distribution. Kapitän z.S. von

* Though Prinz Franz Joseph credits the deception to von Mücke, other sources suggest that the idea was originally Fikentscher's and dated back to pre-war days. It appears that von Mücke alone remembered the suggestion.

1 The armoured cruiser HMS *Hampshire*, commissioned in 1905, was the most dogged of *Emden*'s pursuers. After tracking the German ship for many thousands of nautical miles, *Hampshire* twice came close to catching her; twice, aided by luck as well as skilled judgement, von Müller got away again. Had a battle been fought, *Emden* would have had little to answer the British ship's mixture of 7.5- and 6-inch guns.

This picture of one of *Emden*'s gun crews (not, as yet, identified individually) was found on the ship after the battle. The terrible casualty rate among the gunners suggests that few of these men survived the encounter with *Sydney* – apart from one or two who may have been ashore on Direction island with the Landing Party. By courtesy of the Australian War Memorial, Canberra; negative A02608. 2

Müller was one of the noble band of men who does everything for others while remaining resolutely in the background. He died of pneumonia in March 1923, mourned from the heart by all who knew him. In his strength of character and goodness of heart he was an ideal capitain, always ready to help and – to those privileged to know him well – an excellent, constant and steadfast friend. In *Emden*, as a mere Leutnant zur See, I had no close relations with Fregattenkapitän von Müller; only after 11th November 1914 did I come into prolonged and active contact with him. For as long as he was with us in captivity in Malta, he was the truest counsellor.

As early as 13th August 1914, we had intercepted wireless messages in cypher from a warship signing herself 'QMD'. After much debate, we thought at first of the British armoured cruiser *Minotaur* but later concluded that the source was HMS *Hampshire.* Dutch and Siamese wireless stations gave the latest news from the theatres of war each evening, which caused us to rejoice greatly at our German successes.

The news that the French government had been frightened out of Paris to Bordeaux was received with special acclamation. There were beaming faces aboard *Emden* next day, and our ship's company went about its daily duties with redoubled zeal.

An island group hove into sight on 3rd September, among it being Simaloer and a snug harbour. As we did not wish to enter until the morning of 4th September, speed was reduced accordingly. The bay into which we would run was known as Langini Harbour, though the term 'harbour' did not quite correspond with reality. Langini consisted of an oval bay with a very narrow entrance, protected by several islets. The 'port' consisted of a few native huts. The place was simply a sanctuary: a place in which to coal unseen. Better could not be desired.

We passed by the island in darkness and saw the blink of harbour-town lights to the south of us. All the while our wireless intercepted cypher messages sent by QMD, from the strength of which we inferred she must be somewhere close by. We subsequently learned that *Hampshire* was patrolling daily in a search for our warships, and that very evening had anchored off the south-west point of Simaloer. Had we appeared there early in the morning, we must have run into the guns of a warship powerful enough to have cost *Emden* dear. But a guardian angel still watched over us.

We ran into the quiet bay at 0600hrs on 4th September. It looked heavenly. The narrow entrance was thickly framed by mangroves, behind which the primeval forest in all the magnificence of the tropics was the most superb sight I had ever seen. Beautiful new vistas greeted our eyes as we sailed ever farther in, making an unforgettable impression after our long sea voyage.

It was a fairy-tale land indeed, but the collier we had expected was nowhere to be seen. Once again, our companion *Markomannia* had to help us out. She soon found the marker buoy and anchored to allow us to make fast alongside.

An officer and a signalman were posted in the fore-top crow's nest to keep a precautionary lookout, even though we knew it would be much harder for an enemy to spot us. Coaling began at 0900, with the intention of raising our reserves to a thousand tonnes.

Had the morning been cool, the men would have accomplished the task. However, in the warm humid tropical day – which was particularly noticeable in Langini Harbour – the work proved impossible. Although the men worked willingly and the officers joined in to help, we were exhausted by midday. Coaling continued to 2300hrs that night, after a break for the evening meal, until 450 tonnes had been brought on board. The idea of working all night was soon abandoned; the men simply could do no more. We then turned in, hoping to wake refreshed next morning. Only light war-watches were set in consideration of the men's efforts: one Oberleutnant and the indispensable posts. The rest of us enjoyed a much-needed rest.

Normally, Schall and I shared a cabin on the lower deck – from where we had difficulty reaching our action stations in an alarm. Since the outbreak of war, we had moved our night quarters to the wardroom, where I slept in a hammock with Schall beneath me on a mattress. Our sleep after the strenuous day in Langini Harbour was well earned, deep and quiet. But it was not to last.

At about 0300, I was wakened by the piercing miaow of a cat that is not at ease with the world. The noise was fearful, and my anger at the unwarranted disturbance easily its equal. I cursed most heartily, but the miaowing continued. The cat cared not a jot for the wrath of a Leutnant zur See, worn-out by coaling and desiring only sleep.

At first I could not discover what was wrong. Such a clamour could not have been caused by seasickness: it clearly came from our own ship's cat, for no other animal could have smuggled itself aboard *Emden.* My musing did not put an end to the noise. Indeed, the miaowing became stronger and punctuated with a noise that resembled a child crying.

With the honourable intention of dissuading the cat from her morning song, I took a box of matches from my pocket and tried to light the scene.

What disturbed me most, more even than the cat's behaviour, was that my colleague Schall ignored the concert and went on sleeping soundly. Scarcely had I lit a match, however, than my rage turned to laughter. In the madness of my mirth I broke the silent night more effectively than any feline – even one that had just presented another kitten to the Sumatran world between the legs of the sleeping Schall.

Four healthy kittens and their mother lay curled up in the welcome warmth radiating from my colleague. This was distinctly novel in the annals of *Emden*, and the delightful family picture was highly entertaining.

My laughter achieved what my curses had not. Leutnant z.S. Schall rubbed his eyes and discovered, by the feeble light of my match, the surprise-packet between his legs: the five cats of *Emden.* He scarcely knew whether to laugh or cry at such disrespectful behaviour. So one eye laughed while the other glowered: the comedy was unforgettable.

Mother-cat and her offspring were removed, whereupon Schall turned his mattress over and went back to sleep. The cats were cared for by members of the crew, but the little ones later disappeared.†

† The kittens – five in all – were eventually named after the captured merchantmen: Pontoporos, Lovat-Indus, Kabinga, King Lud and Diplomat (subsequently re-christened 'Little Idiot'). It is believed that they perished, with their mother, during the final battle.

'Der Schrecken der Engländer. Der Kreuzer "Emden" welcher im Indischen Ocean eine grössere Anzahl englischer Dampfer in den Grund gebohrt hat' – a postcard published by Gustav Liersch & Co. of Berlin to celebrate *Emden*'s success against British merchantmen. This is an interesting interpretation; quite apart from the highly questionable rendering of the warship – the funnels are much too short, the sheer aft is much too little – it should be asked where the shell-splash in the left foreground has come from! By courtesy of The Lyon Press archives.

Coaling began again at 0600hrs. It had to be hurried at all costs, for we had to get our full supply aboard and vanish with *Markomannia* before the Dutch discovered us. This was simply because the Netherlands Indies government had ruled that warships of the belligerents could remain in neutral Dutch waters for only a single day in three months. It would be in our interests to get away from Simaloer unseen, as we would still have our unexpended day's grace.

At 0800, however, our lookout announced that a small white steam-yacht flying the Dutch flag was approaching the bay. We had been caught. Soon the boat had anchored right beside us. The government official wasted no time coming across, and we all knew the reason. We were to leave neutral waters: our time was already up. In the presence of the insistent Dutchman, Kapitän von Müller asked our engineering officer, Marine-Oberingenieur Ellerbroek, when the engines of *Emden* and *Markomannia* would be ready for sea.

Catching the hidden meaning of the remark, Ellerbroek replied that at least two more hours would be required. These the Dutchman granted us, accepting whisky and iced soda-water to quiet his conscience completely.

Our men needed no explanation of the urgency of the situation. They guessed it all, fell-to with threefold energy, and by 1100 *Emden* had loaded her thousand tonnes. The crew worked wonders on behalf of its country in the infernal oriental heat.

At the order to cast off from the much lightened *Markomannia*, the Dutch official took his leave, cooler in both body and spirit, and our ships immediately steamed out of harbour. Even after we were away from the threatening gaze of the Dutchman, we kept a south-easterly course. Afterwards, however, we came about and steamed northwards for our real objective: the steamship route from Khota Raja to Colombo.

The weather, which had hitherto been beautiful, suddenly turned to strong and troublesome white squalls. These were welcome, as our fresh water was running very low; now stores were replenished simply by allowing the kindness of the heavens to fill every conceivable receptacle.

Our greatest lack was soap, lauded as the index of civilisation by uncharitable observers who have never endured its absence aboard ship. Soap had become a luxury for us, with each scrap used so exceedingly sparingly that the water in which the men washed was saved for their clothes and then the decks.

The squalls brought a sea with them, and *Emden* dipped her bows deeply and frequently until we finally reached the steamship route on 7th September.

Our war cruise had begun with the aim of missing not a single ship. Eyes and glasses were continually exercised, as everyone wished to be the first to exclaim 'Smoke in sight!'. Like the hunter, however, a sailor also needs luck. For this we in *Emden* seemingly hoped in vain. Hour after hour of cruising brought us nothing. Clearly we would have to search elsewhere, making instead for the shipping lane from Negabatam to Khota Raja on our way to the line between Colombo and Rangoon.

We reached our first objective on 8th September, but several hours of cruising again brought nothing but the conviction that capturing the enemy's merchant ships was not as easy as we had supposed. Not even a single sailing vessel was to be found in the three lanes we had scoured.

As the huntsman's patience must be shared by the seaman, we altered course again toward the important lane from Colombo to Calcutta. Fortune was still against us, but at least she winked. Scarcely had we reached the line, at about 2300 in the friendly darkness, when the lookout reported a light four points on the starboard bow.

Sighs of relief were heard. The order 'Clear ship for action!' ran through *Emden* like a clarion-call. We were away at full speed, with *Markomannia* following faithfully as best she could.

Courage, suspense and rejoicing were mixed within us, with some anger at the delay before we could make out what sort of ship we had found. At last we saw that she was a merchantman. Two blank rounds were fired to stop her, while the signal lamp flashed, in English, 'Stop your engines. Do not use wireless!'

The stranger obeyed at once. A prize crew had been told-off beforehand under the command of Oberleutnant z.S. d.R. Lauterbach. Armed to the teeth, it now rowed over to the stranger and boarded her. Things passed too slowly for the curiosity of us aboard *Emden*, for although our quarry was lit up by our searchlights, her nationality was still far from obvious. We were desperate for Lauterbach to tell us both this and the nature of her cargo.

At last the signal lamp blinked. 'Greek steamship. *Pontoporos*'. There was consternation aboard *Emden*. Our first prize since *Ryazan* was a neutral and must be allowed to go on her way! But Lauterbach had not finished: 'Carrying 6,500 tons of coal for the English Government. Bound from Calcutta to Bombay'. So she was carrying contraband which could be confiscated, and in the form of the coal we could use so well. In time of war, this was better than diamonds and pearls.

The dictates of war were at once followed, the prize crew being enlarged by some of our engine-room personnel while some of the boarding party returned to *Emden*. Lauterbach was put in command of the Greek steamer.

Kapitän von Müller asked the Greek skipper if he would be willing to serve Germany, in the guise of *Emden*, on receipt of proper payment. A signal-lamp message replied to the effect that both he and his command would readily do so. It mattered little to him whether he served Britain or Germany. What did matter was payment.

The Greek's consent simplified matters greatly, as coal could not be taken in immediately. The biggest problem was that *Pontoporos* could not steam at more than nine knots and would undoubtedly hamper our movements.

Lauterbach signalled that everything was in order aboard his charge and so we proceeded onwards in convoy, with *Markomannia* to starboard and *Pontoporos* to port where we could see them both.

We reverted to our course for the Colombo–Calcutta route and redoubled a lookout.

A smoke cloud was sighted to the north at 0800 on 10th September. *Emden* leapt towards it, cutting through the water in fine style. As we came nearer, we could make out a large steamship with an unusual superstructure. That she was British was proclaimed by the Blue Ensign waving proudly at her stern. Had she been chartered by the Admiralty or was she being run by the British government?

She steamed unconcernedly towards us, probably in the belief that *Emden* was a British warship. Her unwary conduct was otherwise difficult to understand. After studying the newcomer carefully, we concluded that she was unarmed. We immediately fired a warning round, simultaneously hoisting the German ensign and the international signal 'Stop! Do not use wireless!'

The British ship harkened to necessity and hove-to in 10°48′N 84°2′E, whereupon a boarding party under Oberleutnant z.S. von Levetzow and Vizesteuermann d.R. Meyer was sent across. After inspecting her papers, von Levetzow signalled 'steamship *Indus*, 3,143 tons, en route from Calcutta to Bombay for the Indian government. Equipped to carry troops and horses, which she is to take to Europe'.

Not bad! *Emden* had caught her just in time, before Indian troops could be taken to Europe to fight against Germany. Of course, it was a pity that the soldiers were not already aboard; then *Indus* would have been an even more welcome prize.

The practical British had supplied their trooper with ample provisions, giving us considerable satisfaction. What pleased us greatest, however, was that she was carrying a fantastic amount of soap. Such rejoicing at sea in wartime may seem surprising, but seafolk like cleanliness and we delighted in the news.

Thanking the British government for its far-reaching consideration and care in supplying us with just what we wanted, our second cutter was immediately called away to collect items from *Indus*.

Complicated arrangements became necessary as a result of our success, as stores had to be shipped to both *Markomannia* and *Pontoporos*. As the former was to receive the crew of *Indus*, Kapitänleutnant d.R. Klopper was sent over to act as navy commander. *Pontoporos* received the first officer of *Markomannia*, to serve as captain, while *Markomannia* received Vizesteuermann d.R. Meyer in return.

Pontoporos

SECOND SHIP INTERCEPTED

Completed in 1913 for National Steam Navigation Company of Greece by William Doxford & Sons Ltd of Sunderland (yard no.462), this 386ft steamship displaced about 7,480 tons (4,049grt) and could make nine knots. Seized on 9th September 1914 while under the command of Captain Polemis, laden with 6,500 tons of Indian coal owned by the British Government, she was recaptured on 12th October 1914 by HMS *Yarmouth*, returned to her former owners and eventually torpedoed by *UC21* in the Bay of Biscay in August 1917. Pontoporos was black-hulled, with red boot-topping and buff masts; her single funnel was buff with a black top above a blue band displaying 'E' on a white circle superimposed on a white saltire. The house flag duplicated the funnel band.

Indus

Board of Trade Registry 118440

THIRD SHIP INTERCEPTED, FIRST VICTIM

Built by C. Connell & Co. Ltd of Glasgow for James Nourse Ltd, London, 3,413grt 350ft single-screw *Indus* was registered in Glasgow with the call-sign VRNL. Chartered by the Indian government at the beginning of the First World War to serve as a troop transport, she was seized on 10th September 1914 while steaming in ballast from Bombay to Calcutta under Captain Henry Swaridge. Nourse's ships had black hulls with red boot-topping, masts and derricks being buff. The funnels were buff with a circlet of red triangles whose tips touched the black top. The house flag comprised a small blue lozenge superimposed on a blue saltire on a white ground.

Lovat

Board of Trade Registry 129401

FOURTH SHIP INTERCEPTED, SECOND VICTIM

Owned by J. Warrack & Co. of Leith, with the call-sign HSKT, this 6,102grt 405ft single-screw steamship was delivered from the yard of Russell & Co. of Port Glasgow in April 1911. Under charter to the Indian government as a troop transport, she was seized on 11th September 1914 while travelling from Calcutta to Bombay under the command of Captain Glegg. *Lovat* was immediately scuttled. Her funnel was black with a narrow white band; upperworks were white, masts were brown, and the topsides showed black above red boot-topping.

Once these arrangements had been completed, we joined forces to transfer provisions. First came the commodity we most needed; soon, soap was piled in mountains aboard *Emden*. Then came fresh provisions and, finally, the navigating instruments. There was never enough of these indispensable tools.

As the men were not familiar with requirements, first officer von Mücke went across to *Indus* about noon to supervise the transfers personally. Kapitän von Müller wished to hasten the transfer as much as possible, but decisions were difficult: faced with the treasures *Indus* had to offer, even for the first officer.

It was 1600hrs before our needs were satisfied. Kapitän von Müller, as ever, knew exactly what he wanted and simply declared the transfer complete once his requirements had been met. Our upper deck looked like a colossal warehouse. There were towels, soap, linen, tinned foods, fresh meat, live hens and ducks, drinks, nautical instruments, charts, pencils, and some very welcome oilskins for the cutters' crews and the watches.

Finally, *Indus* had to be sunk. To bury the ship in open sea, a scuttling party comprising an engineer, a petty officer and three stokers removed the doors between the boiler and engine rooms, and then opened the sea-cocks so that water would flow freely into the lower compartments of the ship. Its tasks completed, the party immediately returned to *Emden*.

The gunners were then ordered to accelerate the process with a few well-placed shells, but *Indus* declined to sink. As we could not afford to waste ammunition, and as the vessel would eventually sink anyway, we left her to her fate. But it was an hour before she began to settle; then slowly she listed, though surely, and began to ship a good deal of water. The bows went under, and all at once *Indus* rushed gurgling into the depths.

The spectacle was eerie. Escaping air made a loud bang, throwing up masses of debris, while the masts sprang several metres out of the water before splashing back audibly. Some of *Indus*'s boats remained afloat, but could neither be taken in nor easily destroyed. This was unfortunate, we reasoned, as they might betray to the enemy that *Emden* had been waging war on merchant shipping in these particular waters. But we could lose no more time, as there were more important things to be done, and so we proceeded on a northerly course.

The captain decided to remain among the steamship routes, capturing as many ships as possible before their disappearance was noticed. Our orders had been to use every opportunity to inconvenience the enemy. War is war!

The night passed quietly, nothing being sighted. The morning of 11th September was devoted to the division of the spoils, with Kapitänleutnant von Mücke sitting on his treasures like a pasha. As the goods were allotted to the Divisions, those which were superfluous were tossed over the ship's side.

Hardly had we finished our simple lunch in the wardroom than *Emden* was felt to turn and increase speed.

Tumbling out on deck, we discovered another ship in sight. At hunting speed we soon came up on our prey. The ensign and the usual 'Stop!' signal were hoisted, the steamship immediately hove-to, and Lauterbach – our most experienced prize officer – was sent over with the boarding party.

She was another Briton: *Lovat*, 6,012 tons, equipped as a trooper and chartered by the Indian government. Her destination was Bombay, but she had been captured in 16°25′N 86°32′E. There had been no scarcity aboard *Emden* since we had seized *Indus* and we had no intention of wanton robbery. All the captain wanted was news, so Lauterbach was instructed to confiscate all the newspapers he could find.

Lovat's crew, as was the custom in a ship bound for destruction, was allowed to pack all its possessions quickly and make ready to leave the ship for ever. The men were then transferred to *Markomannia*, where the captain of *Indus* was ruefully preparing to greet his fellow sufferers.

Lovat was to go the way of her predecessor, though with all her cargo. Bulkheads were bored, sea-cocks opened, and a few of Gaede's shells expended to help her on her last voyage. However, *Lovat* was as obstinate as *Indus*; as darkness fell, we simply left her to an inevitable fate.

The newspapers Lauterbach had brought back were eagerly examined, but were full of stories a baby would have refused to take seriously. We had been kept up-to-date by neutral wireless stations and so, knowing something of the truth of events in the theatres of war, were astonished at the lies the British papers dished out to the Indians. This was understandable from the British viewpoint, of course, as the Indian natives often viewed their masters with something less than enthusiasm; hence they had to be won over, or at least prevented from voicing their discontent too openly.

Much more interesting was news from *Markomannia*, where the chatter of the interned captains, enlivened with whisky and soda, had disclosed some important

Kabinga

Board of Trade Registry 125599

FIFTH SHIP INTERCEPTED

Photograph by courtesy of Laurence Dunn.

Built by Armstrong, Whitworth & Co. Ltd of Newcastle upon Tyne, one of four similar vessels for J.Bucknall Steamship Line, 4,657grt 400ft single-screw *Kabinga* was transferred to Ellerman & Bucknall on 1st January 1914. Registered in Liverpool, she used the call-sign HLCS. Seized on 12th September 1914, while bound for New York from Calcutta via the Suez Canal under the command of Captain Thomas Robinson, *Kabinga* was retained as a 'prison ship' until released on 14th September. The ship was black with red boot-topping and white upperworks. Her funnel was black with a circlet of six white diamonds, signifying the discovery of the gems in southern Africa. *Kabinga* was sold to African & Continental Steam Ship Co. Ltd (as *Lulca*) in October 1938, soon passing to Italy – as *San Leonardo* of Compania Ligure di Navigatori, Genova – but was interned in the USA in 1940. Impressed by the US Maritime Commission and renamed *Reigh Court*, she was sunk in a collision in June 1943.

Killin

Board of Trade Registry 124270

SIXTH SHIP INTERCEPTED, THIRD VICTIM

Built by C. Connell & Co. Ltd for Connell Bros. Ltd of Glasgow, 3,544grt 350ft single-screw *Killin* (call-sign HMPD) was registered in Glasgow. While under the command of Captain J.K. Wilson, she was seized on 13th September travelling from Calcutta to Colombo with six thousand tons of Indian coal. *Killin* was later scuttled. She is believed to have been a black ship with red boot-topping. Her funnel was red with a black top, the house flag comprising a white diamond centred on a halved ground of red (nearest the hoist) and blue.

information. That three more troopships followed behind *Indus* and *Lovat* was immediately signalled over to *Emden*.

This saved us seeking new prey. Now we could simply wait while one British ship after another ran onto our guns. So we set course for Calcutta and steamed slowly along the shipping lanes with lookouts posted.

A light was reported ahead towards 2200. The first of the anticipated ships! She was coming directly toward us, so *Emden* hardly needed to increase speed. This time the customary signal was not accompanied by a blank round, as a blast on our siren proved sufficient. The stranger immediately obeyed our order to heave-to without using her wireless.

We intended to search the ship properly next morning, so a prize crew commanded by Lauterbach and Leutnant z.S. Gyssling went aboard with orders to keep station near *Emden*. The signal came back: 'English ship *Kabinga*, 4,657 tons, with cargo of piece goods. From Calcutta to Bombay, Port Said, Mediterranean and New York'.

Though valuable, the cargo was of no use to us. In addition, most of it was American-owned; if we had sunk *Kabinga*, which we could have done within international law, we (or our government) would have been liable for the neutral cargo. This did not please Kapitän von Müller, who decided to use the ship as a depository – a Lumpensammler or 'dump' – for the crews of the ships we had already sunk. Without the timely intervention of *Kabinga*, with her largely neutral cargo, we would have been bound to use a captured ship for this purpose. She seemed specially designed for our needs! In addition, the master had his wife and children aboard. And though this was scarcely the most important factor in the decision to release *Kabinga*, it did give us the chance to show how Germany conducted war on merchant shipping.

Officers who were not on duty turned-in after *Kabinga* had been quietened. We were all glad of the opportunity to rest, but sleep was short: about three hours later came the order 'Clear ship for action!'

Zum teufel! What was it this time? Seizing my clothes, I rushed to my action station in the torpedo flat. This had the disadvantage that I could not immediately satisfy my curiosity – below, we could see nothing – and had to rely on information gleaned from the conning tower, with which we were connected by speaking tube. I soon learned that we had found another merchantman, so, as there was no work for the torpedomen, I went back on deck beneath the bridge. Here I could see everything without getting in anyone's way. There was too little room on the bridge itself, where it would be easy to obstruct the captain and the officer of the watch.

The new steamer was stopped by siren and megaphone in 17°55′N 86°24′E. Oberleutnant z.S. von Levetzow and Leutnant z.S. Zimmermann went aboard with the search party. Soon came the message 'English collier *Killin*, with 6,000 tons of Indian coal, from Calcutta to Bombay, speed eight to nine knots'.

By this time, *Markomannia*, *Pontoporos* and *Kabinga* had caught up. As the work of careful search and subsequent scuttling had to be undertaken by day, *Killin* was ordered to fall in with our proud little squadron. *Emden* took the van, with *Kabinga* and *Markomannia* on the starboard quarter and *Pontoporos* and *Killin* to port. This formation gave us a good view of our convoy, which was necessary to ensure that black-out was observed. A ship may be betrayed on a dark night by a single light at a great distance: this we wished to avoid, lest our fruitful activities should be prematurely curtailed by hostile warships. The possibility of this increased with the passing of every hour. Our voyage was no life-insurance, as we were well aware that the day would come when gallant little *Emden* would make the acquaintance of the bottom of the ocean. We held the idea in no esteem, but had resolved to sell our lives dearly.

Our cutters' crews began to row British seamen from *Markomannia* over to *Kabinga* in the morning of 13th September 1914. As a swell was running, the work was difficult even after *Emden* had given the oarsmen protection of her lee side. Lauterbach rejoined us, leaving Oberleutnant z.S. Geerdes to carry out the duties aboard *Kabinga*.

The scuttling party, meanwhile, had completed its unpleasant work aboard *Killin*. At about 1000, she was given a few German shells by way of leave-taking and plunged smartly into the depths for ever – though not without the usual sprinkling of flotsam that broke loose, arching out of the water to fall back with a splash. *Killin*'s funnel aspired briefly to heaven, but then sank.

By this time we had unrivalled practice sinking enemy ships, and preparations had become second nature.

As our cruise toward Calcutta resumed, we speculated on what the next surprise would be. The afternoon was peaceful at first. We off-duty lieutenants were playing

Diplomat

Board of Trade Registry 131457

SEVENTH SHIP INTERCEPTED, FOURTH VICTIM

Photograph of a sister-ship, *Explorer* of 1910 by courtesy of the Trustees of the National Maritime Museum, negative P16920. Note the torpedo damage.

One of five similar vessels built in Glasgow in 1904-12 (three by Connell and two by Henderson), 7,615grt/10,825dwt *Diplomat* was completed in October 1912 by C. Connell & Co. Ltd for T. & J. Harrison of Liverpool (Charente Steam Ship Co. Ltd, London). A single-screw twin-deck steamship driven by quadruple-expansion engines, she measured about 470ft overall and could make twelve knots; registered in Liverpool, she used the call-sign HWQM. She was scuttled on 13th September 1914, laden with tea for London and Liverpool from Calcutta, while under the command of Captain Robert Thomson. Like many Harrison ships of this era, *Diplomat* had four widely spaced masts. Her topsides were black, with a pink band separating the red boot-topping; upperworks were white, the funnel being black with three bands (white/red/white). The house flag comprised a red cross formy extending to the edge of a white ground.

bridge, just finishing a rubber when news reached the wardroom that another smoke cloud was in sight. Hastily, we threw in our cards and tumbled out onto the quarterdeck, eager to catch sight of the smoke.

Emden approached the new victim at full speed. She was a good-sized vessel with a big funnel, and soon we could make out the Red Ensign. We were very pleased: it would have been a pity had she been a neutral. The British ship soon stopped, taken in 18°1′ N 86°24′ E. Lauterbach and party went across to report 'English steamship *Diplomat*, 7,615 tons, with ten thousand tons of tea, from Calcutta to England'.

Kapitän von Müller decided to sink the ship on the spot, this time under the direction of the first torpedo officer, Oberleutnant z.S. Witthoeft. The scuttling party was soon assembled, armed with blasting charges and sent aboard *Diplomat*. The British ship's company left, the charges were laid and the sea-cocks opened. Then the blasting-charge fuzes were touched off together and the scuttling party immediately took to its boat. Scarcely had the last man left the ship when the explosion took place.

Meanwhile, *Emden* had sighted another smoke cloud and hared off in pursuit. That the quarry was a steamship was in no doubt, but her flag could not be identified. It had been decided that von Levetzow and I were to deal with her but, to our great disappointment, we made out the mercantile ensign of Italy as we approached. She was not only a neutral but an ally of the Triple Alliance, which made our visit all the more galling.

We boarded the ship with mixed feelings, to be received by her captain with some acidity. Von Levetzow asked for the ship's name and papers, received the necessary information and signalled back 'Italian steamer *Loredano*, en route for Calcutta'. Kapitän von Müller requested that the Italian captain be asked to land the crews of the ships we had sunk – about two hundred men all told.

I, meanwhile, had set guards and taken a look in the hold. The ship did not seem fully laden. Excepting a small cargo of crude wool, there was nothing of importance in *Loredano*.

Von Levetzow called me to him, as the captain spoke no English. I tried to convey von Müller's wishes, but Italian was out of the question: I understood only a few phrases. In French, however, we had more success... if success it could be called, as the Italian did not wish to convey men to Calcutta, even for payment, and remained obdurate even after I explained that we would supply food for them.

We were keen to rid ourselves of all the crews and sink *Kabinga* as well. But friendly words were useless and our

A hazy view of Harrison's *Explorer*, showing how *Diplomat* would have appeared to *Emden*. By courtesy of the Trustees of the National Maritime Museum; negative P16918.

ally remained acid. Levetzow signalled the fruitless discussions to *Emden* while *Diplomat*, with an elegant swing, had taken leave diplomatically and slid quietly to the bottom.

The Italian captain's uncooperative attitude was annoying. Then I hit on a ruse. Word by word in French, I asked him what he would do if we were to cast the crews adrift in open boats. He replied that he would be forced to take them on board. I proceeded cautiously: 'if you are prepared to do this, there can be no objection to your taking them on board immediately. And you would gain by it, too, for if you take them voluntarily you will receive payment and provisions'.

Enlightenment dawned on the Venetian until, after consideration, he agreed to co-operate. Von Levetzow immediately signalled the decision to Kapitän von Müller, but darkness had fallen and the transfer of the crewmen – always awkward – was not desirable at night.

Our captain sent back a message that the Italian's help was no longer necessary, as *Kabinga* would be retained.

There was nothing to do but leave *Loredano*, but not before von Levetzow had demanded the Italian's word of honour that he would preserve strict neutrality and assist in no actions hostile to us. This he gave, whereupon we returned to *Emden* glad to have nothing further to do with him. The two hours aboard the Italian vessel had been no pleasure.

About 1930hrs, *Emden* and her flotilla set course for Calcutta. However, as the untrustworthy *Loredano* steamed away in much the same direction, so we initially moved southward before reverting to a northerly course. Common sense demanded we should now leave the Colombo–Calcutta sealanes.

Loredano

EIGHTH SHIP INTERCEPTED

Completed by Hawthorn, Leslie & Co. Ltd of Newcastle upon Tyne in July 1905 as *Port Caroline*, this 4,149grt 381ft single-screw tramp had been sold to Societá Veneziana di Navigatori a Vapori by 1914. Registered in Venezia (Venice) and commanded by A. Giacopello – cf., *Dandolo* – she was stopped on 13th September 1914 bound for Calcutta. Being neutral, she was released to continue her journey but offended *Emden* by broadcasting the cruiser's presence.

Dandolo

NINTH SHIP INTERCEPTED

Owned by Societá Veneziana di Navigatori a Vapori, and registered in Venezia (Venice) with the call-sign NSCA, this Italian vessel was stopped on 13th September 1914 but released. Built by Cantiere Navale di Muggiano of La Spezia as *Muggiano*, and delivered in 1906, the 4,977grt 377ft single-screw steamship was commanded by Captain E. Giacopello . . . whose brother was in *Loredano* (q.v.). These ships were apparently black with red boot-topping, and had black funnels with two narrow white bands flanking a broad red one. Their house flag was a white lozenge on a green ground, the lozenge containing a golden Lion of St Mark on a rectangular cartouche split horizontally, red over white. The letters S V V N appeared in the corners, reading clockwise from the hoist.

Trabboch

Board of Trade Registry 128025

TENTH SHIP INTERCEPTED, FIFTH VICTIM

Built for Kyle Transport Co. Ltd of Liverpool, where she was registered with the call-sign HQPJ, this 4,028grt 352ft single-screw steamship was completed by A. McMillan & Sons Ltd of Dumbarton in March 1910. She was seized and scuttled on 14th September 1914, bound for Calcutta from Negabatam under Captain W.H. Ross. *Trabboch* had black topsides, red boot-topping and a plain black funnel. Kyle Transport's house flag was a simple white 'K' picked out of a blue lozenge on a red ground.

TRIALS AND TRIBULATIONS

Monday 14th September–Monday 21st September 1914

Our new objective was the steamer lane from Madras to Calcutta, where we hoped for rich booty. At about 2200hrs, the lookout reported a light; we were soon after it, cleared for action. Then we could make out a steamship and signalled "Stop your engines! Don't use wireless. What ship?"

We received a one-word answer: '*Dandolo*'. Another Italian! As we had no wish to be recognized, we simply signalled back 'Thank you. Bon voyage!' And off we went on our way, keeping at first to a fictitious course.

Our discretion had the unwelcome result of losing our companions, who could not follow quickly. In the frantic search for our convoy, we nearly rammed *Kabinga*. A collision was only averted by putting both ships full speed astern.

Safely back together, we laid a course for the Madras-Calcutta steamer lane. The night passed quietly, bringing us welcome rest and the chance to recover from the strain of the preceding days.

The pagoda of Puri came in sight in the morning of 14th September. Fooled by the mirage into believing it to be a ship, we made straight for it. The mistake was only discovered as we neared our goal, whereupon a strong landward current threatened to ground us in the shallows. To escape the beckoning mud banks, we beat a hasty retreat.

Once open water had been regained, *Emden* was stopped to complete the transhipment of the British crews begun the previous day as we had decided to abandon *Kabinga* with all her seamen captives. The work was, as usual, undertaken by the cutters. Finally, the *Kabinga* prize crew and Kapitänleutnant a.D. Klöpper's military commando from *Markomannia* returned to us. Arrangements were complete.

Before *Kabinga* could be released, however, another British-flagged ship was sighted. *Emden* speedily ran down and 'adopted' the newcomer in 19°55′ N 87°10′ E. She was ordered to join our convoy, whereupon the prize crew commanded by Lauterbach and Leutnant z.S. Fikentscher went across in company with the scuttling party under Oberleutnant z.S. von Levetzow.

The ship proved to be *Trabboch*, an empty collier of

Clan Matheson

Board of Trade Registry 121305

ELEVENTH SHIP INTERCEPTED, SIXTH VICTIM

Photograph by courtesy of Norman Middlemiss.

Completed by Furness, Withy & Co. Ltd of West Hartlepool in March 1906 for Clan Steamship Line, London (Cayzer, Irvine & Co. Ltd, Glasgow), the 4,775grt single-screw *Clan Matheson* measured 400ft overall. She was registered in Glasgow, her call-sign being HFQJ. Commanded by Captain William Harris, she was seized and scuttled on 14th September 1914 while bound for Colombo from Liverpool with a mixed load. Clan Line ships had black hulls with red boot-topping. Upperworks were white; masts and derricks were grey. Funnels were black with two red bands. The house flag comprised a red lion rampant on a white lozenge extending to the edges of a red ground.

4,028 tons making for Calcutta from the southern Indian harbour of Negabatam. The British ship's company was quickly transferred to *Kabinga*, which was immediately detached. Our 'dump' took leave politely, giving three cheers for *Emden* before vanishing into the darkness.

The unexpected ovation gave us great pleasure in *Emden* – recognition, we hoped, of the considerate treatment we had extended to our prisoners as far as circumstances would allow.

Trabboch's end made a spectacle quite unlike the others we had sunk. As soon as the prize crew and scuttling party left her, there had been a tremendous explosion accompanied by sheets of flame. The coal-dust in her holds had ignited to provide a wonderful display of fireworks against the blackness of the night.

We proceeded on our original course knowing the collier to be doomed. After about half an hour, a light was reported on the starboard beam. *Emden* was after it like a flash. The stranger must have been warned – or, perhaps, had seen the flames from *Trabboch* – as she had a full head of steam and was making a run for it.

A chase! A chase on the high seas, and in darkness! *Emden* was unquestionably faster and was soon within hailing distance. The signal to stop was given by siren; still the steamer kept on going. A few rounds of blank backed up the order to stop, but our quarry also left this summons unheeded. Our patience was exhausted and a live shell was placed across the steamer's bows. At that she stopped, in 19°55′N 87°11′E.

Emden sent the question, 'What ship?' The answer came back immediately: '*Clan Matheson*' – a British ship and, as she had tried to escape, one that must have a guilty conscience. Lauterbach and Schall were sent over to investigate. They discovered that the 4,775-ton vessel was carrying piece goods from England to Calcutta – and a valuable cargo it was, too, comprising motor cars, railway locomotives, bicycles, typewriters... and even a racehorse, which we later learned to have been entered on the list of the Calcutta Racing Club.

The utmost speed was required for the dispatch of the steamer. Klöpper and his military commando went back to *Markomannia*, while, concurrently, she took the British crew aboard. The scuttling party was also working at full speed.

Everything had been done within 45 minutes, whereupon the British ship and cargo were consigned to the deep.*

Emden now took an easterly course. Our objective was Preparis North Channel, protected by the Andaman Islands, which were especially suitable for the coaling that had now become necessary. We had taken nothing aboard since 5th September.

That night we intercepted a wireless message sent by the Calcutta lightship. Awakening no little anger aboard *Emden*, it read: 'As reported by the Italian steamship *Loredano*, the German cruiser *Emden* has sunk the *Diplomat*, *Kabinga* and *Pontoporos* at 18°1′N 86°24′E'. What an unpleasant business! The Italian captain had not kept his word. A breach of faith and rank betrayal of an ally could have been neither expected nor foreseen. We had not sunk *Kabinga* or *Pontoporos*, but that scarcely mattered. We heard later that the betrayal was sanctified by the Indian government. The Italian captain received a gold watch and chain – a true reward of Judas.

Kabinga, once free of our influence, had broadcasted with rather more truth: "The German cruiser *Emden*, with the collier *Markomannia*, has sunk outside Calcutta the steamships *Indus*, *Lovat*, *Killin*, *Diplomat* and *Trabboch*. The *Kabinga* herself has been abandoned with all the ships' companies".

15th September was a rest day for all of us. We were steaming well away from the shipping lanes, and an interception was as good as impossible. Our gallant men had to be granted their rest, for the previous days had taxed their endurance to the limit.

We officers were also glad of a day's relaxation, allowing us to prepare for the further efforts we knew would be demanded.

That evening we intercepted news sent by the Calcutta wireless station. It was concerned principally with our exploits and ended with the advice 'Look out for the *Emden*'. Clearly, in the Bay of Bengal – the part of the Indian Ocean in which we had done most harm – *Emden* was too well known. After coaling we would have to seek new pastures and, indeed, attempt to work more secretly.

Next morning, 16th September, brought brilliant weather and a mirror-like sea. Kapitän von Müller decided to use the chance to coal at sea. The attempt was to be our first. This time, coal from *Pontoporos* was to be transferred to *Emden*. We went alongside the collier and made fast, placing washboards and improvised fenders ('baskets' and 'elephant eyes') between the ships to ensure our freeboard would escape the worst of the damage as the ships rode together. *Pontoporos* lay to starboard.

After we had made fast, *Emden* went dead slow ahead with the starboard engines, while *Pontoporos* stopped hers. Coaling began from the steamer's after holds at about 0900. The great heat made the work arduous, but slack and dust from the poor-quality coal was all but unbearable. The coal we had been taking from *Markomannia* was Shantung, solid lumps that were not only easily handled but also of good calorific value.

Difficulties began immediately we started to unload *Pontoporos*. We succeeded in boring a hole in a heap of coal, to get at it from both sides at once, then the walls immediately collapsed and the digging had to begin again. We could hardly blame the men for the strings of oaths; indeed, we were in full empathy with the cursing. The work and choking dust were no better for us.

* Prinz Franz Joseph does not relate the story offered by van der Vat, Lochner and others that *Clan Matheson*, after replying to the initial challenge simply with her name, was asked 'English?' – only to retort, indignantly, 'British!' owing to her Scottish ownership. The notion that she was sunk because of her captain's 'insolence', as suggested in several of the 'Emden' books, is apocryphal: von Müller needed to take nothing from her and thus there was only one ultimate solution. The racehorse had been shot to prevent it suffering unnecessarily.

Discretion forced us to hurry and, towards midday, Indian coolies from the crew of *Clan Matheson* were put to work as well. Progress was no quicker, but the reinforcements gave some relief to our exhausted men. At 2200hrs we stopped, having taken aboard 440 tonnes of coal to fill the bunkers and replenish some of the deck stores.

In view of the bad quality of the coal and the great heat of day, our achievement was satisfactory. The defects of the Indian coal, first noticed during coaling, were fully revealed when the coal went into the furnaces. No longer would there be steaming without smoke – the clouds emanting from our funnels would betray us for miles. In addition, coal consumption increased dramatically, and the boilers and tubes became so dirty that cleaning (usually required every ten days) was needed continually. The complaints of Marine-Ingenieur Haas rang in our ears constantly.

To stop using *Pontoporos*'s Indian coal was impossible, as nobody knew when we should meet a collier. *Pontoporos* was our indispensable last reserve. Our captain had other plans for her, however: the collier was to be detached to rendezvous with *Emden*, as I remember, in the neighbourhood of Simaloer Island.

It was necessary to put an adequate guard aboard *Pontoporos*, as the Greek captain could not be trusted without supervision. The first officer of *Markomannia* and Vizesteuermann d.R. Meyer remained at their posts in *Pontoporos*, where they had been since the ship was impressed. Their command comprised a machinist acting as leading artificer, four petty officers and nine seamen.

Kapitän von Müller sent written instructions over to the Greek vessel, whose captain was assured that he and his crew would be set free as soon as *Markomannia* could offload all the coal from *Pontoporos*. Then he would also receive adequate recompense for his efforts.

Emden set course for Preparis North Channel once again, as *Pontoporos* steadily vanished over the horizon. At about noon on 17th September, we reached the intersection of the Madras–Rangoon and Calcutta–Singapore shipping lanes. There we cruised unsuccessfully for some hours. We passed Preparis channel after nightfall, then altered course for the Bay of Rangoon.†

Rangoon, the capital city of Lower Burma, then had about 180,000 inhabitants. We hoped to capture ships at the mouth of its harbour; from daybreak, therefore, we scanned the horizon in all directions. But the weather had changed, bringing white squalls which all too often resembled smoke clouds on the horizon. So often had we been disappointed that, by midday, we were growing impatient.

About 1600hrs we sighted a smoke cloud to southward, in the direction of the Molucca Straits. There was no sense in steaming directly towards the ship, but rather to cut off her way to Rangoon; escape would be difficult, as she was constantly in our sight. *Emden* came up with the steamer at nightfall. The order to stop was given, whereupon Lauterbach, who was a tireless prize officer, boarded the stranger with Leutnant z.S. Schmidt and the search party.

We had been deceived again. She was a neutral, the Norwegian ship *Dovre* of about 3,000 tons. Her captain greeted us warmly in German. Though meeting a neutral was annoying, we were able to rid *Markomannia* of *Clan Matheson*'s crewmen. The Norwegian skipper indicated his willingness to take them for a payment of a hundred Mexican dollars.‡

The transfer of the Britons to the Norwegian ship took place in our cutters, passing, to our mutual satisfaction, without incident. Lauterbach had been conversing with the Norwegian captain, who told him much of what we already knew – but also that he had been examined by the searchlight of a warship the previous night, and had met an auxiliary cruiser off Penang. As he professed to have come from Penang, Lauterbach and Schmidt questioned him closely about the harbour where, or so the Norwegian said, the armoured cruisers *Montcalm* and *Dupleix* were stationed.

The news was most interesting, and gave us the idea for the later attack on Penang harbour. *Dovre*'s captain then told Lauterbach that he would steam slowly into Rangoon, delaying his arrival until dawn so that *Emden* would be well away. The Norwegian captain took his leave as dusk fell.

With Lauterbach and the prize crew back aboard, *Emden* took a westerly course. Lauterbach had brought fresh newspapers with the latest news of the war. The stories of greatest interest to us were naturally those charting our exploits in the Bay of Bengal. The British papers did not belittle our successes, though they attempted to quiet anxious shipping and commercial circles with statements that *Emden* would shortly disappear for good – assuming she had not already been sunk.

Such bravado amused us greatly; far from being destroyed, we had not actually so much as seen an Allied warship.

Unwittingly, the Allied wireless stations gave us useful news. For example, the station at Diamond Point told us that gunfire had been heard at Akyab on the east coast of Burma, considerably to the north of Rangoon. This was very useful, as it clearly indicated districts we should avoid. Allied warships would undoubtedly have been sent there.

Our friend QMD had apparently been in communication with authorities ashore, as we heard a message from an intercepting station asking the identity of the mystery ship. A third had interjected obligingly: 'QMD is the armoured cruiser *Hampshire*'. We rejoiced at this disclosure, flattered that our suspicions about QMD had proved correct.

The weather was favourable enough on 19th September for *Markomannia* to be signalled alongside. We

† Now known as the Gulf of Martaban.

‡ In this era, Mexican dollars provided an acceptable standard currency in the Pacific Basin – a legacy, perhaps, of the one-time Spanish domination. There were still $500 of Mexican currency in the safes recovered from the *Emden* wreck by HM Sloop *Cadmus* in 1915.

Dovre
TWELFTH SHIP INTERCEPTED

This 1,181grt 225ft Norwegian steamship, built for AB Dampskibs 'Dovre' (Bruusgaard, Kjøsterud & Co.) by Trondheims Mekaniske Vaerkstad in 1906, was stopped on 18th September 1914 and instructed to land the crew of *Clan Matheson* (victim 6, q.v.) at Rangoon. *Dovre* was registered in Drammen, used the call-sign MCSB, and was commanded by Ingo Sigveland.

still had spare stowage capacity and, as we could meet an enemy warship at any moment, it was imperative that we had as much coal aboard as *Emden* could carry. We had no way of knowing when another favourable opportunity would present itself.

Coaling began at 0700hrs and lasted until about 1500, a little over three hundred tonnes being transferred. The procedure was similar to the *Emden/Pontoporos* system devised three days previously, excepting that we stopped our engines while *Markomannia* steamed slow ahead.

Finally, we had nine hundred tonnes of coal aboard. In spite of the debilitating heat, our crewmen worked magnificently. However, they were exhausted and it was clear that the next night should be one of rest. As we were no longer on a shipping route, it passed without disturbance.

Late that evening we passed through Preparis South Channel, between Preparis and Great Coco Islands in the Andaman archipelago, and full war watches were set.

During the night *Hampshire*'s wireless was so loud that our radio-telegraphists estimated she could be no more than ten nautical miles distant. After midnight, once through Preparis South Channel, we altered our course for Madras.

Madras was then the capital of the Presidency of the same name, the most important town on the east coast of India with a population of 517,355. It was also the country's third largest port, the seat of the Governor, and lay along the flat beach for about 23 kilometres with a breadth of about ten. On the beach in the middle of the town lay old Fort St George. The harbour was protected by a large mole and sported, on its southernmost tip, the storage tanks of the Burmah Oil Company.

The principal objective of our attack was to unsettle the Indian inhabitants, but we also wished to destroy the oil tanks and – if possible – the ships lying at anchor.

Sunday 20th September brought us Divine Service and an afternoon of rest. Off-duty officers either sat in the wardroom playing cards or occupied themselves reading the latest English papers. On the basis of the news these contained, the first officer gave a lecture to the petty officers and men about the events of war.

On Monday 21st September, we held a big action-station practice, supervised by Kapitän von Müller in person. We had not had an exercise for some time, owing to lack of opportunity; now the day seemed especially favourable, particularly as we intended to attack Madras the next evening and were liable to meet an enemy warship.

At the very least, we had to reckon that our fire would be answered by the St George battery. Our nautical handbooks suggested that it had six-inch guns. Although they would be old – or so we assumed, as the fort dated from the 1880s – six-inch shells were never to be underestimated. Even if they were completely up-to-date, however, the decision had been taken; the plan would be carried out, come what may.

Surprise would be in our favour and we should be able to hinder British counter-battery fire with our powerful searchlights. Who dares, wins...

Madras

A HOT NIGHT IN MADRAS

Tuesday 22nd September 1914

On 22nd September 1914, the German submarine U9, commanded by Kapitänleutnant Otto Weddigen, sank the British armoured cruisers *Aboukir*, *Cressy* and *Hogue* some twenty nautical miles north-west of the Hook of Holland and returned safely to Wilhelmshaven.

In our official war annals, under the same date, appears: 'the German light cruiser *Emden* is also noteworthy. From 10th September onward she made war on British merchant shipping in the Bay of Bengal and caused losses to the British flag to the extent of twenty million Marks'.

After listing names and descriptions of the individual ships, the annals continue: 'when...*Emden*, on 22nd September, also set fire to the oil tanks of the Burmah Oil Company in Madras, and escaped despite the fire from the fort, even greater anxiety was aroused in Britain'.

The Times noted that the courage of our cruiser deserved recognition, as officers and men alike must have been aware that – sooner or later – *Emden* would be caught and shot to pieces. Escape was simply impossible.

The *Daily Chronicle* wrote that "*Emden* has had a momentous cruise. The ship's company have proved their gallantry. We admire the sportsmanship shown in their exploits as much as we heartily wish that the ship may soon be taken".

So much for the chronicles of war. It is important to return to the reality of the attack on Madras, as official news is usually much too colourless to present an accurate picture.

22nd September 1914 was a really beautiful day, the like of which is experienced nowhere but in the tropics. We had plenty of work to occupy us all day: flammable articles were stowed beneath the armoured deck, then more ready-use live ammunition had to be brought up for the guns.

An officers council was convened after lunch under the presiding eye of the first officer, von Mücke. It was necessary to reiterate the importance of our shipboard duties, and to give us instructions should the captain and the first officer fall in the attack on Madras. Every eventuality had to be discussed.

The men were given the opportunity to bathe in fresh water and ordered to don clean clothes, hygienic measures designed to keep wounds as clean as possible. This foresight was doubly necessary in the tropics, where festering was far more rapid than in European climes.

Markomannia was detached at the appointed spot late that evening, signalling us 'Wish you the best of luck!' Now we were alone once more.

'S.M. Kleiner Kreuzer "Emden" beschiesst Madras im Golf von Bengalen. 22 1
Sept. 1914.' This is an interesting, if somewhat fanciful postcard published 2
by 'E.P. & Co. AG, L[eipzig]' after a painting that had appeared in the *Illustrierte Zeitung*, Leipzig, in 1914. It is suspiciously similar to a contemporary watercolour by the renowned German marine artist Willy Stower (below), but it is not clear which is the older. The Hohenzollern memoirs indicate that *Emden* entered the Gulf under the guise of a British cruiser, with the dummy fourth funnel raised throughout the action. This is not evident in either picture. By courtesy of The Lyon Press archives.

Our fourth funnel was hoisted at nightfall. The engines were 'all clear for full speed'; each and every boiler had a full head of steam, so that maximum speed could be used at will.

Towards 2000hrs, the Madras light came in sight. We were astounded that it should still be burning, proof of the unwariness of the British authorities. They cannot have expected an attack, perhaps regarding as impossible the chance that a fortified harbour would attract impudent Germans. So much the better for us: surprise was our best ally.

Another shock awaited us as we approached the town. The harbour lights were all burning, and Madras was a sea of light. How different it would be in Germany, we mused. Lighthouses on the German coast had been extinguished at the beginning of hostilities and an effective blackout was enforced in the coastal towns.

As 2100 approached, we came close enough for the order 'Clear ship for action!' to be given. Searchlights and guns were manned at once. As there was little chance that our torpedoes would be required, I stayed for a while in the after battery with my friend von Levetzow. Naturally, I wished to see something of our splendid undertaking. My guess that torpedoes would not be fired proved accurate.

We rushed toward the harbour at seventeen knots, steering, thanks to the Madras lights, so that the oil tanks and battery would be in line when we opened fire. At 2145 we were still about three thousand metres from land. *Emden* then turned to port and stopped. Immediately came the order: "Switch on for'ard searchlight. Open fire!" It was a heart-stopping moment.

A few seconds later the first salvo blazed out, but went over. The second salvo – hard on the heels of the first – found its mark, and tongues of flame soared from the oil tanks. One shell struck a steamer lying at the mole.

Von Levetzow and I were very anxious about the return fire from the Fort St George battery but, to our astonishment, not a shot was fired. A few shells fell about a hundred metres short of us, but we could not determine whence they came. I suspected there was a gun on the

mole, as this seemed to be the origin of the shells. I admit I had imagined our baptism of fire would be livelier.

When 125 rounds had been fired, Kapitän von Müller ordered 'Cease fire!'. The results of our night shooting were that the oil tanks had been set alight, a few shells had done some damage in the town and one ship had been struck.* *Emden* had received no hits.

A few Madrassi had been killed, we later learned, though this had been unintentional. The attack was directed only at important targets. However, the town may have been consumed by the flames of the oil tanks had the wind been anything but westerly. Fortunately, the fire stood out seawards.

The effect of our raid on Madrassi morale was encouraging, newspapers subsequently informing us that many people left the town the next day by rail. We must have made quite an impression!

Searchlights were extinguished after the cease-fire and our electric lights were directed to port. Fully visible, we steamed on a fictitious northerly course. It was vital to mislead the enemy at this point; had we taken our true course at once, there was little doubt that enemy warships would soon be on our tracks.

We steamed northward for a short time, then extinguished all lights, turned about and made off to the south. The night passed with the least disturbance, the horizon lit like some giant torch by the fire we had kindled. Even next morning, at a distance of sixty nautical miles, we could see the smoke pall from burning oil – a sure sign that our work was completing itself unassisted.

* One of *Emden*'s shells hit British India Steam Navigation Company's steamer *Chupra* (Barclay Curle & Co., Glasgow, 1906: 6,175grt), moored in the harbour. A seventeen-year old cadet, Joseph Fletcher, was killed by splinters; Cadet Wheeler was seriously injured, while three other boys were slightly wounded.

SUGAR AND SPICE AND ALL THINGS NICE

Wednesday 23rd September – Monday 28th September 1914

In the early morning of 23rd September, we again fell in with *Markomannia*. The collier's company was immediately given a brief account of our success.

Between 0500 and 0600 we passed the French harbours of Pondicherry and Cuddalore, in whose roads we had hoped to surprise some ships. But our hopes were dashed.

As there was nothing for us in this neighbourhood, we sought other fields for our activity. We had searched the Bay of Bengal so thoroughly, indeed, that we could expect nothing more. The anxiety of the British was such that some harbours lost their trade completely for a while. Rangoon and the Burmese Peninsula, for example, were blocked for fourteen days: nothing could enter or leave. Our reputation was an effectual deterrent by itself.

We congratulated each other at this news, for where was the Royal Navy, mistress of the seas? Nowhere had we encountered Britannia's representatives.

Our next objective was the island of Ceylon, past which we intended to steam at an appropriate distance and board any ships we met. In the wardroom, we freely expressed two of our greatest wishes – that the first ship we met should be carrying the best coal; the second, the latest newspapers. *Emden* was in great need of good coal, as Shantung in *Markomannia* was diminishing rapidly and the pitiful Indian stuff in *Pontoporos* caused only anxiety. Anyone who has had to work with Indian coal will understand the daily prayer of chief engineer Ellerbroek to surprise an Admiralty collier with Cardiff coal.

I had a feeling that we should come across such a ship within a few days, but Ellerbroek met my guarantee with scepticism. But I was soon proved right.

It may sound strange, but rarely do several men have identical premonitions only to be proved wrong. Of course, there was some logic behind my guarantee. I reasoned that colliers must be on their way to Singapore and Hong Kong, where there would be many British warships in need of fuel. Why, then, should we not have the luck to encounter one?

By 24th September we were on patrol. Particularly lively wireless transmissions were intercepted in the evening, but, as they were in cypher, we could only tell that warships were communicating with each other in the vicinity.

In the hope that ships would be more plentiful along the coast than at sea, we edged nearer Ceylon on 25th September. At midday, we sighted the lofty mountains of southern Ceylon with their beautiful and varied scenery. We cruised along the coast at a distance of twenty nautical miles, where we would undoubtedly spot any steamer coming towards us while remaining invisible from the shore. A reversion to Shantung coal minimized the smoke emitting from our funnels.

We drew ever nearer the Colombo–Penang–Singapore steamship lane, the most important link in the whole Indian Ocean between Britain and her East Asiatic possessions. Soon after lunch we spotted a smoke cloud. Without increasing speed we slowly but surely approached the ship. As we neared her, we could see she flew the British mercantile flag. So we immediately hoisted our own ensign.

I would have given anything to see the expressions on the Britons' faces. *Emden* went close and ordered the steamer to stop. Lauterbach and Leutnant z.S. Schmidt went aboard with the prize crew, and sent back: 'English ship *King Lud*, 3,650 tons, in ballast, from Suez to Calcutta'. She had been taken in 5°47′N 79°46′E.

As *King Lud* was to be sunk immediately, the torpedo officer and the scuttling party went aboard as well. Under the direction of our steward and his men, we took a splendid supply of stores from our captive. The meat and potatoes, in particular, were of great value.

The transfers were completed in an hour, during which the ship's company had been moved to *Markomannia* along with Kapitänleutnant Klöpper's commando.

By about 1600hrs, *King Lud* was so disabled that she could be left to the mercy of the deep. Her last voyage into the depths could be watched as we went on our way. Our orders were to pass Colombo in darkness, as the harbour was one of the largest in the East and was sure to be well defended.

By 2000 we were about thirty miles south of Colombo. The British here did not wish to repeat the mistake of Madras: searchlights played over the horizon constantly and we assumed that ships would be patrolling outside the harbour.

An hour later we sighted a ship to port, steaming with all lights burning. *Emden* made towards her, leaving *Markomannia* holding our original course. Approaching the vessel, we saw her to be a large oil-tanker with the quirky funnel-aft appearance of all her kind. Overtaking her from the stern, we hailed her by megaphone. Back came her response: 'Norwegian steamship *Oceanis*'.

As we had no wish to be recognized, *Emden* hastily responded 'Proceed. Bon voyage!' and steamed back to rejoin *Markomannia*.

Our next objective was a small island west of Colombo, on the steamer lane from Colombo to Minicoy, where a lighthouse served as a beacon for Colombo harbour. Every ship coming to Colombo from the west passes Minicoy.

Towards 2200, the lights of a ship were seen off the starboard bow. We gained the impression that she had come straight out of Colombo harbour. How well silhouetted she was by the searchlights!

Moving quietly along our original course, we were bound to meet the ship at a safe distance from the coast. At 2300, in 7°10′N 79°21′E, Lauterbach and I went over with the prize crew. Soon we discovered our captive to be the 3,500-ton British ship *Tymeric*, on passage to England with 4,000 tons of sugar – a fine cargo to sweeten the seawater!

Tymeric was instructed to follow *Emden*, as we did not wish to sink her too close to Colombo harbour. We also intended to give the British crew time to pack its belongings.

However, when Lauterbach ordered the captain to follow *Emden*, both he and his chief engineer refused. What were we to do? Naturally, Lauterbach flashed the news to von Müller. Hardly had the message been dispatched than *Tymeric*'s captain, enraged by running into our hands right outside Colombo harbour, began to curse the 'damned Germans'.

With such a fellow the shortest way was best, so Lauterbach asked permission to sink the ship immediately. Von Müller granted it at once, sending additional men over from *Emden* to reinforce our prize crew. The British captain and engineer were transferred to *Emden*, while the remainder of the crew was taken over to *Markomannia*. Owing to the change in plan, *Tymeric*'s men had not been able to pack their things.

I was present when the captain expressed a wish to pack up his belongings. In the event, there was time only to take his mess jacket and some underclothes. Of course, he deserved such treatment for his insolence, yet I was sorry in the knowledge that his personal effects would soon be prey to the waves. However, a strict example had to be made – especially as, after capture, a master and his crew were under German martial law.

I could also understand his anger at the Royal Navy staff in Colombo which, as the irate man explained, had solemnly guaranteed that the coast was clear. He had his countrymen to thank for this dubious advice. We had nothing to do with it.

The British crewmen were aggrieved with their captain, whose intransigence had lost their possessions. Their oaths to make him suffer at the first opportunity amused us greatly.

The Britons were no sooner aboard *Markomannia* than *Tymeric* had been readied for sinking. Firstly, however, the abundance of fresh provisions discovered aboard our captive were transferred to the cutters and a rapid-but-effective search had found recent newspapers. Their accounts of our exploits proved very entertaining.

While Lauterbach and I were carrying out our duties with the prize crew aboard *Tymeric*, *Emden* had sighted another ship. However, it could be safely assumed that this was the neutral Dutch mail steamer *Konigin Emma*, which had previously wirelessed her impending arrival in Colombo. We let her go unchallenged.

Once the Dutch vessel had passed by, Lauterbach reported to *Emden* that *Tymeric* was readied for sinking. I returned to *Emden* with the prize crew, followed by von Levetzow and his successful scuttling team. We did not wait for *Tymeric* to sink after the explosion, but proceeded at once on our previous course. By this time, the

King Lud

Board of Trade Registry 124273

THIRTEENTH SHIP INTERCEPTED, SEVENTH VICTIM

Built by J.L. Thompson & Sons Ltd of Sunderland for King Line Ltd, delivered in November 1906 and registered in Stockton-on-Tees with the call-sign HJRB, 3,650grt 350ft *King Lud* was seized and scuttled on 25th September 1914 while travelling in ballast from Alexandria to Calcutta. She had a black-topped buff funnel and buff masts. Topsides were black; boot-topping was red.

Oceanus

FOURTEENTH SHIP INTERCEPTED

Hailed and hove-to, but released when her nationality was realized, this tanker was a neutral Norwegian.

Tymeric

Board of Trade Registry 113930

FIFTEENTH SHIP INTERCEPTED, EIGHTH VICTIM

Built by Russell & Co. of Port Glasgow for Tymeric Steam Ship Co. Ltd (managed by A. Weir & Co.), this 330ft 3,314grt single-screw tramp had been delivered in January 1901. She was seized and scuttled on 25th September 1914, while bound for Falmouth under the command of Captain John J. Tulloch. Her cargo was largely sugar. *Tymeric* had a black hull with red boot-topping. Her uppers were buff, the funnel being buff with a black top.

captain and engineer of *Tymeric* had been lodged under restraint on *Emden*'s middle deck. Later they were transferred to the Minenhellegat,* where they were watched by pistol-carrying guards.

Although it was past midnight, we officers immediately rushed for the newspapers. They contained plenty about the war at home, though most of the reports were garbled. We were most interested in the reports of our exploits off Madras and learned for the first time how our enemy saw our activities.

The papers were preoccupied with the damage to the oil-tanks and their contents, claimed to amount to the large sum (for those days) of twenty million gold Marks. We also read claims that inhabitants were leaving for the interior in droves, many of them travelling on the roofs of the railway carriages.

Naturally, we wished that the feeling of insecurity and the general mood of unrest should spread to the interior of India. The papers freely blamed the inactivity of the Allied warships for the troubles, opining that the Royal Navy should have been able to catch *Emden* with the larger number of cruisers at its disposal.

For *Emden* herself, and for Kapitän von Müller in particular, there was nothing but praise. The papers talked enthusiastically of 'fair play' and talked of our captain as a real sportsman – great praise indeed, from a nation where sport is a national obssession.

There were many articles about us, all offering similar opinions. One paper was particularly witty. Among its advertisements was one for a common soap, accompanied by the legend: 'this... is so good that even the *Emden* took it from the *Indus* and used it'. I firmly believed that the joke would be appreciated by the British.†

We were still scanning the papers at 0100, when suddenly a night alarm rang out. A new victim was in sight: proof that we were on the right route. Lauterbach and Leutnant z.S. Zimmermann went over with the prize crew, with instructions to take command of the vessel and follow astern of *Emden*.

We were naturally curious about the new prize. She turned out to be the British steamship *Gryfevale*, travelling from Aden to Colombo in ballast. Kapitän von Müller immediately decided to use her as a dump.

When all was clear, we resumed course for Minicoy. Our lookout sighted a Dutchman passing distantly at dawn on 26th September, which suited us admirably as we did not wish to be recognized in the neighbourhood. As the Dutch steamer had a wireless, she could easily have put hostile cruisers on our track. Around 1200, the ship's smoke cloud disappeared over the horizon. We hoped we had not been seen.

Soon afterward, however, we intercepted a call from a British ship asking the Dutchman if she had seen anything of *Emden*. We were greatly relieved when the Dutch ship answered 'for reasons of neutrality, answer refused'. It is not clear to this day whether we had been seen. But at least the Dutch captain conducted himself as a true neutral.

Intercepted wireless messages then announced the impending arrival of the Danish motor-ship *Fionia*, which steamed past us in the early evening clearly lit as befits a large passenger vessel. We did not trouble her. Lauterbach and the captain of *Gryfevale* offered the opinion that she was a British India liner, but our captain had no wish to chase an unknown – and very fast – ship proceeding towards Colombo.

Early in the morning of 27th September, at about 0300, we saw another ship coming our way. Her lights seemed those of a merchantman. As she approached us, however, the lookout suddenly announced the presence of another vessel steaming unlit behind the newcomer. 'Clear ship for action!' was ordered as we sheered off to port. We had no wish to fall into a trap. Thank heaven! The mystery ship was a dark smoke cloud, presumably thrown out by the stranger while cleaning fire and then stoking up again.

Assured that we were not running into a hostile warship, we halted the steamship in the usual way. Von Levetzow and Gyssling went aboard with the prize crew, signalling back: 'English steamship *Buresk*, 4,350 tons, cargo 6,600 tons first-class Cardiff coal, chartered by British Admiralty, from England to Hong Kong'.

Great was the joy aboard *Emden*. At last we had some decent coal, and better than Welsh we could not do. Most pleased of all was Marine-Oberingenieur Ellerbroek, who hugged me enthusiastically; after all, I had prophesied the prize. The priceless collier had been taken in 7°24′N 76°41′E.

We now had sufficient coal for the foreseeable future. As *Markomannia* would soon be empty, the captain decided to appoint *Buresk* our Hilfsschiff or 'follower'. She was also quite speedy for a collier, being capable of ten knots. I was later told that she could occasionally reach twelve.

Gallant *Markomannia* had accompanied us faithfully since 6th August, and had given us good service in many differing ways. When we learned that *Buresk* held 1,600 tons more coal than *Markomannia* had had when we left Tsingtau, our hopes of being able to rely on her increased dramatically. We decided to exhaust *Markomannia*'s Shantung coal immediately and then abandon her.

To achieve this, however, *Buresk* had to be properly manned. Kapitänleutnant d.R. Klöpper was given the command, with Leutnants z.S. Gyssling and Schmidt as officers of the watch. Torpedomaschinist Wittkopf, whom we had taken from *Cormoran* in Tsingtau to make up our war complement, was appointed chief engineer. Two Maschinistenmaaten, two seamen and three stokers were also sent over. The Arab crew of *Buresk* was retained – partly because we did not wish to send over too many of our own men and, second, because it was desirable to have experienced men aboard.

All the British crewmen were transferred from *Markomannia* to *Gryfevale*, the appointed dump. Britons from

* The Minenhellegat was a small flat in which the minesweeping gear was prepared.
† In *The Last Corsair*, Dan van der Vat names the soap-brand as 'Elysium'.

Gryfevale

Board of Trade Registry 121326

SIXTEENTH SHIP INTERCEPTED

Delivered in April 1906 to Gryfevale Steam Ship Co. Ltd (managed by A. Crawford, Barr & Co.) by Grangemouth & Greenock Dockyard Co., the 4,437grt 370ft single-screw *Gryfevale* was registered in Glasgow with the call-sign HGCQ. Out of Aden, bound for Colombo in ballast under the command of Captain J.W. Steel, she was seized by *Emden* on 26th September 1914 and retained as a 'dump' until released two days later. On 21st October 1917, *Gryfevale* was chased onto the coast north of Cap Blanco by a U-boat and became a total loss. Black hulled, with red boot-topping and white upperworks, she had a plain black funnel with three narrow bands (blue/black/blue). Masts and derricks were grey, while the house flag comprised a large blue 'C' on a plain white ground.

Buresk

SEVENTEENTH SHIP INTERCEPTED, EIGHTEENTH VICTIM

Painting by courtesy of Laurence Dunn.

Built by Richardson, Duck & Company of Stockton on Tees — yard no.638 — for Buresk Steam Ship Co. Ltd (Burdick & Cook) of London and completed in May 1914, this single-screw 4,337grt 380ft steamship displaced about 7,880 tons. Registered in London, her call-sign was JFMK. *Buresk* could make a mere ten knots at full speed. Laden with 6,600 tons of Welsh coal, she was seized on 27th September while travelling from Barry to Hong Kong under the command of Captain Frederick Tayler. The German prize crew scuttled her on 9th November 1914 to avoid being challenged by HMAS *Sydney*. *Buresk* had a plain black funnel, brown masts, white uppers, black topsides and red boot-topping.

Buresk were also to be transferred, but the master and chief engineer then asked to remain aboard.

Kapitän von Müller did not object, but, as so often happens, the initial request was followed by others. The second engineer, a steward and the Norwegian ship's cook all asked to remain with their captain. What had been said to one must also be said to another; in this case, the requests could all be granted without anxiety. The five Europeans were unlikely to pose much danger to our own men in *Buresk*. We did not quite understand the requests, as the men would be prisoners of war. Faced with the same circumstances I, for one, would have taken my freedom. But an old sea dog is not always easily separated from his floating home, so we let the men stay.

Once von Levetzow had returned to *Emden*, we proceeded on our course – once again steaming in the famous echelon, with *Buresk* to port and *Gryfevale* to starboard. *Markomannia* brought up the rear behind *Gryfevale*.

27th September was another exquisite day, being particularly clear and pleasant. The sea was like a mirror. Divine Service was held in the morning, as customary on Sunday. As there was no chaplain on small cruisers, Divine Service was celebrated by the senior Protestant naval officer; in *Emden*'s case, this was our captain. After Divisions, church was piped by the Bootsmannsmaat, whereupon the Protestant crewmen who were not on duty assembled on the middle deck aft. The band played a hymn, which was followed by readings from the Bible, a sermon, the Lord's Prayer and a closing hymn. The Catholic service was held in the forecastle. The senior officer was the adjutant, Leutnant z.S. von Guérard; however, he was usually on duty in the wireless room and so the task fell to me. The Epistle and Gospel were read, followed by meditation and prayers.

Divine Service was given as ceremonial a character as possible, though the ceremony itself had to be kept simple in the restricted space aboard a ship of *Emden*'s

Ribera

Board of Trade Registry 118484

EIGHTEENTH SHIP INTERCEPTED, NINTH VICTIM

Built by J.L. Thompson & Sons Ltd of Sunderland for Bolton Steam Shipping Co. Ltd, and registered in London with the call-sign HBDR, 3,500grt 336ft single-screw *Ribera* was seized and scuttled 27th September 1914 while travelling in ballast from Alexandria to Batavia. She had been under the command of Captain James Isdale. Bolton ships were black-hulled with red boot-topping, buff masts and plain black funnels. The house flag comprised a red 'FB' on a white lozenge on a red ground.

Foyle

Board of Trade Registry 115800

NINETEENTH SHIP INTERCEPTED, TENTH VICTIM

Built for Mercantile Steam Ship Co. of London by J.L. Thompson & Sons Ltd of Sunderland, being completed in April 1902, the single-screw 4,147grt 345ft *Foyle* was seized and scuttled on 27th September 1914 while travelling in ballast from Port Said to Rangoon under the command of Captain William Gibson. She had been registered in London and had the call-sign THPG.

Djocja

20TH SHIP INTERCEPTED

A Dutch (neutral) vessel, belonging to the Batavia Line. Stopped, but allowed to proceed.

type. Neither was there much time for preparation, but we had to be content. The plentiful goodwill enabled us to give the men spiritual edification. Our captain placed great importance on the Sunday services, as they gave the Lord's Day a different character from weekdays even though strenuous work was all too often unavoidable. We were at war, after all.

Once Divine Service was over, the men were allowed off duty whenever possible. However, a ship would often intercede and men were required for the prize crew or scuttling party. As most of them regarded a prize as a fit substitute for relaxation, there were few complaints.

27th September had begun perfectly and looked like continuing well – a day of rest in beautiful weather – when Lauterbach in *Gryfevale* signalled: "Captured ships' companies are making trouble through drunkenness. Some fighting. Have put several men in irons. Urgently request reinforcement".

Emden sinking the British steamer *Ribera* – an atmospheric but dramatized view in which the perspective and detailing of the cruiser are questionable. The wings of the bridge, for example, are much too wide in relation to the charthouse, and the anchor is not only too big but too close to the stem. The steamer's name is wrongly rendered as 'Riberia', and her funnel was actually black. By courtesy of the Bundesarchiv, Koblenz; Bild 134-C2331.

Lauterbach's humanity, which had induced him to allow some of the Britons to take drink with them from their ships (whisky was favourite), was well rewarded. He was immediately ordered to confiscate the liquor – not that much was left. *Emden* approached *Gryfevale* so that von Müller could hail Lauterbach.

The excitement soon subsided. The British captains apologized for the antics of their men and there the matter ended. *Gryfevale* took up her previous position and we hoped to get some Sunday rest after all.

No sooner had we sat down to our sumptuous midday meal – soup, corned beef with rice, stewed fruit! – than we noticed *Emden* was increasing speed. Steaming at full speed meant one thing. That was enough for us. Leaving the soup standing, we all dashed to the bridge and quarterdeck to see what was happening.

The usual smoke cloud on the horizon cleared to reveal a steamship with a single funnel.

Our prize crew, under the command of Oberleutnant z.S. Geerdes and Leutnant z.S. Schall, was immediately piped away in the duty (port) cutter. We had stopped the 3,500-ton British steamship *Ribera* in 7°30′N 75°26′E. Though she was travelling in ballast, we still found plentiful provisions and a complete signal book aboard. Some of the food was transferred to *Emden*, while the remainder went over to *Gryfevale* with *Ribera*'s crew.

To give Kapitänleutnant Gaede's gunners some practice, our captain decided to dispatch *Ribera* by shellfire. Everything went smoothly and she sank very quickly.

Then we inspected the signal book. On her last voyage to the Indian Ocean, we discovered, *Ribera* had met a British troop convoy sailing for Aden. Consisting of seventy ships, this had been escorted by the British battleship *Swiftsure* and the Russian armoured cruiser *Askold*. This we knew as *Ribera* had exchanged signals with both of them.

Again we set course for Minicoy, hoping to surprise a few ships on the way but also feeling that it was time we vanished. Coaling was once again necessary. At nightfall came the report 'Steamship in sight on the starboard bow!'

We allowed the new victim to approach quietly, whereupon von Levetzow and Fikentscher were sent over with the search party, closely followed by Marine-Ingenieur Haas and the scuttling team. Von Levetzow signalled back: 'English steamship *Foyle*, 4,147 tons, without cargo, from Aden to Colombo'. We had stopped her in 7°56′N 47°5′E.

Foyle was being readied for immediate sinking when a brightly lit ship was sighted. Consequently, von Levetzow was ordered to follow *Emden* and her train of merchantmen – *Markomannia*, *Buresk* and *Gryfevale* – as we went to investigate the newcomer. A profusion of lights raised hopes of a rich mail-packet, as a result of which Zahlmeister-Applikant Bordeaux was added to the prize crew to act as a Teller should a large sum of money be forthcoming.

We were due a severe disappointment. The ship was a mail packet, but a neutral Dutch one. *Djocja* belonged to the Batavia line. Geerdes and Schall were able to buy some good cigarettes, which had long been exhausted in *Emden*, but the supply was so small that they kept all of it!

Von Levetzow had readied *Foyle* for sinking, meanwhile, and the ship's company and its belongings were transferred to *Gryfevale*. After the blasting-cartridge fuzes had been lit, von Levetzow and his men returned to *Emden* and *Foyle* was left to her fate. As we had transferred the captain and chief engineer of *Tymeric* to *Gryfevale*, Lauterbach and his party were recalled to let our 'dump' be abandoned.

Gryfevale was released about noon, after the Britons – to our great surprise – had given three cheers each for Kapitän von Müller, his officers, and *Emden*. The steamer left for Colombo while we steered south toward the Maldives.

THE DELIGHTS OF DIEGO GARCÍA

Monday 28th September – Thursday 15th October 1914

28th September found us laying a southerly course taking *Emden* as far as possible from the scene of her most recent exploits. The non-arrival at Colombo of the ships we had sunk would awaken suspicion, and if the British should learn where we had last been busy they would undoubtedly send warships after us. A secretive disappearance was advisable.

The need to coal was also pressing, forcing *Emden* to seek some unfrequented spot. In the afternoon, we were cleared for coaling and the day passed in complete tranquility. This was welcomed by the ship's company as the destruction of the second group of ships had meant working day and night.

We intended to take in coal under the protection of the Maldive Islands on 29th September. A party was dispatched to *Markomannia* in the early morning to clear her for coaling. The advantage of this preparation lay in the fact that we had only to go alongside for the transfer to begin.

The islands came in sight at 0800hrs, and towards 1100 *Emden* and her train were navigating the straits that separated them. We then went alongside *Markomannia*, made fast, and began coaling about noon. *Emden*'s engines were stopped, *Markomannia*'s screw being rotated sufficiently to give us steerage way.

Coaling continued until 2100, by which time we had transferred 570 tonnes – not much, perhaps, but the heat made it impossible to do more. *Emden* then cast off and cruised the neighbourhood; the next day was also to be used for coaling.

30th September was a day of parting. *Markomannia* was to be abandoned. In the early morning, our new companion, *Buresk*, made fast alongside *Markomannia* to take on stores of oil and fresh water. The men were given the chance to send letters home, as *Markomannia* was to make for a port in the Dutch Indies and would be able to deliver the mail. The men were naturally forbidden to write about *Emden*'s exploits. Secrecy was so important that some measure of control had to be exercised, the officers having the pleasure – if that was the word – of reading the crewmen's letters in the capacity of censors.

We had barely completed our own letters when those of the men began to pour in. Many howlers came to light, which amused us greatly. But it was refreshing to see in all the letters the enthusiasm of the men for their duties, and how proud they were of belonging to *Emden*. There were no complaints of overwork or bad food. Almost every letter contained the desire for further successes against the enemies of the Fatherland.

In view of such enthusiasm, our irritation at having to act as censors was rapidly turning to pleasure. The labour was its own refreshment. It was a delight to work with such a ship's company and the outcome of the censorship was a renewed and enthusiastic confidence in the trustworthiness and capability of our men.

Everyone naturally wrote in the hope that the letters would reach home, though this was by no means certain – *Markomannia* might easily be attacked by enemy warships and it would be unlikely that the captors would forward the mail to Germany. I later learned that only a few of the letters ever reached their destinations.

At about 1400hrs, *Emden* went alongside *Markomannia* and the arduous work of coaling continued until about 1930. By this time we had over a thousand tonnes aboard.

Zahlmeister-Applikant Bordeaux went over to *Markomannia* with our mail and £50 Sterling. His errand was to purchase items needed aboard *Emden* in a neutral port.

Markomannia was first to meet *Pontoporos*, fill up with her coal and then run for a port in the Dutch East Indies. Here she was to take in as many provisions as possible, leave secretly and steam to a clandestine rendezvous with *Emden*. We reckoned on meeting her again early in November, giving her four weeks to complete the allotted tasks.

It was hard to part from our faithful companion, under the diligent command of Kapitän Faass, for *Markomannia* had shared *Emden*'s joys and sorrow for more than two months. She had been faithful and diligent. Would we ever meet again? How easy it would be for harm to befall either of us.

Such doleful thoughts did not occupy us for long, as it is always far better to face the future cheerfully.

The farewell to *Markomannia* took place towards 2030hrs, when her ship's company gave us three cheers. We never saw her again. She now rests on the sea bed.

As long as *Markomannia* was in sight, we cruised up and down, heading for our new objective – the Chagos Islands – only when she was over the horizon. The archipelago had been selected for several reasons. It was important, and indeed necessary, to vanish from the scene of our previous exploits. Not only was the enemy likely to appear, but *Emden* needed overhauling. It was not possible to dock her, of course, but we could heel over far enough to expose and then remove some of the incrustation below the waterline. This was composed of small mussels, which encouraged rust and reduced our speed.

Parts of *Emden* badly needed repainting. A lengthy sea-cruise and frequent coaling had done nothing for the appearance of our gallant ship. Once so perfect, nothing was now to be seen of the paint. Most of the life-rails had been bent by the weight of the coal stored on deck, and practically no linoleum remained on the quarterdeck. There could be no question of replacement: the spare rolls had been put ashore in Tsingtau. We comforted ourselves with the thought that the beauty of the ship did not matter as much in wartime as the fitness of the ship's company and the perpetual readiness of her weapons.

Our engines needed overhauling, however. Oberingenieur Ellerbroek and Ingenieur Haas – together with Ingenieur Andresen, who looked after our electrical equipment – had already done as much as was possible during the cruise. Unfortunately, Ingenieur Stoffers was still incapacitated in the sick bay and could not lighten the load on his colleagues. He was the one case that gave Stabsarzt Dr Luther and Assistenzarzt Dr Schwabe cause for concern. Otherwise, health aboard was more than satisfactory.

Another part of the Chagos plan concerned the mercantile war. The steamship routes from Australia to Suez and from Mauritius to Calcutta pass southward of the Chagos Archipelago; according to the captain of *Ribera*, the troops being taken from Australia to Europe must also pass this point. To surprise such a transport at night would be good sport for us. In addition, meat ships also followed this route to Britain. We had been short of fresh meat for some time, so a capture would have benefitted us at Britain's expense.

Emden cruised slowly toward the sea-lanes – slowly, because all but four of our boilers were being overhauled. The weak point, the tubes, were changed as far as possible. A thorough overhaul of the auxiliary machinery was also underway and the main engines were stopped alternately to allow work on bearings and glands to proceed. Worn parts were replaced. The condensers, a most important part of the ship, were also thoroughly cleaned. Some of the salt they removed from the feedwater settled on the condenser-tube walls and had to be scraped out occasionally. If this was not done regularly enough, saline feedwater entered and subsequently corroded the boilers. The engineering staff had work enough!

The sailors began to repair the body of the ship. New lines had to be fitted to davits, for example, and there were many other small-but-vital tasks. The ship's company was given as much free time as practicable to repair

'Geschützter Kreuzer "Emden"...'. Taken from an original photograph by Arthur Renard, Kiel (on which the pastiche below was based), this screened postcard states that it comes from 'Kirchhoff [author], Der Seekrieg 1914-1915'. By courtesy of The Lyon Press archives.

'Kreuzer "Emden"...': an interesting commemorative card produced by E.A. Schwerdtfeger, Berlin ('Original-Aufnahme 178') at the end of 1914. It is a clever combination of the preceding picture, taken from the starboard quarter in the Kaiser-Wilhelm-Kanal, with a faked seascape into which a distant squadron of pre-dreadnoughts has been dropped. A head-and-shoulders portrait of von Müller – the Greve picture reversed! – appears in a rope border, insigned on an Imperial flag and some laurel sprigs. The card was sent from Neu-Ulm to Günzburg a/D by D. Spring of Reserve-Infanterie-Regiment Nr.12, Ersatz-Bataillon, 5.Kompagnie, 26th May 1915.

their clothing, new garments being issued from store where necessary.

Our military duties had not been forgotten. The small-arms, usually so carefully stowed away, were taken out and cleaned; and the Maxim machine-guns kept under the armoured deck were also set in order. Their crews were given the opportunity of renewing acquaintance with the weapons, infantry exercises being carried out as expansively as the size of the ship would allow.

Then there was gunnery. *Buresk* towed a target at which practice ammunition was fired. Finally, simulated battle manoeuvres were tried under the supervision of Kapitän von Müller, *Buresk* naturally playing the part of the enemy.

Reserves were also given training during these evolutions; thus stokers were taught how to man the guns. This was vital, for the guns were our principal weapons and had to be in as good practice as time would allow. If men fell out of the firing line, others had to be ready to take their places without fire slackening.

Next to the gunners in importance came the magazines' crews. This seemed a major weakness: ammunition could not be brought to the guns under cover, and we reckoned to take heavy losses at this point in a fight. Thus the most reserves had to be trained for magazine duty.

In our last fight, on 9th November 1914, our experiences were bitter – for the impossibility of getting sufficient ammunition to the guns ensured we were so easily and quickly dispatched. Our light cruisers, excepting the newest, were all built more for extended cruising than cruiser warfare. And neither had they been designed to fight in the tropics.

Later, in captivity, led by Kapitän von Müller, we designed a new type of cruiser for foreign service. The basic improvement was heavier guns. We had only 10.5cm quick firers, whereas 15cm guns would be an improvement on all counts. Better side armour was also desirable. The ready-use ammunition supply points were to be better protected and more favourably placed, while the new cruiser should have more powerful engines and boilers that could be fired with coal or oil.

In *Emden* we considered ourselves inferior in armament and speed to almost every enemy cruiser.* However much we would have liked to enjoin battles with enemy warships, this had to be avoided; we believed we

* Though Prinz Franz Joseph does not say so, it is probable that he refers here to *British* vessels: it is unlikely that the German crew would have felt inferior to the obsolescent French vessels stationed in the Far East. How else can the willingness to take on *Dupleix* and *Montcalm* in Penang harbour be explained? Prinz Franz Joseph himself ventures in Chapter Twelve the comment that *Emden* was prepared to take on a bigger, faster and slightly more powerful British cruiser such as *Newcastle* on more-or-less equal terms off Direction Island.

would be rendered incapable of further warlike action even if *Emden* was not completely finished in such an encounter.

Our success was due to the outstanding qualities of our skipper, though the splendid spirit of our crew was also of inestimable value.

Repairs and renovations took the best part of a week. Finally, at about 0700hrs in the morning of 9th October, we ran into the harbour of Diego García, the southernmost island in the Chagos Archipelago. This miniature paradise of coral beaches, fringed by lofty palms, has a value based on coconut oil and copra. Its sheltered bay cannot be seen from the seaward side and was particularly suited to our purposes.

We passed carefully through the narrow harbour entrance, followed by *Buresk*, and anchored in close to our companion. The anchor had scarcely bedded when we sent a party over to *Buresk* to prepare for coaling. Some of our lower forward compartments were then deliberately flooded to raise our stern out of the water and scraping began. Once the incredible profusion of crustacea had been hacked and chipped away, the ship's sides had to be scrubbed and then painted. First officer von Mücke took charge of the operation, ably assisted by Bootsmann Müller.

The appearance of two ships in the quiet harbour was a great event for the native population. We had been lying there for about half an hour when a native rowboat approached us. Aboard came the under-manager of the oil company exploiting Diego García, a Madagasque whose mastery of language extended only to French. The captain initially spoke with the newcomer, who later came into the wardroom for some excellent practice with our iced whisky and soda. The conversation took a most interesting turn when we realized that the inhabitants of Diego García, to a man, had no idea that the world was at war.

Though initially surprising, the explanation was simple. Only once in three months did a sailing ship ply between Diego García and Mauritius. As the quarterly visit was imminent, it was clear that the inhabitants, ignorant of everything that had happened since July 1914, had no inkling of the war. This useful ignorance gave us an opportunity to replace our stores.

The disadvantage of ignorance, an insatiable hunger for news, was brought home thoroughly to us in the wardroom. The man questioned the very souls out of our bodies! Willingly or not, we had become tellers of tales; a beautiful tableau of non-existent incidents was created for him.

The oilman could hardly be blamed for wishing to know why we had stopped at Diego García, so far to the south of the shipping lanes. Urgent repairs forced us into the harbour, we claimed by way of an excuse. They would be completed in two days.

Then the under-manager wanted to know where we were going and what a German ship was doing in the vicinity: an awkward question to which we simply had to find a convincing answer. A true seaman is never at a loss for long; resourcefulness is a rule of life at sea, so our inquisitor was told that we were taking part in 'world manoeuvres' in which the united fleets of Germany, Britain and France had their principal operational base in the Indian Ocean.

We were pleased that the man believed us so readily. But then he wanted further news of the world. We answered evasively; we had been at sea so long we could hardly remember what was new and what was old. Perhaps, however, Herr Unterdirektor did not yet know that Pope Pius X was dead? His expression showed he was not a little delighted with the news.

The pleasant conversation was in full swing when Mr Spender, manager of the oil company, came aboard to be invited to the captain's cabin. Here this gentleman also asked for news, only to receive the same dish as we had previously set before the under-manager. There were awkward moments, for the manager was English, inquisitive and more forceful than his subordinate. He asked Kapitän von Müller why our ship presented such an unkempt appearance, so our our captain, who always had an appropriate answer, regaled a tale of a terrible storm from which the ship had escaped only with the greatest difficulty. The credulous Englishman said that he had deduced so from our appearance.

At the end of the entertainment, the manager ventured a request. His motorboat – a good boat, made useless by the islanders – was in need of attention. Could Kapitän von Müller send some of his technicians ashore? The captain immediately ordered Maschinistenmaat Kluge and his men to assist. Kluge attended to our own motorboat in peacetime, and had the manager's vessel working again in no time.

The manager was so delighted that he sent von Müller an invitation to breakfast ashore. Politely but firmly, our captain declined the offer. There was too much to be done aboard *Emden*. The manager remained grateful. He sent a large live pig for the wardroom, an enormous heap of fish for the men, and a whole boatload of fruit. We could do nothing other than accept the gifts. As we did not wish to be under an obligation to an enemy, we sent Spender back a few bottles of wine, whisky and some cigars. I doubt whether the Diego García people had ever entertained such generous visitors. They had intended to catch lobsters for us the next day, but time was short and we could not wait. This we all regretted, as we would have gladly welcomed such delicacies on our modest table again.

We weighed anchor and made fast alongside *Buresk* for coaling at about 1400hrs. This lasted until midnight, but the tropical heat made it impossible to take in more than four hundred tonnes; we would have to coal the next day, too. So we simply remained alongside our collier and the night passed without disturbance.

Coaling resumed at 0600 on 10th October. By 1000 a thousand tonnes had been transferred and the strenuous work ended. At 1100 we left the hospitable island, steering a fictitious course to the north-west. We then steered north-eastward, cruising along the steamship route from Australia to Aden.

We had no luck, so *Emden* was turned westward of the Maldives with the ultimate intention of going north. Our real plans were to go directly from Diego García to Penang and surprise the warships lying there.

Soon we had intercepted a wireless message from a British ship inquiring about the security of the Colombo to Aden line. The answer, probably from Colombo, said that there was no danger and that the route was once again safe for shipping. This eminently favourable announcement encouraged Kapitän von Müller to change his plans and head for the hunting ground north of the Maldives. For maximum security, however, we needed to take on as much coal as we could carry.

As this was the time of the north-east monsoons (October to March, north-easterly; April to September, south-westerly), we looked for a quiet place west of the Maldives, but the swell was so strong that we dared not make fast to *Buresk* even in the straits between the islands. The east side near to the islands offered some shelter, but we were not to coal until we reached the end of the island chain.

The intervening period was once again filled with battle exercises, though the men were given as much free time as possible to prepare themselves for the strenuous work which – we hoped – would occupy them in the new hunting ground.

Miladun-Madulu atoll, almost the most northerly of the Maldives, was reached on 15th October. *Buresk* made fast alongside us, with *Emden*'s engines turning over very slowly. Coaling began at 1100hrs, in fine weather, and continued until 280 tonnes had been taken in. The men worked marvellously, enabling us to set a record on our war cruise: ninety tonnes of coal in an hour.

Only the greatest admiration can be expressed for the way in which *Emden*'s ship's company coped with the difficulties of coaling at sea in the equatorial heat. The captain gave special recognition and his thanks for the outstanding efforts.

Clan Grant

Board of Trade Registry 115683

21ST SHIP INTERCEPTED, ELEVENTH VICTIM

Photograph of sister-ship *Clan Chattan* by courtesy of Norman Middlemiss.

Built for Clan Steamship Line, London (Cayzer, Irvine & Co. Ltd, Glasgow), by William Doxford & Sons Ltd of Sunderland, 3,948grt 355ft twin-screw *Clan Grant* was a single-screw turret-deck steamer of a pattern specifically designed to make best use of Suez Canal tariffs by minimizing deck area. Registered in Glasgow, with the call-sign TKBG, she was travelling from Liverpool to Calcutta via Colombo – under the command of Captain Norman Leslie – when seized by *Emden* on 15th October 1914. *Clan Grant* was scuttled the following day.

Ponrabbel

22ND SHIP INTERCEPTED, TWELFTH VICTIM

Completed in May 1914 by Ferguson Bros. (Port Glasgow) Ltd for the Marine Board of Launceston, this 473grt twin-screw dredger was stopped and sunk on 16th October 1914. She had been sailing for Tasmania from the Clyde and Barry Dock under the command of Captain Edwin Gore.

AN EMBARRASSMENT OF SHIPS

Thursday 15th October – Tuesday 20th October 1914

As 1500hrs approached and work had been completed, we set course for Minicoy and the shipping lanes that passed near it.

Minicoy Light came in sight at 2230, causing us to proceed carefully as it was also the principal beacon for ships approaching Colombo from the west.

The area was well known to us, as we had rendered it unsafe barely two weeks previously. As midnight approached, so did the lights of a steamship probably Colombo-bound out of Aden. *Emden* went towards her at full speed, intending to approach in the way that will have become familiar, when we spotted two dark shapes behind her.

We believed the shadow to be a warship steaming without lights in order to entrap us. At once, we wheeled about. Something similar had occurred shortly before the capture of *Buresk*, so we had become extra-cautious. Everything was immediately cleared for action. The first torpedo officer was just clearing a second tube when the shape metamorphosed into a thick smoke cloud. It was easy to be deceived on a dark night, but better safe than sorry.

Again we turned towards the steamship, ordering her to stop in 8°10′N 73°11′E. Lauterbach and Fikentscher went over with the search party, to report: 'English ship *Clan Grant*, 3,948 tons, piece goods, from England to Colombo and other Indian ports'.*

Further investigation revealed a cargo of live cattle, flour, cakes, a substantial quantity of provisions, beer and cigarettes. We were delighted. We could use such a plentiful addition to our household supplies, for we had only the absolute necessities aboard. The greatest joy, however, was expressed by our cigarette smokers. The wardroom stock had long since been exhausted – even though, as it was my responsibility, a large stock had been brought from Tsingtau and then augmented from *Prinzess Alice*.

The unexpectedly plentiful supply of provisions made our captain order *Clan Grant* to follow us. Several days were to be spent emptying her – as much to our advantage as possible.

Slowly we steamed along a course for Colombo. At 0700 on 16th October we stopped, lowering the pinnace and some of the boats, to transfer steward Färber and seventeen men to *Clan Grant*. Discovery after discovery ensued: crockery, which we badly needed; table linen; typewriters in fantastic numbers; case after case of cigarettes; tools of all sorts; fire-bricks, which were vital for our furnaces; oil; live cattle. A large warehouse could not have had a more varied stock. As *Clan Grant* contained items of more use to us than mere provisions, several officers went aboard to represent their own departments.

While we were still hard at work, *Emden*'s lookout reported another smoke cloud to westward. Lauterbach, the very model of a prize officer, was recalled from *Clan Grant* and the cruiser then left the convoy and her boats to head for the smoke cloud at full speed.

On closer inspection, the situation seemed peculiar and possibly even dangerous. The mast that rose above the horizon could have been borne only by a torpedo-boat or a monitor. When the stern of the vessel came in sight, it still suggested a warship. Though the hull was rolling in the swell quite harmlessly, 'Clear ship for action!' had almost been ordered when we saw our mistake.

The ship that had presented such a martial aspect was a deep-sea dredger! How we laughed; now there was no need of Lauterbach's skill. The order to follow proved sufficient. With a new victim taken in 8°21′N 72°24′E, *Emden* rejoined the convoy.

I should have liked to see the faces of those left behind when we returned with a dredger captured on the high seas. There was more merriment in store when Lauterbach and Schall, without the prize crew, went aboard her. There they discovered that *Ponrabbel* was on her way from England to Tasmania.

It was strange enough to meet such a vessel in mid-ocean, but Lauterbach was even more surprised to find the ship's company packed and ready to leave. How was this?

The dredger's master provided the explanation, with a broad grin. They had already learned of *Emden*'s exploits and how we treated the crews of captured ships. When *Ponrabbel*'s crewmen saw us approach, there could be no doubt who we were. So they had all packed their belongings and stood by the rail ready to go. As the captain continued his story, Lauterbach realised why everyone seemed so delighted to fall into our hands. *Ponrabbel* was the second dredger to be sent to Tasmania. The first had gone down in a storm, and the present crew, master included, had demanded wages in advance as compensation for the danger of navigating such a small vessel on the high seas.

The voyage had been dreadful. As they had already been threatened with the fate of their predecessor more than once, the men were only too grateful at being deli-

* The ship shown by Dan van der Vat in *The Last Corsair* as 'Clan Grant' is the wrong vessel: it is, in fact, the third *Clan Grant*, built by Hawthorn Leslie & Co. Ltd in 1912 as *Port MacQuarrie*, but not purchased by the Clan Line until 1929.

Benmohr

Board of Trade Registry 129416

23RD SHIP INTERCEPTED, THIRTEENTH VICTIM

Photograph of *Benrinnes*, a near-sister of *Benmohr*, by courtesy of Laurence Dunn.

A Leith-registered single-screw steam freighter belonging to William Thomson & Co. Ltd of Leith (Ben Line), call-sign HWNV, 4,806grt 403ft *Benmohr* had been completed by Scott's Shipbuilding & Engineering Co. of Greenock in September 1912. Her elegant clipper stem was one of the last to appear on a British-built steamship. Carrying a mixed cargo from London to Penang and Yokohama under the command of Captain James Larchet, she was seized and scuttled on 16th October 1914. The Ben Line ships had black hulls, with red boot-topping and brown upperworks; funnels were buff. The house flag displayed a blue anchor on a white rectangle edged in red.

Fernando Po

24TH SHIP INTERCEPTED

Hailed and hove-to, but released when her nationality — neutral Spanish — was realized.

vered from drowning. Without exception, they expressed gratitude to *Emden*'s crew!

Hardly had the dredger cleared our lee than Gaede opened fire. At the third shell she turned over with astonishing speed, floating bottom upward like a great whale. As *Ponrabbel* had capsized so quickly, however, air had been trapped and she would not sink. A few more shells allowed the air to vent, whereupon the dredger slowly vanished beneath the waves. Thus perished the second dredger sent from England to Tasmania. One wondered whether the British would dispatch a third. In view of the war, such an act would be most unlikely. The dredger's crew settled as happily as possible in the overcrowded *Buresk*.

By the time *Ponrabbel* had gone under for the last time, our men had transferred many of the necessities from *Clan Grant* into the boats, emptied them aboard *Emden* and returned for more. I was sent over with a few extra hands, to speed the process, but we were overcome when we got to the holds. Donnerwetter! What a choice of fine things awaited us. We realized that time must be spent making the best choice, but also that Kapitän von Müller did not wish to wait. As if to hurry our thoughts, the scuttling party began its work while we were still stowing goods in our boats.

The scuttling party initially pierced the bulkheads between the holds and the engine room, as there were no interconnecting doors. Charges were then laid as deep as possible against the ship's sides while everyone except the scuttling party then left the ship, *Clan Grant*'s company was already on its way to *Buresk*. The sea-cocks were opened, the charges were fired and the scuttling party returned to *Emden*. *Clan Grant* did not wait while the steam pinnace and the boats were hoisted aboard. Slowly she settled, then turned on her side and rolled into the depths.

We proceeded on an easterly course. However, this cruise did not last long – lights were sighted on the port bow at about 2300. We steamed slowly towards them.

When *Emden* was within hailing distance, the steamer was ordered to stop. Lauterbach was sent over as usual, with his party and Leutnant z.S. Schall, and soon signalled: 'English ship *Benmohr*, 4,806 tons, with piece goods from England to China and Japan'. She had been stopped in 8°16′N 72°55′E. The captain ordered her to be sunk immediately, and over went the scuttling party.

We later learned that the ship had a valuable cargo of motorcars, railway locomotives, bicycles, engines, and a brand-new motorboat.

The ship's company of *Benmohr* was sent over to *Buresk*, to Klöpper's alarm; he simply did not know where to put the extra men. He even requested Lauterbach, through the megaphone, to provide mattresses and provisions from the captured ship. There usually seemed to be plenty of provisions laid in aboard *Buresk*, for where there were any pickings there was certain to be a foraging party from the collier. This was not to their discredit, of course, as the absence of a proper 'dump' meant that far too many men were aboard *Buresk*. But I am of the opinion that they all ate very well!

After complying with Klöpper's request to the best of his ability, Lauterbach returned to *Emden*. Soon afterward, *Benmohr* disappeared into the depths for ever.

Hopeful of more good luck, we continued to cruise about thirty nautical miles westward of Minicoy. 17th October passed quietly. Our first officer divided the booty between the different branches, during which there were many amusing incidents. As always, everyone could use something different and very little was wasted.

Proceeding leisurely eastward, we passed Minicoy to the south. Next day we intended to turn north again, as nothing could be achieved where we were.

During the night of 17/18th October, between midnight and 0100, those of us who were off duty were awakened by the engines quickening. Hurriedly, we ran out onto the upper deck. To starboard, we saw a fully-lit ship whose entire appearance suggested a very large mail-packet. This probability her high speed reinforced.

We signalled in morse once we were near enough, only to receive the answer 'Spanish steamship *Fernando Po*, from Manila and Colombo to Barcelona'. Another neutral! We thanked her and vanished once more into the night, relieved that we had not been recognized. For safety's sake we sailed on a fictitious southerly course until the Spaniard had vanished over the horizon, then returned northward.

As we had discovered nothing on the shipping routes, we decided to search north-east of Minicoy in the hope of encountering ships on the route from Colombo to Bombay. We had not previously threatened this lane. Victims would be sure to present themselves.

And here we followed a lucky star. 18th October was a Sunday, so there were Divisions followed by Divine Service. After Church, off-duty officers gathered in the wardroom for a customary cocktail or glass of port, and the captain visited us for a chat. In the middle of conversation, however, a smoke cloud was sighted four points off the starboard bow.

Rushing to the bridge and quarterdeck, we examined the new quarry through our telescopes. It was an hour before anything of the ship could be seen above the horizon. Then we saw a huge funnel, which told us only that she was a merchantman. Soon afterwards came a blue streak betraying that the ship belonged to the Blue Funnel Line; this pleased us greatly, for we knew the company owned only large vessels. A choice morsel was undoubtedly before us.

Emden approached the steamer at full speed, leaving the convoy to plod on along its original course. Lauterbach and Leutnant von Guérard went over with the search party. We'd taken the British steamship *Troilus* of 7,562 tons, with a cargo of copper, tin, rubber and piece goods bound for England from Colombo. A valuable prize! The value of the cargo alone was estimated at twenty five million Marks at the then-current rate of exchange.

Troilus carried a few passengers, including a lady. As usual, Lauterbach was first aboard – in full warpaint. Once he had reached the deck, the lady approached him with the words 'Mr Lauterbach, how are you?' It suffices to say that he was speechless.

With great verve, the lady explained that she had spent several days aboard Lauterbach's previous command, *Staatssekretär Kraetke*. Naturally he did not remember her: his ship carried many passengers. But the Englishwoman must have been impressed by Lauterbach's martial appearance, for she recognized him at once. I cannot say what effect her greeting had on Lauterbach. However, typical of her race, the lady was very amused by the capture of her ship by *Emden* in general and Lauterbach in particular. To use an English expression, it had been proof of a small world.

The captain of *Troilus* was furious. He had asked the naval staff in Colombo for a route avoiding the accursed *Emden*. He had been advised to steam thirty nautical miles north of the usual shipping lane, as that route was 'absolutely safe'. And precisely on this 'safe' track had he run into us. It was easy to understand his anger at the Royal Navy, as brand-new *Troilus* was on her maiden voyage.

What gave us most pleasure about his anger was that he blurted out the useful information that the British believed the safest route to be thirty miles north of the Colombo–Aden sea lane – precisely where we lay at that moment. We could, therefore, simply stay to await ships sent out on the route recommended by the Royal Navy.

All of us rejoiced at the capture of *Troilus*, except the admirable Klöpper... who inquired where in the small and simple *Buresk* he was to accommodate not only a large number of seamen but also a lady who would need a cabin of her own.

Troilus, meanwhile, was ordered to follow. She would be sunk later. We did not wish to lose time in this favourable locality, but to continue the hunt without delay.

Claims on our patience were great, as we hoped for – indeed, expected – great things. But the whole afternoon passed without incident, and not until the late evening was a light seen on the port bow. We could not tell what we now shadowed, as the ship showed no lights. The usual alarm was sounded for safety's sake and, ready and armed for any emergency, *Emden* approached the intended victim. *Buresk* and *Troilus* were ordered to follow.

Only when we had drawn near could the harmlessness of the ship be assured. She was a merchantman with a single funnel, and immediately obeyed our signal to stop in 8°16′N 75°7′E. Over went Geerdes and Fikentscher with the search party. Another British ship, her identity was revealed as the 5,596-ton *St Egbert*, laden with

Troilus

Board of Trade Registry 135552

25TH SHIP INTERCEPTED, FOURTEENTH VICTIM

Photograph of sister-ship *Mentor*, built by Scott's Shipbuilding & Engineering Co. of Greenock in 1914, by courtesy of Laurence Dunn. Note the thin auxiliary pipe for the donkey boiler ahead of the funnel, characteristic of many Holt ships of this era; this provided power when the ship was in port.

Built by Hawthorn Leslie & Co. Ltd of Newcastle upon Tyne in 1914, for Ocean Steam Ship Co. Ltd (Alfred Holt & Co. Ltd, Liverpool), this 7,562grt 455ft single-screw steamship was conveying passengers and valuable mixed cargo from Yokohama back to London under the command of Captain George W. Long. She was seized on 18th October 1914 and scuttled a day later. *Troilus* – call-sign JFHB – was on her maiden voyage. She was one of ten sister-ships built in 1913-17 (including a second *Troilus*) and sailed by Holt under the flags of Blue Funnel Line, Ocean Steamship Company, and China Mutual Steam Navigation Co. All Holt's ships had characteristically large black-topped blue funnels, their hulls being black over red boot-topping. Upperworks were generally white; masts and derricks were buff; and the house flag comprised a black 'AH' monogram on a white lozenge in a blue ground.

St Egbert

Board of Trade Registry 135563

26TH SHIP INTERCEPTED

Built by Russell & Co. of Port Glasgow for the British & Foreign Steam Ship Co. Ltd (managed by Rankin, Gilmour & Co. Ltd), this 5,596grt 423ft single-screw steam freighter was registered in Liverpool with the call-sign JFCT. The command of Captain William Barr, she was stopped on 18th October 1914 while New York-bound from Colombo with an American-owned general cargo. *St Egbert* was a black-hulled ship with red boot-topping, her uppers being white and her masts a tan colour. The red funnel had a black top above three narrow bands (white/red/white). The house flag was white, edged top and bottom in red, with 'RG' (also in red) in the centre.

sugar and piece goods bound for New York from Colombo.

Though the ship was British, her cargo was neutral and had to be respected whether or nor we wished to do so. This misfortune had one great advantage; *St Egbert* could be used as a dump. Klöpper must have been relieved, as he was having a difficult time packing British sailors aboard *Buresk*.

Geerdes was ordered to follow in his prize, owing to lack of time and the darkness in which nothing else could be done. Steaming in echelon, with *Buresk* and *St Egbert* to starboard and *Troilus* to port, we reverted to our previous course – but not for long, as the lights of another steamer were spotted on the port bow soon after midnight.

Emden was after the vessel at high speed, leaving the convoy to follow at its own leisurely pace. Soon we caught the newcomer in 8°39′N 75°7′E. This time von Levetzow and I had the pleasure of the capture. We were rowed over in the lifeboat, to climb aboard the steamer with some curiosity. The prize crew was posted, whereupon von Levetzow and I went to inspect the ship's papers.

A pleasant surprise awaited us. *Exford*, a British ship of 4,542 tons, was laden with 5,500 tons of the best Cardiff coal. Like *Buresk*, she had been chartered by the Admiralty and was on passage for the East. Quickly we passed the news back to *Emden*, for we wished our colleagues to get it as soon as possible. Once again we had coal aplenty of the best type. With this we could work for a whole year.

We were ordered to follow between *Emden* and *Troilus*. Von Levetzow saw to this, while I revisited the sentries and ensured that a proper blackout was maintained. Returning to the charthouse, I informed the captain of the fate of his ship and advised him to pack his belongings. His men were to be told to do the same.

It was a difficult night. The engine-room telegraph worked poorly, forcing us to make constant speed adjustments to maintain the distance to *Emden*. All would go well for a time, but then the old tub began to steam too fast and there was a danger of passing the cruiser. Though we signalled a change, *Exford* had too much way before any effects were visible. So we signalled again, and she slowed too greatly. Thus *Exford* surged back and forth continually. It was no easy matter to steam in convoy when one's ship had such antiquated equipment.† The problem may seem minor, given the simplicity of a merchantman, but a clear idea of it could only be appreciated aboard.

† In spite of these disparaging comments, *Exford* was comparatively new. She was just three years old, but could not have been in especially good repair.

Geerdes, in *St Egbert*, had an even worse time of it than we did. He lost touch completely during a tropical rain storm in the dead of night, suddenly finding himself alone on the high seas. Not knowing what to do, Geerdes and Fikentscher decided to heave-to for the day. The British crew saw what was happening but kept quiet – though, for safety, Geerdes placed sentries at all the important points to prevent anything being laid to his charge should the captured ship be lost.

When all was finally clear, he resumed his original course in search of *Emden* and the convoy. Fortunately, he found his way back to us at 0700 on 19th October. We had lain in wait for him. During the pause, *Emden* had launched the pinnace, the cutter and both lifeboats to transfer all the captured ships' companies (plus those in *Buresk*) to *St Egbert*.

The plentiful provisions in *Troilus* went largely to *Buresk*, where there were mouths to fill. This took time, but the calm sea was in our favour. The difficult task of transferring the men fell to the first officer in person. Kapitänleutnant von Mücke immediately went over to *Troilus*.

If *Emden* had been surprised by an enemy warship at this moment, Kapitän von Müller would have been caught fair and square, for most of his officers were divided among the captured merchantmen.

Buresk had supernumerary officers and men, so she can be discounted. However, *Troilus* had Lauterbach and adjutant von Guérard, plus about ten men and Kapitän-

Exford

Board of Trade Registry 128527

27TH SHIP INTERCEPTED

Photograph (as *Assunzione*) by courtesy of Laurence Dunn.

Built by Craig, Taylor & Company of Stockton on Tees, as yard no.144, the 4,542grt – or about 8,270dwt – 380ft single-screw *Exford* was completed in May 1911 and could make about twelve knots. Owned by Tatem Steam Navigation Company (W.J. Tatem & Co. Ltd) and registered in Cardiff with the call-sign HSRW, she was seized during the night of 18/19th October 1914 while laden with more than five thousand tons of Welsh coal bound from Britain to India under Admiralty charter. Recaptured by AMC *Himalaya* (q.v.) on 11th December 1914, *Exford* was renamed *Brendon* before being sold to Italy in 1922, then became successively *Valnegra*, *Assunzione* and *Santa Elisabetta* before going to the breakers in 1953. As a Tatem-owned ship, *Exford* would have been painted black, with red boot-topping and buff masts. Her black funnel bore a white 'T' on a red band, the house flag being a white 'T' on a red ground.

Chilkana

Board of Trade Registry 136315

28TH SHIP INTERCEPTED, FIFTEENTH VICTIM

Photograph of sister-ship *Chinkoa* (5,222grt), built by W. Gray & Co. of West Hartlepool in 1913 and scrapped in 1937. She has clearly unloaded forward but remains laden aft, allowing the exposed portion of the hull to be repainted. By courtesy of Laurence Dunn.

Possibly the unluckiest of *Emden*'s victims, the 5,146grt 400ft single-screw steamship *Chilkana* was merely a few days old when seized and scuttled in Nine Degree Channel in the Arabian Sea on 19th October 1914. She was bound for Calcutta out of the Tees and London with a mixed cargo. Built by W. Gray & Co. Ltd of West Hartlepool, one of four similar vessels dating from 1912-14 (three by Gray and the other by Henderson), she had only been delivered to the British India Steam Navigation Company at the beginning of September! Registered in Glasgow, she had the call-sign JGFM. Her service speed was about eleven knots, 12.75 being made on trial. The hulls of BISN ships were painted black with a white band, and had red boot-topping. Upperworks were white above stone, boats were black, while masts were buff or brown above black. Funnels were black with two narrow white bands, while the house flag – in the form of a swallow-tail – comprised a red saltire on a white ground.

leutnant von Mücke; *St Egbert* had Geerdes, commander of the after battery, plus Fikentscher and ten men; *Exford* had von Levetzow and me, second gunnery and second torpedo officers respectively, plus ten men. In addition, there were the crews of the pinnace and three rowboats – about 32 in all. Thus there were seven officers and 62 men out of *Emden* – leaving only the captain, gunnery officer Gaede, torpedo officer Witthoeft and two lieutenants.

A smoke cloud came into sight toward 0900. *Emden* had time to hoist in one cutter and surged off at full speed towards the new target, which had come from the direction of Aden. Owing to the shortage of men, the search party comprised Leutnant z.S. Zimmermann and very few others. The new ship, stopped in 9°22′N 75°4′E, was the British steamer *Chilkana* of 5,220 tons, belonging to the British India Steam Navigation Company. Her cargo comprised piece goods and provisions being hauled from England for Indian ports. Like *Troilus*, she was brand new and on her maiden voyage.‡

Emden returned with *Chilkana* in her wake. In *Exford*, meanwhile, we transferred our Britons to *St Egbert*. Only the Chinese stokers remained aboard, as they were willing to work for the German flag provided they were paid. This was desirable, as our stokers were better employed on *Emden*.

The other ships had transferred their captives to *St Egbert*, and those held aboard *Buresk* had also gone over. In the course of time our peculiar sea voyage had proved too much for them, though most had originally followed our activities with interest.

The strangest piece of luggage belonged to the captain of *Troilus*, who asked von Mücke if his harmonium could go with him to *St Egbert*. Our Kapitänleutnant consented. Unfortunately, I was not near enough to hear the comments our men made about this 'furniture removal'.

‡The identification of *Chilkana* has been complicated by confusion with the earlier *Chilka*, a 1910-vintage 3,952grt product of Barclay Curle & Co. In his book *Die Kaperfahrten des Kleinen Kreuzers Emden*, even the authoritative Lochner gives an approximation of *Chilkana*'s tonnage with *Chilka*'s date. There is no doubt that it was the former *Emden* sank. She was then only about forty days old!

All in all, the day's activities would have been worthy of a comedy film.

Chilkana had come alongside us, to allow the transhipment of her ship's company to begin. It, too was destined for *St Egbert*. As the provisions in our most recent prize proved to be more plentiful even than those in *Troilus*, Kapitän von Müller ordered provisioning from the latter to cease. Kapitänleutnant von Mücke, accompanied by his staff and Lauterbach, promptly went over to offload *Chilkana*. Three fully laden boats of food were shipped to the dump, which was being readied for release.

The blasting and scuttling party went over to *Troilus*, while a careful search of *Chilkana* revealed that the brand-new ship had a fine wireless installation. Adjutant von Guérard and his experts promptly dismantled the equipment, rebuilding it aboard *Exford* so that our new collier had the most modern methods of signalling. A good stock of medicaments was also discovered in *Chilkana*, the removal of which was overseen by our two doctors.

The boats that had taken the ships' companies to *St Egbert*, but were now free, came alongside *Chilkana*. *Buresk* also sent Gyssling with two boats; nobody wished to miss out on provisioning.

The division of stores was undertaken so that *Emden* and her convoy received them in proportion to the individual complements. As soon as the boats were full, each departed for its destination, unloaded, and returned for more. Drinks, crockery, cutlery and linen – there was plenty aboard *Chilkana* – were divided between *Emden* and *Buresk*.

A fully laden rowboat was a comical sight. There were whole hams; sausages; tinned goods of every kind; sacks of table linen; whole baskets filled with plates, cups, teapots and coffee-jugs, saucepans and frying-pans, knives, forks and spoons. It was as though we were at a giant fair. Other boats carried tea, chocolate in all its forms, cases of bottled beer or hundreds of boxes of condensed milk.

On the side that was free of traffic, *Emden* had meanwhile opened fire on *Troilus*. The ship was very well built and would not sink. Several salvoes only encouraged her to settle a little deeper. She seemed to have no intention of disappearing beneath the waves.

The spectacle was carefully watched by the people in *St Egbert* – she looked for all the world like an emigrant ship – and many photographs were taken.

We in *Exford* lay close to *Emden*, from where we could watch the whole show with great enjoyment. A sharp lookout had to be kept, however, for the ships were constantly shifted by wind and current and our engines had to keep turning. Von Levetzow, who was in charge, was once even forced to hail *Emden*: 'Please go full ahead. My engines do not function astern!'

This was a perpetual problem with *Exford*'s engines. If the cruiser had not immediately speeded ahead, we would have planted *Exford*'s bow in her stern. Safe navigation was impossible in our old tub, though the worst defects were later rectified by our engine-room staff.

We received no more provisions, as we were already well stocked – though *Emden* took some of our flour, and *Buresk* sent oil in exchange. Between 0100 and 0200, *Exford* received a new ship's company. Kapitänleutnant Gropius, *Emden*'s navigating officer, had been given the command. His place aboard the cruiser was being filled by Lauterbach.

Leutnant z.S. Schall and Bootsmann Müller came over as officers of the watch, Maschinist Fischer was chief engineer, and there were a Steuermansmaat, three Maschinistenmaate, a signalman, three seamen and four stokers.

Once von Levetzow had handed his temporary command to Gropius, he and I returned to *Emden* accompanied by our prize crew. We arrived just in time to witness a fascinating spectacle.

Gaede was shooting a standard service rifle at the sharks that clustered round the ship. His white topee suddenly fell overboard, floating enticingly in the water until the largest of the sharks rushed eagerly for the bright lure – probably in the hope of a tasty titbit. As the monster raised its head, Gaede got in a fatal shot. The shark vanished into the depths in his death agony, his kindred followed and suddenly all was quiet again.

It was now 1500hrs, and still the unsinkable *Troilus* would not disappear. This was largely due to the fact that the newest ships were especially water-tight, subdivided below the waterline into so many more compartments than their predecessors had been. We had to fire shell after shell into sturdy *Troilus*; not until 1800, indeed, did she take her final leave.

Unloading *Chilkana* was finished by 1600. The boats had shuttled back and forth at least four times apiece. Now we had plenty of provisions aboard all our vessels, and were that much farther from starvation. *Chilkana* was given over to von Mücke, Zimmermann and their merry men: sea-cocks were opened and the blasting charges fired. At 1630 we fired a few rounds into *Chilkana*, encouraging her to sink so quickly that she had gone before *Troilus*.

Soon, Geerdes and his men returned from *St Egbert* and reported that, according to orders, he had instructed the captain not to put into Bombay, Colombo or any other Indian port. If he failed to heed the instructions, Geerdes had told him, his ship would be sunk without mercy. Apparently the British captain – who had not taken the order too unhappily – had given hearty thanks for the way in which he and his men had been treated, and also for sparing their ship. However, no particular thanks were due to us; he was, after all, carrying a neutral cargo.

Von Müller was greatly surprised by Geerdes' report, as he had wished *St Egbert* to go directly to some small Indian port, where offloading 500-600 men would create discontent among the native population.

The effect of the misunderstanding was not serious,

but *St Egbert* had already steamed away. By 1830 we had hoisted all our boats and, followed by *Buresk*, chased after *St Egbert* to give her the correct orders. We later heard she put into Cochin safely.

We took our now-standard ficitious course, but in a special way. Starting in a southerly direction, but while still in sight of *St Egbert*, we turned northwards. Only after nightfall did we take up our true southerly course.

'Fregattenkapitän v. Müller. Der heldenmütige Kommandant S.M.S. "Emden"...' – a good-quality sepia photo-card of the head and upper torso, published by Gustav Liersch & Co., Berlin SW (no.7144), from an original photograph by Carl Greve, Hofphotograph, Blankenburg a/H. By courtesy of The Lyon Press archives.

An alternative view of the destruction of *Zhemchug*, published by Gebr. Lempe, Kiel, under the 'NPG' trademark – 'Die Taten der Emden. Hafen von Pulo-Penang. 30.Oktober 1914. Die Emden vernichtete den russischen Kreuzer "Szhemtschug" und einen französichen Torpedojäger'. The illustration is a cunning pastiche of the fore-part of the standard Lempe photo-card of *Emden*, a photograph of an oriental harbour, and a painted-in Russian warship. Odd mistakes include the omission of the fourth dummy funnel, which should have lain immediately abaft the bridge; the lateral puff of smoke from guns that are trained fore-and-aft; the lack of a bow-wave and smoke drifting forward rather than back (*Emden* would have been travelling at considerable speed). The name 'Emden' has been added to the bow above the starboard anchor: in reality, it appeared aft. *Zhemchug* is shown with her original three masts, rather than the simpler rig fitted by 1914. By courtesy of The Lyon Press archives.

ASSAULT ON PENANG

Tuesday 20th October – Wednesday 28th October 1914

For this night all captures were to be eschewed. The lookout did sight the lights of a ship at about 0100, but no notice was taken. *Emden*'s men had to rest after the strain of the previous few days, and it was Kapitän von Müller's intention – encumbered as we were by the ponderous *Exford* – to get as far from the shipping routes as possible. Our new cruise must not be discovered, for our captain wished to mount a surprise attack on Penang.

Another ship was sighted at 0200, unlit excepting for her side lights. She passed us at great speed and, as she was very large, we speculated that she was an enemy warship. We later discovered that the British armed merchant cruiser *Empress of Russia* was cruising the locality at this time.

A ship passed astern of us at about 0300. We could not determine whether she was a merchantman or another auxiliary cruiser. That we were not detected proved the efficacy of our black-out arrangements. During the night we lost *Buresk*, but soon found her again.

We kept to a southerly course during 20th October, keeping south of the shipping lanes from Aden to Colombo, where we were to turn east. Most of the day was claimed by the first officer, Kapitänleutnant von Mücke, who wished to divide the booty among the Divisions. There was a lively scene aboard *Emden*, with von Mücke enthroned on the finery he was dividing among the Messes. It was soon clear that we had a surfeit of some goods and a shortage of others. Events were soon to resolve our problems.

Emden hove-to in the morning of 21st October, allowing Marine-Ingenieur Haas to go over to *Exford*. The steamer's engines and boilers were in such a bad way that they needed a thorough refit. While we were stopped, von Mücke took the opportunity to exchange provisions with *Exford*. The rapidity of the transfers attempted two days previously had prevented proper distribution.

As *Exford* was to be detached, with orders to meet us at a pre-arranged point, an exchange of personnel was also undertaken. Leutnant z.S. Schall and signalman Lindner returned to *Emden*, while nautical instruments and charts were sent over to the collier with instructions telling *Buresk* to remain at the rendezvous until lack of provisions forced her to run for a neutral port. She left us towards evening.

22nd October was the Kaiserin's birthday. Our masthead flags were flown in honour in addition to saluting the colours, which took place every day at 0800. At 1000 there were Divisions in Sunday dress, and then an address by Kapitän von Müller. He spoke briefly of the anniversary and recalled the contribution the Kaiserin had made to welfare and hospital work. Her Majesty had shown herself a true mother of her country. She was to be remembered with especial gratitude on her birthday, for during the war she would be especially active in the Fatherland's good works. This we were to express in true seaman's fashion: three hearty cheers, given from good German hearts. We joined in enthusiastically. The band played the national anthem. It was all very stirring.

Toward noon we altered course to eastward. There was a memorable meal in the wardoom, in honour of the day, and von Mücke remembered the Kaiserin with a few well chosen words.

During the afternoon we arrived in the southern part of the Bay of Bengal, but stood off to southward of the shipping lane from Colombo to Singapore. There was to be no interference with enemy shipping; the men deserved rest, as they needed to recuperate from the exertions of previous weeks.

The following day also passed without incident, our time being filled with battle practice. These were vital, as enemy warships were certain to be lying in Pulo Penang harbour and a fight was to be expected. As we had no battle practice for some time, the men had to be thoroughly reminded of their action stations. After a few exercises, however, the men had become so well versed in their duties that the work passed with splendid smoothness.

The gunlayers, gunnery specialists and range-takers were given an opportunity for additional practice on a target towed by *Buresk*.

Our next objective was the Nicobar Islands, where *Emden* was to take on as much coal as possible. One never knew when there would be another opportunity.

The Nicobars came in sight on 26th October; at 0700 we ran into Nancowry Harbour. *Buresk* anchored first, whereafter we went alongside her and made fast. Coaling began soon afterwards. The men worked marvellously, reaching an average of sixty tonnes an hour. By about 1600hrs the five hundred tonnes we required had been taken aboard. Anticipating a fight in Penang, it was no longer stowed on deck where – if scattered by a shell – it would have presented an additional danger to the gun crews.

Our ship was now in an unusually beautiful bay. Nancowry Harbour lies on the south side of the island of Nicobar, possessing the luxuriant tropical vegetation that was a joy to see after a long voyage. During our stay,

Buresk was robbed of her name and port of registry to hinder recognition. Her captain, Klöpper, was instructed to steam away to a rendezvous west of the island of Sumatra and there await us as long as his provisions held out. The orders were similar to those given to Kapitänleutnant Gropius aboard the collier *Exford*.

We cast off at 1615, whereupon *Buresk* weighed anchor and put to sea. *Emden* followed her out of the bay, but then started for Penang at twelve knots as *Buresk* slowly vanished over the horizon.

That evening we cruised along the shipping lane from Calcutta to Singapore but met no ships. Actually, we had no intention of taking them and would simply have avoided any we saw. To mount an effectual raid, we had to get to Penang unseen and unexpected.

The night passed without disturbance until, early in the morning of 27th October, we accelerated to fifteen knots. Kapitän von Müller met the officers in the forenoon to give us the details of his plan of attack. The assault was to be mounted the next morning. Each officer received precise instructions for every conceivable emergency, for we had to reckon on the disablement of each and every one of us... and maybe even the captain.

Our men, meanwhile, had cleared the ship for action. Anything that might be a hindrance was stowed away, and large amounts of ready-use ammunition were placed at the guns. We also had a thorough 'Clean ship', which *Emden* badly needed. During the afternoon the men were given a change of clothes and the opportunity to bathe. Everyone was to go into the fight as clean as possible.

At 1700hrs came the order 'All hands aft!' The captain briefly told the men what he expected of them the next morning and hoped that every man would do his duty. Enthusiasm could be seen in the faces of our brave crewmen. Thank heavens we could trust the ship's company so thoroughly; without it the tasks would never have been carried through.

The greatest wish of everyone aboard *Emden* was to meet an enemy warship. Sinking merchantmen was acceptable, but required no deed of arms and engendered little pride. A fight against a similarly armed enemy, however, gave everybody satisfaction – a trial of strength of the ship, her officers and men. This fervent wish was about to be granted. When we asked our men whether they were pleased about the forthcoming morning's events, to a man they replied 'Of course, for now we shall get to grips with the *real* enemy'.

It may seem strange that we had not sought out enemy warships from the beginning. This, however, is not the primary duty of a cruiser on foreign station. Our orders were specifically to destroy the enemy's trade. To execute them with the greatest effect for as long as possible, *Emden* had to remain undamaged. This could only be achieved by avoiding enemy warships as best we could.

So why did we now seek a fight, and enter the lion's den to get it? The answer is simple. As we had done enormous harm to British trade during the preceding weeks, we had fulfilled the greater part of our task. The danger of being annihilated in Penang did not seem too great, as our principal weapon would be surprise. The maxim that attack is the best form of defence would thus be valid. We were certain that we could deal with an enemy warship before being spotted. Our fourth funnel would play a great part in deception by substantially changing our appearance. We hoped to buy enough time to destroy other shipping anchored in Pulo Penang as well.

Our plan was well conceived, and so we had great hopes of success. Success would bring a double victory – physical as well as moral.

At 2000hrs we increased speed to seventeen knots. We wished to gain our objective by dawn; the entrance to Penang is narrow, making a passage in darkness impossible. Without light, we would probably run aground. We also assumed that vigilance would diminish at dawn, for the sharper it is by night the more certain a reduction will be at first light.

The attack was nothing if not bold. Coming out of the Straits of Malacca from the west or north-west, a channel – perhaps a thousand metres broad – had to be negotiated between the island ('Pulo') of Penang to westward and the sandy coast of the Malaccan Peninsula to the east. To enter harbour, a ship rounded the north side of Pulo Penang with her helm hard-a-starboard, taking great care not to run too far to port and aground on the flat shore.

Once this corner had been negotiated, the bottleneck mouth of the harbour hove into view. There was an additional opening to the south, suited only to shallow-draught ships, but it would not accommodate *Emden*.

On the island itself, inside the bay, lay Georgetown and the harbour buildings. On the north side stood an old fort, which we reckoned to be obsolete and no real threat.

It is necessary to imagine a warship entering the harbour to engage vessels at anchor, and then turning in the narrows to leave again. The success of our commerce-raiding activities meant that many merchantmen would lie in harbour, restricting our turning space. If a torpedo-boat lay in some corner – which was easily possible – she could undoubtedly creep far enough toward *Emden* unseen to fire a torpedo. Even if we sighted the torpedo-track in time, we would have neither the time nor the space to avoid it.

There were many great risks in our attack-plan. Success would only come by cold-blooded calculation followed by ruthless execution. There would be no time for second thoughts or hesitation.

We had not a moment's doubt about victory, for we all knew the character of our captain. He was the very man to lead us to success in such a perilous venture.

It was pleasing to know that at least one torpedo played a part in our plan of attack, to be used to sink an enemy warship before she had time to offer resistance. Light war-watches were mounted until midnight, but then full watches began.

An anonymous – and questionably rendered – *Emden* sinks an equally poorly drawn *Zhemchug* in Penang Harbour, showing the dummy fourth funnel in its correct position between the bridge and the forefunnel. This illustration is additionally interesting in that it shows the Russian ship rigged with only one mast. By courtesy of the Bundesarchiv, Koblenz; Bild 134-C136.

The light of Pulo Penang hove into sight about 0200 in the morning of 28th October. Everyone aboard *Emden* was roused. After washing, our men had a hearty breakfast of milk soup intended to satisfy the inner man before the fight began. The watches coming off duty also washed and fed. Our fourth funnel was already hoisted, looking quite imposing as it rose from the deck. We were ready.

Soon we saw the lights of a steamship entering the harbour. But the moon still shone brightly, increasing the danger of being seen by a signal station atop the hill. *Emden* turned away and cruised until the moon went down.

Then we turned about again, approached at eleven knots and then – boldly – turned toward the harbour mouth. This manoeuvre was greatly assisted by the lightbuoy, the brightness of whose lantern greatly astonishing us. Soon we passed the ship we had previously sighted, but was now presumably waiting for a pilot. At 0430 came the order 'Ready!' We passed an islet in the harbour mouth, especially suitable to conceal guardships, and then sighted fishing boats keeping such a poor lookout that we nearly ran one down.

Scarcely had we passed the islet than a pilot boat approached to within twenty metres of us. What he made of our appearance I do not know, though he was unlikely to take us for a hostile warship.

We entered the bottleneck at 0450 and again received the order 'Ready!' We rushed for our action stations; mine was the torpedo flat, where I checked the arrangements yet again. The torpedoes were already loaded and the electric release-gear was connected. We were ready to fire.

Communication had to be established with the conning tower, the order 'Clear ship!' being obeyed as adroitly in the torpedo-flat as elsewhere. Communications, however, meant principally the transmission of news from above. In the flat we could see nothing, but wished to be kept abreast of progress with the attack. At 0505 we received the order 'Clear away starboard tube!', and waited in some suspense for instructions to release the torpedo.

At 0518 the torpedo-flat telegraph lit up: 'Fire!' The fish was out and away. We waited in suspense, holding our breath. There was dull bang.

Cheers and congratulations echoed across the flat. We had no doubt that the torpedo had struck home. The guns above us had opened fire almost simultaneously with the final thud of the torpedo hit. The noise of the salvoes was deafening, but we could see nothing.

News came from the conning tower: 'Torpedo got home well under the waterline, but has not completely dealt with the Russian cruiser *Zhemchug*' – this, then, was our target – 'and another torpedo is to be fired'.

No sooner had we reloaded the starboard tube than we received 'Clear away port tube!' The electric release-gear was connected and, once again, we awaited the order to fire. *Emden* heeled. Clearly, she was turning sharply. The electric signal inquired 'Ready?', to which we replied 'Everything ready!' Shortly afterward came 'Fire!'

The torpedo hissed out of the tube. At once there was a fearful crash, which also gave *Emden* a considerable shock.

Amid rejoicing, we greeted the noise as proof that the torpedo had struck home in the magazine or torpedo flat of the Russian ship. There was no other way in which the tremendous explosion could be explained.

Soon we received word from the conning tower that *Zhemchug* had vanished, and that we were leaving harbour. Now that my presence in the torpedo-flat was no longer necessary, I rushed up to the deck. A cloud of yellow smoke rolled where the Russian ship had once been. Nothing of the cruiser remained excepting the mast-tops and some flotsam.

Soon I found my friend von Levetzow, who told me the story as seen from the upper deck.

At about the time I had gone down to the torpedo flat, 0450, dawn was just breaking and the coast – mainland to port, Pulo Penang to starboard – could already be distinguished. Georgetown was still brightly lit, unwittingly helping to guide our approach. Marker buoys provided exact bearings.

Before entering harbour we reduced speed. Four lights were spotted to starboard, giving the impression that we had to deal with torpedo-boats, but the mistake was soon recognized. It was a warship with several masts and funnels.

As day broke, *Emden* had mast-head flags proudly flying. The enemy had been identified as the Russian light cruiser *Zhemchug*, about the same size and power as our ship and, therefore, a worthy opponent.

The first torpedo officer, Oberleutnant z.S. Witthoeft, immediately hurried to the conning tower and gave the orders to clear away the torpedo tubes. *Emden* went so close to the Russian that we could not miss, firing at no more than 375 metres. At exactly 0518 there had been a muffled report, at which the Russian ship rose for a moment only to sink back up to her deck at the stern. Simultaneously, our starboard guns had opened fire with a frightful crash. Their objective was *Zhemchug*'s forecastle, which contained the men's flats, to incapacitate the gun crews before they could man their weapons.

It had been a fearful sight, so von Levetzow told me. In no time at all the fore part of the Russian ship was aflame. Her side was pierced like a sieve, aglow from the fires within. The scene had been at once awful and enthralling.

Soon after the first torpedo had been launched, *Emden* turned sharply to port to avoid the merchantmen anchored closest. Torpedo officer Witthoeft – who was also in charge of battle tactics – had given the order to reload the starboard tube and clear away the port one. A second torpedo was to be fired to prevent the Russian ship firing one at us.

While Witthoeft had been asking von Müller for permission to fire the port tube, a few shells passed over us. Some appeared to have come from *Zhemchug*, where a few gallant men had manned the after guns and returned our fire. Other Russians, however, had preferred

A fanciful representation of the destruction of *Zhemchug* by the watercolourist A. Hubert. The rendering of *Emden* at least shows the fourth funnel, though it seems to have been added abaft the third rather than ahead of the first. The sinking Russian cruiser is much too far inshore, has too many masts, and the three funnels all appear to lie ahead of the mainmast. The third funnel was actually abaft the mast. By courtesy of The Lyon Press archives.

Zhemchug

29TH SHIP INTERCEPTED, SEVENTEENTH VICTIM

Comparable in size and power to *Emden*, though somewhat older, the protected cruiser *Zhemchug* — one of two ships of the Izumrud class — was originally distinguished by a unique combination of three funnels and three masts. By 1914, however, she had apparently been re-rigged with only a single mast between the second and third funnels.† Laid down in 1901 and completed in 1904, *Zhemchug* was a product of the Nevski shipyard in St. Petersburg. She displaced 3,103 tons at standard load draught, measured 364ft overall and could attain 24 knots when new. By 1914 she mounted eight 12.2cm, six 5cm and two 3.7cm QF guns, plus three 45cm torpedo tubes. Surprised by *Emden* in Penang Harbour on 28th October 1914, while under the command of Captain Second Class Baron Cherkassov, she was blown apart by gunfire and two torpedo hits without landing so much as a single shell on her opponent.

† There is confusion over the precise rig in 1914, and even Prinz Franz Joseph refers to a ship with 'several' masts and funnels. It is generally agreed — but not conclusively proven — that the foremast had been removed by this time, and possibly also the mizzen to leave only the original mainmast.

to jump overboard and swim for the safety of the shore. Other shells came from interior of the harbour. The miscreant was soon located: French torpedo-boat *d'Iberville*, lacking the courage to show herself. We promised to be back for her as soon as we had finished off *Zhemchug*.

We remained unscathed, though a Japanese ship behind us was hit in the funnel by shells that went over us. By this time we had approached to within seven hundred metres of the crippled Russian. As our guns raked the length of *Zhemchug*, her gunfire slackened and then ceased. Torpedo-officer Witthoeft pressed the firing button, whereupon we released the port torpedo to hiss out of its tube and rush unerringly towards the enemy. A few seconds later there had been a frightful bang, and *Zhemchug* had been literally torn in half. Huge chunks of metal had flown skyward, only to splash back noisily into the water. The spectacle lasted but a few seconds, then a thick cloud of yellow smoke blanketed the scene of destruction. Green and yellow flames darted erratically from this cloak, accompanied by bangs and crashes; it had been a memorably weird and wonderful episode.

The veil of smoke had lifted after several minutes, but nothing of *Zhemchug* was to be seen apart from the tops of her masts. The whole attack had lasted about fifteen minutes.

We were contemplating turning to deal with *d'Iberville* when a vessel was sighted in the harbour mouth. Believing this to be a torpedo-boat bent on blocking our escape, we turned quickly to port and pelted towards the entrance at full speed.

I watched the quarry from the quarterdeck. Irritatingly, smoke clouds hid her from us. As the smoke would not clear, we opened fire at about 5,500 metres. The bad mirage that morning hindered our shooting, but we were glad when we saw the 'torpedo-boat' to be a harmless government launch. We ceased fire immediately.

Insignificant as the little ship had been, her unwitting intervention had saved *d'Iberville* and her companions from destruction. Kapitän von Müller had decided to deal with the French torpedo-boat and then sink the merchantmen. Now that *Emden* was outside the harbour, however, he did not wish to re-enter. So our mast-head flags were hauled down and the men released from their action stations.

Somewhat later, Kapitänleutnant von Mücke called the men aft and explained the progress of the fight to them. This was worth doing, because many had their action stations beneath the armoured deck and had seen nothing. They all expressed great satisfaction

Finally, Kapitän von Müller gave a short speech in which he said that we should remember the War Lord in the hour of success, and renew our loyalty by giving His Majesty Kaiser Wilhelm II three rousing cheers. We gave them with enthusiasm and joy. We were uplifted and refreshed by the thought that something had been contributed toward the greater glory of the Fatherland. The men were released to breakfast, and then to wash. The guns were cleaned, fresh stocks of ready-use ammunition were brought up and the searchlights were made fast.

At about 0700, when the men had already vanished from the waist of the ship, the order 'Clear ship for action!' brought them rushing back again.

What had happened? A very large ship whose flag could not be distinguished from the fore-top had appeared on the horizon. The range was taken and passed to the guns, and *Emden* turned slightly so that the entire port broadside could be employed. Everyone waited for the order to fire. But the order never came.

Everyone on the bridge had initially agreed that the newcomer was a big auxiliary cruiser. The nearer we moved, however, the smaller the image became. Finally it had shrunk into an ordinary merchantman. But this ordinary steamer flew the yellow flag showing her cargo to be explosive.

The mirage had played a second trick on us. Though no harm had been done, there was no reason to respect the powder ship and we proceeded to stop her according to our well-tried recipe. Over went Lauterbach and the search party. The order to sink the ship was accompanied by a message for her captain to pass on at the earliest opportunity. *Emden* had not saved men from *Zhemchug* as many boats had been nearby, and the government launch had been attacked under the misapprehension that we were dealing with a torpedo-boat. Kapitän von Müller wished to express his regrets.

So noble was our captain that he wished to apologize! Had the situation been reversed, I suspect we would have awaited an apology for a very long time.

Lauterbach was posting his men aboard the 'powder keg' – which was revealed as the British steamship *Glenturret* – when *Emden* signalled him to return at once. Lauterbach and his men returned in our cutter, which was hoisted aboard with all speed. We had to be clear for action as soon as possible, which meant that *Glenturret* was now granted an unexpected reprieve.

The cause of alarm was a suspicious vessel sighted to starboard; in spite of the distortion due to mirage, there was no doubt that the newcomer was a warship. It was simply her size we could not determine.

On the order 'Clear ship for action!', everyone had rushed to their action stations. I had gone down to the torpedo flat, only to learn from the conning tower that the stranger had been identified as a French torpedo-boat. As torpedoes would not be used against such a small target, I could return to deck. There I found *Emden*, with mast-head flags flying, steaming towards the new enemy at full speed. Our first salvo was fired at 4,500 metres; by turning to port, the entire starboard battery could be brought to bear.

Our little enemy was injudicious. She did not steam straight for us, as a torpedo-boat should have done, but turned and fled at the first salvo. In so doing, she presented us with the splendid target of her whole length.

The first salvo was somewhat high, while the second fell short. But the third could not have gone more exactly to plan. One shell shot down the Tricouleur while another had found the boiler room. Huge clouds of steam were enveloping the French ship.

Though severely damaged, our enemy managed to launch a torpedo which passed several hundred yards astern of us. Her main gun – which stood ahead of the conning tower – was also brought into action. It must have been a large machine-gun, for it fired with astonishing rapidity. But it hit nothing. Most of the shots went high, humming over *Emden* like a monstrous swarm of bees.

Our gunnery was excellent. Once the range had been found, every shell thumped home. The French ship was now in desperate straights. Her superstructure was shot to pieces; her hull was a wreck. After our twelfth salvo, the torpedo-boat disappeared in a cloud of yellowish smoke. Kapitän von Müller ordered a cease-fire.

When the smoke cleared, the French vessel was still afloat and showing no signs of surrendering. So we

Glenturret

Board of Trade Registry 106031

THIRTIETH SHIP INTERCEPTED

Built for Glen Line Ltd, London (McGregor, Gow & Co. Ltd) by London & Glasgow Shipbuilding Co. Ltd, 4,696grt 400ft *Glenturret* had been delivered in September 1896. Registered in Glasgow, with the call-sign PLGH, she was stopped in the entrance to Penang harbour on 28th October 1914 while laden with explosives. Fortunately for Captain Jones and his crew, the approach of *Mousquet* (q.v.) forced von Mller to release *Glenturret* to sail into Penang with an apology for shelling a pilot-boat! Glen Line vessels were black, with red boot-topping, white upperworks and brown masts. Funnels were plain red with a black top, while the house flag comprised the Union superimposed on a red/white diagonally quartered ground. This was flown below a small blue pennant bearing a white cross at the hoist.

Mousquet

31ST SHIP INTERCEPTED, SEVENTEENTH VICTIM

Built by Chantiers de la Loire of Saint-Nazaire under the 1900 programme, this 298-tonne torpedo-boat destroyer of the Arquebuse class was launched in August 1902. Measuring about 58m on the waterline and capable of 28 knots when new, *Mousquet* carried one 6.5cm and six 4.7cm QF guns, plus two torpedo tubes. Under the command of Lieutenant de Vaisseau Théroïnne, she was sunk off Penang by gunfire on 28th October 1914.

opened fire again, ten more salvoes ensuring the torpedo-boat would never again move from the spot. 'Battery cease fire!' was ordered, whereafter *Emden* came to a standstill abaft the shattered vessel to prevent our victim launching another torpedo.

As we manoeuvred into position, the French ship dipped her bow beneath the waves – gradually sinking deeper until her stern stood vertically out of the water. Soon the stern had also vanished into the deep.

Nothing was to be seen but flotsam and swimming survivors. We approached to within about two hundred metres of the spot where the torpedo-boat had sunk. While the mast-head flags were being run down, our second cutter was lowered with an officer and the surgeon's assistant in addition to her usual crewmen. The first cutter soon followed; she had been made fast for the fight, and casting-off had taken time.

We began to rescue the swimming Frenchmen with all speed. If we thought the task would be easy, we were very wrong. The uninjured men would simply not let themselves be taken from the water. This mad refusal made no sense. I speculated that the men had been fed such horrendous anti-German propaganda that they would rather risk their lives trying to swim to the neighbouring shore than fall into the hands of 'man-eating barbarians'.

We later learned that one Frenchman had indeed reached Pulo Penang, which was a quite a task for a swimmer.

Once the French seamen saw the care with which their wounded were hoisted into the boats, their attitude changed. Eventually, we saved a sublieutenant and 36 men.

When the cutters came alongside *Emden*, the uninjured men came in over the boom. As it was necessary to get the wounded aboard without causing them too much pain, we simply hoisted the cutters amidships. Here the Frenchmen were carefully lifted out and taken forward to berths in the sick-bay in compartments XI and XII.

The poor sailors, who had fought bravely for their country, were a pitiful sight. I can always picture one of the men when I think of his pain. He had been hit so badly in the stomach that his entrails were hanging out.

Our doctors went to work straight away, though it was unfortunate that the wounded had been in the water so long. The salt quickly aggravated their wounds. Two of the wounded men had their legs shattered and, as the wounds had already begun to fester, required immediate amputation.

The uninjured were accommodated in the starboard waist, which made a tolerable lodging with the help of an awning made from a breadth of sail cloth. It was certainly more agreeable than 'tween decks near the engines, where the heat was suffocating. Anyway, we had no room between decks for prisoners. Sentries were placed to prevent the Frenchmen swarming all over *Emden*, whose construction naturally interested them greatly. We learned that the torpedo-boat had been named *Mousquet*. This was confirmed by a lifebelt retrieved by one of the cutter's crew, a trophy that had been hung proudly on the quarterdeck.

As we treated them quite well, the Frenchmen became talkative and told us of their movements during the previous night. Some of the story was particularly interesting.

Mousquet had been on patrol duty at the north entrance to Penang harbour, her station being near the islet we had passed in the early morning. The men said they had seen a cruiser sail by, but had been duped by our fourth funnel into believing us to be British.

We could not understand the behaviour of the Frenchmen. If *Mousquet* had been lying in wait behind the island, she was clearly not keeping a lookout or had neglected her duty by not hailing us as we passed. She could also have reported our presence to the harbour. Only by hailing us could the officer of the watch aboard *Mousquet* be certain of our identity.

When our first torpedo had exploded against *Zhemchug* – so the Frenchmen said – *Mousquet* had hurried into the harbour to discover what was happening. As she entered, *Emden* was encountered once again; *Mousquet* had kept silent, still thinking us to be British.

And so it must have been in the open sea, as *Mousquet* would not have run confidently toward a cruiser she knew to be German. The Frenchmen had been brought to their senses by our first salvo. Such a rude awakening had robbed *Mousquet*'s captain of his senses, making him imprudent enough to turn to flee – exposing his entire flank to us when he should have come head-on to attack.

Asked about events aboard *Mousquet*, the Frenchmen said that part of her company had offered stout resistance. Some members of the crew had been hurled overboard, however, to be followed by others who had mistaken their colleagues' predicament for an order to abandon ship.

Confused as the French captain had been by the realization that he had confronted *Emden*, he remained courageous to his dying breath. After his legs had been shot away in the course of the fight, he had had himself lashed to the bridge and went down with his ship – a hero's death for his fatherland.

Most of the Frenchmen had saved nothing but their lives, so we gave them underclothes and uniforms from our stores. The prisoners were treated as well as possible. The attitude of our crewmen bordered on touching, as they brought the Frenchmen chocolate, cigarettes and many a refreshing drink. The prisoners' expressions showed that they were grateful and content with the change in their fortunes.

The French sublieutenant was severely wounded, and had to be given a special room in the sick-bay. I paid him a visit after an operation to amputate his right foot. He was content, but complained of frightful pain. I told him how many of his men we had rescued and what had befallen him. This quieted him. He was grateful that he did not need to worry about his fellow prisoners.

Many news items were gleaned from the Frenchmen, including the fact that Japanese warships were lying at Singapore. From this we guessed that the British ships had been sent home.

We also learned that HMS *Yarmouth* had escorted *Pontoporos* into Singapore on 14th October. We assumed that *Markomannia* had scuttled, as she should have been lying with *Pontoporos* off Simaloer.

Conversation between our men and *Mousquet*'s survivors was limited, as the Frenchmen were aware that our men would report important news. However, we discovered that the French officers had told their men that Germans killed all prisoners. This explained why some of the Frenchmen refused our offer of rescue and tried to swim to the shore. The joy of those we saved was heightened by the good treatment they received.

I confess that I did not understand the policy of saying nothing but bad about your enemy. If – as in *Mousquet*'s case – men drowned as a result of this propaganda, then the responsibility lay solely with the French authorities. Perhaps these men believed their sailors would fight better under such circumstances. I shall assume, in honour of our enemies in 1914, that this poor reflection on the French navy is incorrect.

Meanwhile, a new enemy had appeared off the entrance to Pulo Penang. Keeping a respectful distance from us was the torpedo-boat *Fronde*, a sister of *Mousquet*. Our new opponent had been anchored in Penang harbour.

What good spirit had protected us? Had we approached *d'Iberville*, her compatriot *Fronde* could easily have cut off our exit. Our destruction would have been certain.

Now we endeavoured to get away, steaming northward at 22 knots to escape from *Fronde*. This was truly a strategic retreat. We had good reason to withdraw, for we knew from interceptions that the wireless station had broadcast '*Emden* at Penang!' and a description of our exploits in the most modest terms possible.

These broadcasts would certainly bring all our enemies to the neighbourhood. Many hounds are certain death for the hare, so our best course was to flee. At 1030 our wireless intercepted additional messages, replies from enemy warships to the news of *Emden* at Penang.

We could not know the position of our enemies, though distance could be roughly gauged from the strength of the messages.

Fronde obstinately insisted on following us, keeping a prudent distance, while mouthing incessantly like an old slut. With astonishing fierceness she shrieked to the world that she dogged the course of the 'fearful' *Emden* which had so terribly 'assassinated' her sister *Mousquet*. She continually broadcast our course and speed in the earnest hope that a ship of the Entente would give chase. Periodic interceptions showed that she was denouncing us wildly.

She could not be silenced by gunfire, but our wireless was so much more powerful that we could confuse her messages almost to the point of obliteration. We could also reckon on *Fronde* losing breath – her fuel would certainly run out! Such a small ship carried too little coal to keep up a chase for long.

Emden delighted her talkative pursuer with a certain amount of cunning, steaming on a fictitious course west-northwest. The weather-god also favoured us, sending a violent squall to blind *Fronde* completely. In the midst of the squall we turned north-northwest. When the sun returned fifteen minutes later, there was no sign of our pursuer. The horizon remained clear, the best eyes and sharpest glasses finding nothing. We had lost our tormentor.

Now we could reflect and rejoice at our success. How much *Emden* had achieved! And what luck had accompanied our enterprise. We had made the difficult passage into Penang harbour to destroy an enemy cruiser. Three times had we been fired on without suffering the least damage. For this we were a little sorry, as *Emden* could have afforded a trifling (but honourable) memento...

As a finale to a crowded hour, we had sunk an enemy torpedo-boat. It was victory indeed; and it must have had a devastating effect on enemy morale. Every man in *Emden* looked back on that day with a feeling of gratitude.

In the torpedo branch, we were particularly proud; we had, after all, delivered the coup de grace to *Zhemchug* ourselves. Without the effectual launching of the two torpedoes, *Emden* could not have achieved her success so quickly.

What rankled was that we had not been able to sink any of the merchantmen in Penang harbour. The large ships among them would have made excellent ornaments at the bottom of the sea!

OUR FINAL PRIZE

Wednesday 28th October–Sunday 8th November 1914

Our objective was now the shipping route from Penang to Rangoon. We hoped to force a ship to take our prisoners to a neutral port. Speed had been reduced to seventeen knots after we had escaped from *Fronde* in the squall.

We remained on our course until 1600hrs, but as no ship had showed we turned to port and headed west-southwest. By evening, *Emden* was to reach the familiar neighbourhood of the Nicobar Islands. We were to pass St George's Channel in darkness. The channel lay some way south* of Nancowry harbour, where we had coaled before the attack on Penang.

At about 1800, the islands came in sight. Soon, *Emden* was in the middle of St George's Channel, formed by the islands of Great and Little Nicobar. The strait, bordered by wooded heights, presented a splendid appearance. After the strain of the day, we enjoyed the scene twice as much. Our Frenchmen showed great anxiety, however, and their behaviour changed so greatly that we inquired the reason. They feared we would leave them to their fate on one of the lonely islands, but were soon reassured when we told them that no such thought had occurred to us. We were greatly surprised by the existence of such a fear. Had our roles been reversed, perhaps the French would have marooned us!

At 2000 we had the beautiful channel behind us, whereupon *Emden* turned to port on a south-westerly course. The port engine had run hot, owing to a fault, and was stopped that night for repair.

During the night of 28/29th October, two Frenchmen died of their wounds. When this was reported to Kapitän von Müller, he ordered that a ceremonial burial at sea would take place at 0800 on 29th October. Full naval honours would be conferred on the sailors, as they had died after fighting bravely for their country.

A speedy burial was necessary; decay starts with astonishing rapidity in the tropics, and it would not be beneficial to the health of the ship's company to keep the bodies aboard for long.

At 0800 we were ordered to fall-in on parade, the officers wearing ordinary service dress and their decorations. The uninjured Frenchmen were placed in the starboard waist. Leutnant z.S. Schall was on the quarter-

* The original English-language memoir erroneously states the direction as north.

HMS *Yarmouth* is seen here leaving the Grand Harbour, Valetta, Malta, in June 1927. Unlike the ships of the Bristol class, which had two 6-inch and ten 4-inch guns, the succeeding Weymouths — *Yarmouth* being one — had eight 6-inch guns. Note that there are three large guns between the masts instead of five smaller ones. By courtesy of Wright & Logan, Portsmouth.

deck in command of the guard of honour, which was to fire the final salute.

Wrapped in sailcloth and covered by the Tricouleur, the two bodies were placed on the starboard boom and our men assembled in a half-circle. Kapitän von Müller made a short speech in praise of the fallen heroes in German, repeating it in French.

As the Lord's Prayer was recanted, *Emden* hove-to. When both engines had stopped, the bodies were consigned to the deep as three salvoes were fired over the seamen's grave.

Our ship's company dispersed glumly, whereupon the engines roared into life again and we rejoined our course. The remainder of the day was devoted to ordinary tasks. The preparations for the fight in Penang harbour were cleared away, and back went the deck awnings so that the men could sleep under cover in the fresh air. The heat in these regions – always great – is particularly unbearable in warships, whose all-steel construction is a very good conductor.

The balmy weather improved the humour of everyone aboard. Our French prisoners were content with their lot, as their good treatment continued. The concern of our men was really quite touching. They continued to bring the French sailors cigarettes, chocolate and the other little things that make life tolerable.

The wounded Frenchmen were the subject of much anxiety, however. Although our doctors looked after them as well as circumstances would allow, the sick-bay was cramped and the atmosphere was much too humid. The sole surviving officer had had a leg amputated and was suffering severely. We did all we could to ease his pain.

Our dearest wish was to surprise a ship so that the wounded could be taken ashore for further treatment as soon as possible. But another wounded man died in the night of 29/30th October. The efforts of our doctors had been in vain.

Towards 0630 on 30th October, we spotted a smoke cloud and gave chase. The stranger was a good-sized ship, which relieved the anxiety about the condition of our prisoners. Lauterbach went over with the search party. She was the British steamer *Newburn*, about 3,000 tons, hauling a cargo of salt from England to Singa-

Newburn

Board of Trade Registry 118634

32ND SHIP INTERCEPTED

Photograph by courtesy of the Trustees of the National Maritime Museum, Greenwich; negative P12015.

Built by Swan, Hunter & Wigham Richardson Ltd of Newcastle upon Tyne, for the Newcastle Steam Ship Co. Ltd, 3,000grt single-screw *Newburn* was delivered in June 1904. She was a black ship with red boot-topping, her funnel being black with a white band displaying a circlet of black diamonds. The house flag comprised three black diamonds extending to the edges of a white ground. Under the command of Captain William Richards, *Newburn* was seized on 30th October 1914 while hauling salt from England to Singapore under a pre-war German charter. Richards was instructed to land French sailors from *Mousquet*.

pore. Best of all was news that the cargo was destined for a German company in Singapore! Sinking the ship did not even enter our heads.

Emden stopped. The British captain, meanwhile, was learning his task from Lauterbach. He accepted it readily, realizing that taking the Frenchmen to Khota Raja would guarantee the safety of his ship.

Khota Raja, a small town on the north tip of the Dutch island of Sumatra, not only had a well-appointed hospital but was also the nearest port. We could not have chosen better.

The Frenchmen agreed, giving their word of honour not to fight against us again during the war, and transhipment began immediately. The uninjured men went across to *Newburn* first, taking me with them to reinforce Lauterbach. The lightly wounded men followed, their transport raising no insuperable difficulties. The transfer of the severely wounded was undertaken under the supervision of Stabsarzt Dr Luther in *Emden* and his assistant, Dr Schwabe, in *Newburn*. The casualties were lashed to hammocks, which made handling them easier, but the whole process was very awkward.

The last of *Mousquet*'s survivors to leave us was the officer, who gave his grateful thanks for the kindness shown to his men aboard *Emden*. We later learned that he died of his wounds in hospital.

The wounded were stowed as well as possible in *Newburn*. The British skipper received precise instructions from Dr Schwabe for their treatment, then Lauterbach, the doctor, myself and our men left *Newburn* for *Emden*. By our calculations, the steamer should reach Khota Raja about 2200 that evening.

We set a fictitious course for Colombo, but then turned southward as we intended to meet *Buresk*. At 0900 on the morning of 30th October, we committed the dead Frenchman to the sea with the same honours accorded to his comrades.

As *Emden* ran for the agreed rendezvous, the men were given nothing but light duties, being allowed to wash and mend clothes in the afternoon. We were to meet our companion *Buresk* on 31st October and had come so close to the rendezvous early in the morning that we expected to sight our collier at any time. Great care was necessary, however, as there was every possibility that *Buresk* had been captured by an enemy warship which now lay in wait for us. There was considerable excitement, therefore, when the stern of a dark ship came in sight at about 0430.

As the huntsman stalks the buck, so we quietly approached this dark and questionable object. Many sharp eyes strained to distinguish the characteristics of this unknown ship through the darkness. One thing was certain; she had one funnel and could indeed be *Buresk*.

And *Buresk* it was, thank heaven. We had our companion again. Her loss would have been a hard blow, for a well-trained auxiliary is invaluable in the open sea. She was immediately signalled by morse lamp to follow *Emden* on a new course. We steamed close to her in order to convey important news by megaphone. When Kapitän von Müller told of our exploit in Penang, the answer was a shout of joy.

We now steamed eastward at ten knots. In *Emden* we had a thorough 'clean ship', during which the officers assembled in the captain's cabin to discuss promoting some of the men. Kapitän von Müller, mindful of events at Penang, wished to reward some of the senior men who had rendered *Emden* especially good service. The cutters' crews deserved recognition, as they had borne the brunt of capturing the merchantmen and deserved to profit by it.

As 1st November was a Sunday, the usual Divisions were followed by Divine Service. The order 'Everybody aft!' was then given. The promotion of forty men was announced, among them the very capable Torpedo-Maschinistenmaat Pyttlik to Torpedo-Maschinist. He was already acquainted with his new duties, of course. All of us in the torpedo section were naturally delighted at his well-deserved fortune, which reflected credit on us all.

In a short speech, the captain emphasized that he could not promote everyone, even if he wished to do so, but could only reward a few. He then repeated his thanks for the good service rendered by the entire ship's company.

After the gathering had been dismissed, we were invited back to the captain's cabin for a glass of champagne. This we downed in joyful remembrance of the attack on Penang.

1st November was an anniversary aboard *Emden*. We were now three months into our cruise. The engines had made ten million revolutions, as we had put 30,000 nautical miles behind us at a cost of six thousand tons of coal. Apart from a few minor troubles, our engines had coped with the extended cruise marvellously. We could be grateful to Marine-Oberingenieur Ellerbroeck for the diligence of his staff, without whom we would have had no success.

We had a total rest in the afternoon. The orchestra played, many men danced and the night passed without incident. On 2nd November, in the early morning, we made clear for coaling and went alongside *Buresk* at 0800. By now we were close to the Poggy Islands, west of Sumatra and not far from the town of Padang.

Coaling began punctually at 0900, being favoured by splendid weather and a flat calm. Five hundred tonnes were taken in, raising our stocks to 950 tonnes. But a very unpleasant accident happened among my men. We were in full swing when a hoist broke loose high over the hold. A few sacks of coal fell onto the left leg of Torpedo-Obermatrose Possehl, breaking his thigh. The poor fellow was immediately taken by stretcher to the sick-bay, where Dr Luther soon splinted the leg.

This was the only accident I remember occurring during coaling exploits. I am sure that none of the men was responsible for it, as the security of the hoist was examined before each lift.

At midday, during the meal hour, a sailing boat came alongside and aboard came an officer in greenish-khaki

Dutch uniform. The boat, which had an auxiliary motor, made fast to the port boom. The newcomer – a captain in the Netherlands Indies Army – wished to ascertain if *Emden* lay outside the three-mile limit. We were able to assure him of this with a clear conscience. His duty done, he gratefully accepted a whisky and soda. His stock of news was meagre. The news that Portugal had also declared war on Germany awakened no great excitement aboard *Emden*: the Dutchman had a sense of humour!† He wished us bon voyage, and left *Emden* at 1500hrs.

Coaling lasted until 1700, when we cast off from *Buresk* and steamed away westerly. When out of sight of the island, *Emden* turned southward. Our next objective was the Sunda Straits, where we hoped to cruise for a few days and take some more merchantmen.

We reached the straits on 3rd November. We ran through and then back, but found nothing. That not a single ship was to be seen was largely due to our own activities. We had made the Indian Ocean as unsafe as possible, though this was little compensation for our boredom.

As we cruised we came across the well-known volcano Krakatoa, which had blown away most of its former glory thirty years previously. Now, broken open almost down to sea level, it looked no more exciting than a giant hollow tooth.

Our cruise was unsuccessful largely because British ships no longer dared to navigate the Indian Ocean alone. Something of value we did get, however, was interceptions of Dutch wireless messages telling us that *Newburn* had run into Khota Raja and delivered the survivors of *Mousquet* to the Dutch authorities. We were really glad that the wounded had reached safety.

The cruise finished on 5th November, and *Emden* turned towards the appointed rendezvous with the collier *Exford*. The latter had been sent on ahead to wait for us. We steamed west, the days passing all but unnoticed. The sea was rough, however, and gallant *Emden* rolled appreciably in the swell. Seamen are accustomed to this and the change in conditions made little impression; for the mess steward carrying dishes, it was quite another problem.

We reached the rendezvous on 7th November, only to find no trace of *Exford*. This made us fear an enemy attack, even though the rendezvous was far from the trade routes.

The area had to be searched thoroughly until, early in the morning of 8th November, a smoke cloud finally metamorphosed into our long-sought collier.

An exchange of personnel was now possible. Kapitänleutnant Gropius, our navigating officer, was to return to *Emden*; Lauterbach, who had served as navigating officer during the attack on Penang, where his local knowledge had been invaluable, took command of *Exford*. Leutnants z.S. Fikentscher and Schall went to *Buresk*, replacing Gyssling and Schmidt. The latter pair was to take part in our sortie against the Cocos Islands, and thus in at least one martial operation before our cruise ended. The Signalmaat from *Buresk*, who was to install the wireless, exchanged with the *Exford* Signalgast.

Assistenzarzt Dr Schwabe visited a case of sickness aboard *Exford*, while special attention was taken to synchronize chronometers in all three ships. The differences between two of them had prevented *Exford* being at the rendezvous on time.

Accompanied by the colliers, we set off south-westerly. *Exford* was detached at 1600hrs, after a new rendezvous had been fixed in the western part of the Indian Ocean. Kapitän von Müller intended to continue our war on merchant shipping in the neighbourhood of the Island of Socotra.

Setting course for the so-called Direction Island, the principal settlement of the Cocos Group, we steamed off in the company of *Buresk*. Soon speed was reduced, as we did not wish to appear at Direction Island before daybreak. Our plan was simple but audacious. A landing party under Kapitänleutnant von Mücke was to go ashore on Direction Island to destroy the wireless and cable stations. The local cable station was especially important, being a relay for the Australia–India and Australia–Zanzibar–Africa links. Were these to be severed, disquiet would be aroused in Australia as well. However, the enterprise was not so simple in reality. To render a marine cable useless it is necessary to cut and then hide the severed end. The objective is attained if the two parts can only be found with time and trouble.

Wrecking the wireless station would be much easier, as we would only have to destroy the wireless mast and the transmitting apparatus.

Much of 8th November was spent on telling-off the landing party. Commanded by Kapitänleutnant von Mücke, supported by Leutnants z.S. Gyssling and Schmidt, the party comprised 30 seamen and seventeen technicans (including two from our wireless staff). Including officers, therefore, the raiders were some fifty strong. The seamen included most of our 'nine-year men': those who aspired to becoming petty officers, and had undertaken to serve for nine years.

Buresk was detached at 1900hrs. She was to wait at a distance of thirty nautical miles from the Cocos Islands and to make for Direction Island only on receipt of the signal 'Close up!' We had to proceed with all possible caution, taking into account that enemy warships may lie off the Cocos Islands. Only without *Buresk*, did we have the necessary freedom of movement.

† The reason Prinz Franz Joseph found this so amusing was that his elder sister Augusta-Victoria had married Manuel II, the one-time king of Portugal who had been deposed in 1909. He did not believe Portugal to pose much of a threat.

THE LAST BATTLE

Monday 9th November – Tuesday 10th November 1914

At 0600hrs on 9th November 1914, we approached Direction Island with our fourth funnel raised in the hope that we could complete our major tasks before we were recognized. We anchored in the harbour mouth and immediately piped away the landing party. The steam pinnace and our two cutters were lowered into the water ready-laden. Kapitänleutnant von Mücke commanded the party from the pinnace, with Leutnant z.S. Gyssling in the first cutter and Leutnant z.S. Schmidt in the second. Each cutter was armed with two machine-guns.

The steam pinnace set off for land towing the cutters, all boats flying the German flag. The party reached the shore shortly before 0700.

As the weather was favourable, Kapitän von Müller decided to coal. The order to close up was immediately wirelessed to *Buresk*. No answer came. The island's radio station then asked us who we were. Naturally we did not answer, ordering our wireless staff to jam the messages being sent out from Direction Island. However, the station did manage to transmit the message 'Strange ship in harbour'.

This was annoying, and could have been avoided had we opened fire on the station before landing. However, our captain wished to avoid unnecessary bloodshed and had directed that the wireless station alone be destroyed.

Almost immediately, the lofty wireless mast of the land station was seen to topple. Transmissions ended once and for all. This was timely, as only a few minutes later had we intercepted a message from an unknown ship calling the land station. Measurements showed the ship to be 250 nautical miles distant, so there was no danger.

As *Buresk* had been called up by wireless, we expected to meet her at about 1000hrs. When our lookouts sighted a smoke cloud at 0900, this was assumed to be our collier.

The work of the landing party, meanwhile, was taking an inordinately long time.

We cleared for coaling. The smoke cloud to northward suggested that *Buresk* was approaching, as we expected her from that direction. Lookouts kept the approaching smoke-plume under continual observation, reporting that the ship had a funnel and two masts. As this was like *Buresk*, we did not worry unduly. Leutnant z.S. von Guérard went up to the crow's nest and confirmed the report.

At 0915, a signal was sent to the dilatory landing party ordering it to hurry its work to a conclusion. But no sooner had this been done than the lookouts reported that the approaching vessel, which had been taken for

HMS *Newcastle*, the cruiser the Germans initially thought they faced. The photograph shows how easily *Newcastle* and *Sydney* could be confused from a distance, particularly at angles where the shape of the bow and the disposition of the midships 4-inch guns in the Bristol class were not obvious. By courtesy of the Trustees of the Imperial War Museum, London; negative Q 21564.

Buresk, had the tall masts of a British warship. Soon the White Ensign was visible.

There was now no doubt. We faced a stiff fight with the Royal Navy.

However hard the fight, our confidence in the efficacy of our ship and the proven leadership of our captain was so great that every man aboard *Emden* hoped to bring the fight to an honourable conclusion and gain victory.

Kapitän von Müller ordered 'Clear ship for action!', three blasts on the siren sounding the hasty recall of the landing party. But minutes were precious and the clock could not be turned back. There was no time to await the return of von Mücke and his men. Steam was being raised frantically in all boilers, as we would need *Emden*'s full speed.

At 0930 we weighed anchor and steamed out towards the enemy. All this I could see from a vantage-point on deck, but then duty called me to my action station in the torpedo flat. Everything there had been readied for action, a fact I relayed to the conning tower. The electrical firing apparatus was tested once again with dutiful thoroughness, anticipating the solemn joy of battle.

Vibrations of the ship, caused by the rapidity with which the engines were working, told us that we were going at high speed. Soon our guns had opened fire. We waited in suspense for a reply, but, at first, nothing could be heard of the enemy's shells. We judged the British ship to be shooting badly.

Towards 1000 there were a couple of hits near the torpedo flat and I had soundings taken in the double bottom to ensure water was not coming into the bowels of the ship – the only way to gauge the effect of hits below the waterline.

A raking hit on the armoured deck beneath the waterline came at 1020. The explosion and shock were such that our Torpedo-Maschinist, an unusually large and powerful man, measured his full length on the plates. So comical was this that we could not restrain our laughter, even though our situation was so serious.

This shell gashed the armoured deck, allowing water and gas to enter the torpedo flat. We immediately donned our smoke bandages to minimize the effects of the gas, as proper masks were not then known.

My men tried to shore up the rupture in the armoured deck, using canvas and planks that were stored in the flat. This was nothing but an expedient. I asked for carpenters to be sent below, but they were busy with more important tasks elsewhere. Our temporary repairs were not enough. Water and gas were bound to enter in time. I released some of the compressed air from the reservoir used for recharging the torpedo tubes, in the hope that it would expel the gas. The atmosphere improved immediately. However, the reservoir now had to be replenished. I ordered the port auxiliary engine-room to activate the torpedo air pumps, but received no answer. This could only mean that this particular area had been hit, a fact I reported to the conning tower. The hits on *Emden* proved that the British had now got our range. Shells landed on the armoured deck all around the torpedo flat. The noise was incredible. Indeed, we were surprised that the deck held under such a pounding. But it was impossible to get news from the conning tower, which caused us great anxiety even though we knew that the officers there had more important work to worry about than communicating with the torpedo flat.

Occasionally we were called, answering 'Torpedo flat all clear!' An order to ready the starboard tube came at 1025; this was done immediately. We were greatly encouraged, hoping to be able to join the fight with our weapons as well. Unfortunately, the opportunity never came.

My men worked splendidly. The work proceeded as if at drill, though hindered by the water in the flat. We were already ankle-deep. As *Emden* twisted and turned, the water splashed back and forth like a small wave. This would have made reloading the tubes hazardous; the work had to be accomplished quickly and men could easily slip.

At about 1045 we received a tremendous shock. This was too dull to be a direct hit and we correctly guessed that the foremast had been shot away. Still the torpedo flat avoided danger; though several shells exploded above the armoured deck in our vicinity, none but the first full hit pierced it.

Another enemy shell struck the armoured deck beneath the waterline towards 1100. All our lights immediately failed, but the emergency lighting was activated and we could assess the damage. The narrow hole was about forty centimetres long. Through it we could see water shining. Then water and gas began to pour into the flat again.

Three of my men had received shell splinters in the feet but, thank heaven, were only slightly injured. We could make nothing of the large hole; so many noxious fumes had entered that the torpedo flat was no longer tenable. The danger of gas poisoning had become too great and the gas bandages had ceased to be useful. I reported to the conning tower: 'Forced by danger from gas and water to abandon the torpedo flat!' I ordered the men out.

We tried to leave through the armoured hatch, but the hatch cover would not open. The 20cm-high coaming, preventing water entering the torpedo flat should the hatch-seal fail, had been bent over and now threatened to entomb us. There was nothing left but to get on deck by way of the torpedo-loading hatch. I ordered the armoured hatch to be secured before we left, preventing water in the flat rising higher.

The men nearest the transport hatch rushed to the port torpedo tube. The first man was hoisted up to loosen the securing nuts, whereupon the hatch was lifted clear by men summoned to our assistance on the deck above. We lifted the first man as high as we could, until he could be pulled up through the hatch. The rest of us followed, until I could order the transport-hatch cover to be replaced, the bolts fastened and the whole thing secured from above.

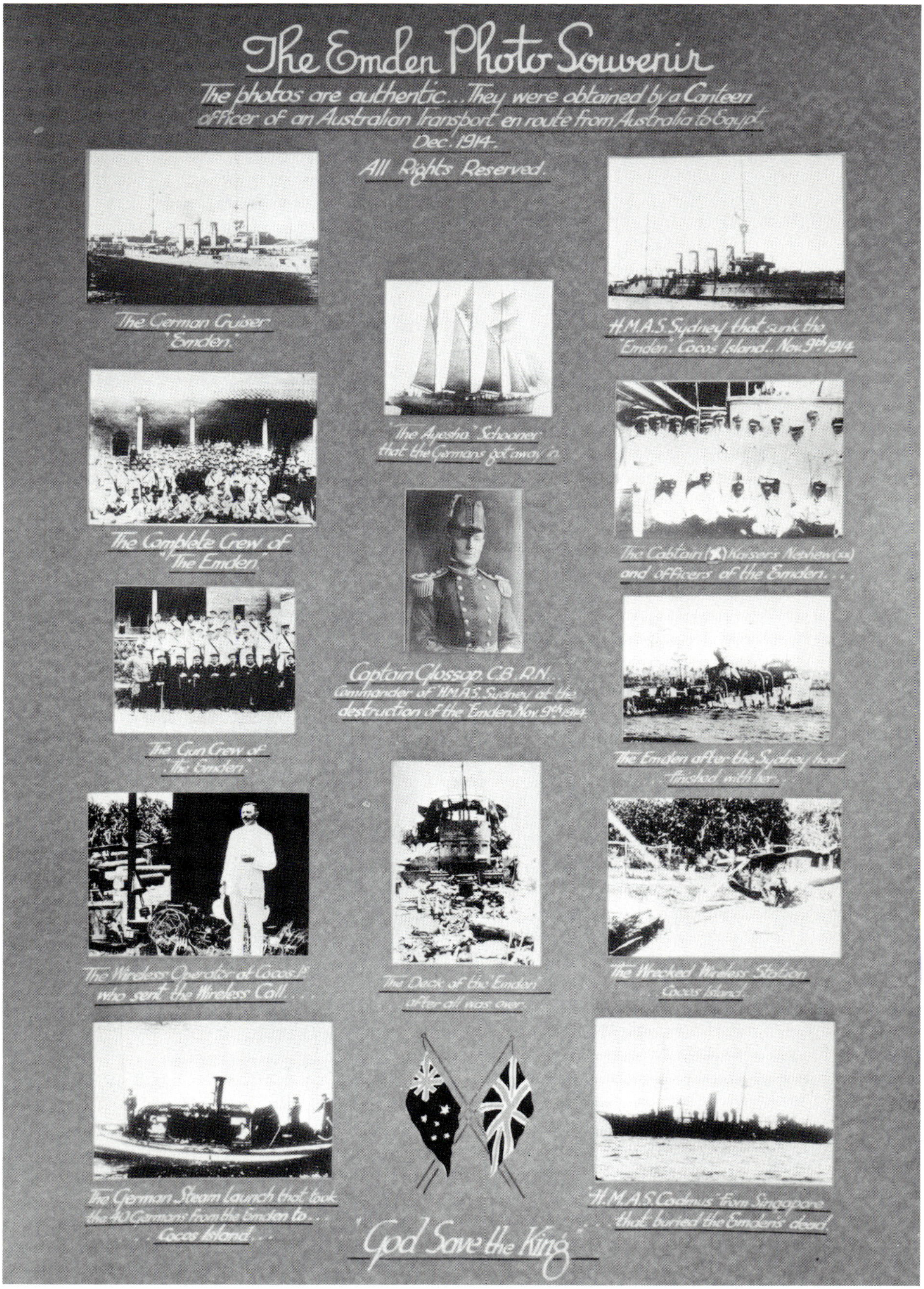

By courtesy of the Naval Association of Australia, New South Wales Section.

In the ship's waist I found wounded being bandaged by Oberhoboistenmaat Wecke, who told me how things looked in our beloved *Emden*. Going forward along the upper deck I could see the extent of the damage for myself; everywhere there were dead and severely wounded men – groaning, moaning and plaintively crying for help. Most distressing was the realization that I could do nothing to help. First aid was lacking, as the sick-bay in the steering flat could not be reached.

In the fore battery I found Oberleutnant z.S. Geerdes, who was wounded; he pointed out gunnery officer Gaede. Mortally wounded, Gaede lay at the No.1 port gun; though his uniform was red with his blood, he recognized me still. But he lapsed into unconsciousness as he thanked me for my meagre words of comfort and was carried to the forecastle. There he closed his eyes for ever and his body, according to seamen's custom, was committed to the deep.

Emden, shot to pieces but with her engines still turning, was meanwhile being run aground on the southern shore of North Keeling Island.

On deck, a terrible picture met my gaze. Wherever I looked I saw nothing but holes in the side, bent metal, burning rubbish and ashes. Our once-trim *Emden* was now a ghastly sight. Everything was tossed together; two funnels were down, while the foremast, thrown over the port side by a direct hit, lolled across the railing to drag its tip in the water. I learned that Leutnant z.S. von Guérard and a signalman had been thrown overboard from the fore-top.

The worst part of the ship was the stern, where the whole deck and the ship's sides glowed red. The fires that burned everywhere barred the passage aft.

I was very anxious for the safety of my friend von Levetzow, whose action station was in the after battery. To search for him was clearly impossible. Near the conning tower I found Kapitän von Müller, to whom I immediately reported the news that all my men from the torpedo flat – excepting a few minor wounds – were safe. He was visibly glad to see me again, for he had believed the torpedo flat to have been seriously hit. Of course, we were hardly beauties: our faces were blackened by soot

The final battle. SMS *Emden*, in the foreground, vainly challenges HMAS *Sydney* (on the horizon, left centre) in Claus Bergen's oil-painting. Unlike many rival marine artists, Bergen could usually capture not only the essence of warships but also something of the dash of their actions. He was a skilled observer; here the elevation of the aftermost 10.5cm gun and the tiny speck that is *Sydney* immediately convey that naval actions are fought at such great range that hits are difficult to obtain. And his dynamic handling of smoke and swell capture something of the tension of the occasion. *Emden* is accurately observed, but not with such slavish attention to detail that the eye is distracted from the overall composition. Owned by Meinrad, Prinz von Hohenzollern-Emden, this painting currently graces the wardroom of *Emden* V. Photograph by courtesy of Fregattenkapitän Walter Reichenmiller.

Taken on the forecastle, looking aft, this photograph was taken immediately after *Sydney* had returned to take off the surviving members of *Emden*'s crew. The bridge is open to the sky, while the downed foremast can just be seen behind the bridge on the right side of the picture. By courtesy of the Australian War Memorial, Canberra; negative EN0238.

and our uniforms had been stained lemon yellow by the fumes from the exploding shells.

Once the uninjured officers assembled, I saw that more than half our number was missing. For the first time I learned of the experience of the men on deck, much of which I and my men had missed during our confinement below in the torpedo flat.

After 'Clear ship for action!' had been ordered at 0930, Kapitän von Müller had gone into the conning tower accompanied by gunnery officer Kapitänleutnant Gaede, torpedo officer Oberleutnant z.S. Witthoeft (who had responsibility for battle tactics) and Leutnant z.S. Zimmermann, assisting Gaede.

There they had a Feuerwerksmaat, a seaman to pass orders to the gunners, the action helmsman and others whose action stations were in the conning tower. In the 'fire lee' – on the side of the conning tower away from the action – were the navigating officer, Kapitänleutnant Gropius, the helmsman and a signalman. On the quarterdeck, directing the after guns, was my friend Oberleutnant z.S. von Levetzow; Oberleutnant z.S. Geerdes commanded the fore battery, while the adjutant, Leutnant z.S. von Guérard, was ordered up to the crow's nest with a signalman. His duty was to observe the fall of shot and pass information down to the conning tower. Thus alterations of direction, range and deflection could be passed to the guns. Orders were passed to the individual guns by electric transmitters, though there were emergency speaking tubes.

Our chief engineer, Marine-Oberingenieur Ellerbroeck, had command of the engine room and boilers. Under him, Ingenieur Andresen supervised the caulking party in the midships flat; Ingenieur Haas was in direct control of the boilers; and Ingenieur Stoffers, who was recovering from illness, went under cover in a boiler room.

Stabsarzt Dr Luther was in charge of the dressing station, his action station being in one of the boiler rooms. Dr Schwabe had his station in the sick-bay in the steering flat, which was the reserve dressing station, assisted by Oberzahlmeister Woytschekowsky.

As *Emden* left Direction Island with flags flying, von

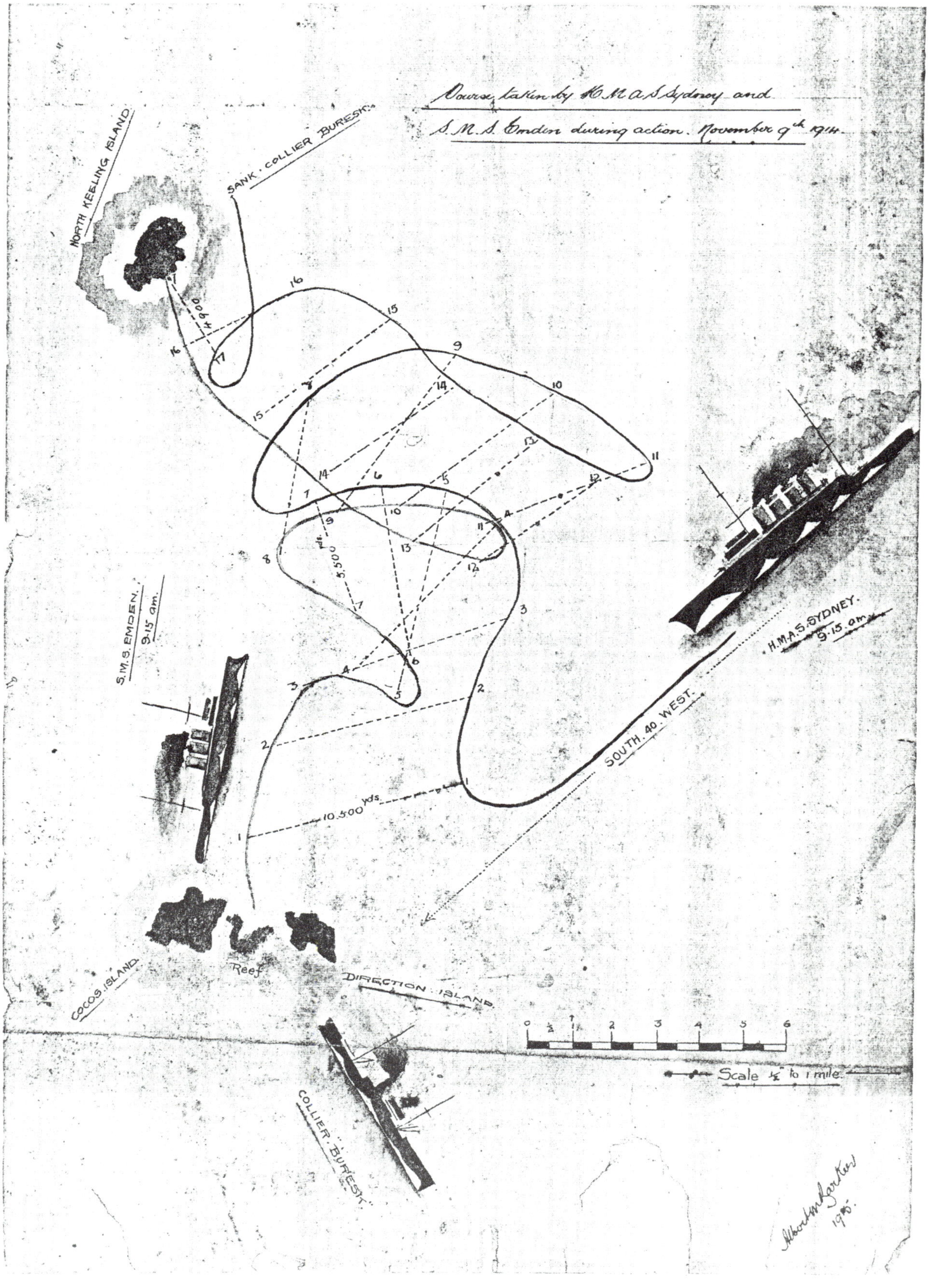

A sketch map of the final battle, drawn by Albert M. Barker RAN, a member of *Sydney's* crew, early in 1915. By courtesy of the Naval Association of Australia, New South Wales Section, Sydney.

Müller had set a north-westerly course. The British cruiser, approaching *Emden* at full speed, was initially thought to be HMS *Newcastle* as she had four funnels.* Ships of this class were slightly superior to us in speed and armament, but under favourable circumstances we could have settled with her without great loss or damage.

At 0935 the British ship turned to starboard, forcing us into a running fight. The direction of the wind still favoured us.

By 0940, when the range had come down from 12,000 to 9,000 metres, Kapitän von Müller ordered 'Open fire!' *Emden*, in spite of her inferiority, had begun the fight. Our faster opponent clearly had steam up in all her boilers; *Emden*, however, had only had a short time to raise steam. It would be a quarter of an hour before we could reach top speed.

Hardly had we begun to fire than the British ship shot back, using her fore and aft guns for ranging. This confirmed the belief that we faced *Newcastle*.†

Our first two salvoes went over, together with all but one shell from the third. We later heard that it had destroyed the British ship's rangefinder and its control gear. Our fourth salvo was short, but then we found the range. To allow our 10.5cm guns to operate more effectually, Kapitän von Müller turned two points to starboard after the first salvoes. At 0953 he turned two more points to starboard.

The British ship shot badly at first; seven or eight salvoes went over, then several fell short. Short salvoes were a great hindrance to our observations, as water continually splashed down on our ship. The columns of water showed us that our opponent's guns were all of the same bore . . . six inches! Clearly, we did not face a ship of the *Newcastle* class,‡ but a more modern vessel. We only discovered her identity after the battle had been lost.

Once we emerged from the shelter of Direction Island, the Pacific swell was very noticeable.

Our eighth salvo caused a fire aboard the enemy cruiser. One shell had ignited ready-use ammunition, but the explosion was not great enough to inflict mortal damage. Our gunlayers shot very well. Had we been armed with 15cm guns, the fight would have been much more in our favour. Soon, however, the British gunlayers got into their stride. The first hit landed on *Emden* soon after 1000. It struck the wireless cabin, which disappeared to leave nothing but dust and ashes. The men on duty died instantly. The second hit exploded near the conning tower, between the foremast and the after side of the forecastle. A splinter hit helmsman Monkediek in the left forearm, wounding him severely. The arm was quickly bound up, however, and the helmsman continued his duties.

* The original memoir erroneously states here that *Newcastle* had three funnels, perhaps temporarily confusing her with the larger Monmouth-class armoured cruisers.

† Light cruisers of this type had only two 6-inch guns, one on the forecastle and the other on the quarterdeck. The 4-inch guns ranged on each beam amidships.

‡ Officially known as the Bristol class.

Almost at the same time, a third shell landed just forward of the conning tower with terrible effect. The guns' crews on the forecastle were disabled, in addition to some of the signalmen. Unfortunately, no help could be brought to the wounded, as the first-aid party was fully occupied elsewhere and the remainder of the ship's company so tied to the posts that it could not offer assistance.

Now that the British gunners were shooting well, shell after shell struck home on our poor ship. Scarcely a minute passed without news of some fresh disablement at or near a gun.

Soon, the electric transmitters to the guns failed. This was a great loss, as the gunnery officer had to relay his orders through the speaking tubes; as these had been perforated in several places, Gaede had increasing difficulty getting messages through to the guns. Our previously excellent battery shooting deteriorated perceptibly. The sporadic fall of shot made shot-observation difficult and reduced the effectiveness of our fire still further.

The enemy ship now had command of the situation. With an advantage in speed and gunpower, she could shoot effectually without running the risk of receiving damaging hits from us. From the beginning, our disadvantage had been weaker armament. The maximum effective range of our 10.5cm guns was 7,000-8,000 metres. If our opponent stood off far enough, we could offer no threat while the British ship's 6-inch guns could destroy us completely.

More casualties were reported, and then both our electric lighting circuits were shot away. The steering telegraph and the steering gear in the conning tower broke down, as their cables had been destroyed elsewhere in the ship. *Emden* had to be directed from the steering flat, while the engine-room telegraph was worked from the midships flat under the supervision of Marine-Ingenieur Andresen. From here he also directed the caulking party. The midships flat would normally have been the action station of the first officer, but Kapitänleutnant von Mücke was ashore on Direction Island with the landing party and engineer Andresen had to substitute for him in a very important post.

Some minutes later, the forward funnel was thrown over to port by a direct hit. This was particularly serious as the smoke from the boilers could no longer be drawn off properly and the updraught necessary to keep the furnaces fully ablaze was reduced. As the heat of the furnaces dropped, so did steam propagation. Thus *Emden*'s speed, already lower than her opponent's, declined further.

The continuous hail of shells, together with losses among the gun- and magazine-crews, was so severe that the guns could hardly be manned. Yet still they shot with astonishing accuracy and rapidity, though this was not to last much longer. Ammunition was now reaching the guns sparingly, forcing fire to slacken until only a few guns were in action. The guns themselves were intact, but most of the munitions hoists had been shot away and great efforts were required to get ammunition up on deck.

The mechanical appliances had all been destroyed, making it necessary to move shells manually. This involved large numbers of men, working virtually without protection, and resulted in terrible losses. Reserves had all been used. Soon there would be no more men to bring ammunition to the guns; or, indeed, even to man them.

At many of our 10.5cm guns there was now no more than a single man, who served on in the face of death. The devotion of these men was plain to all: the heroes stayed at their posts until the bitter end. Several worked imperturbably in spite of severe wounds, including a Bootsmannsmaat whose right arm had been shot away. This warrior continued to serve his gun with his good arm, as if nothing untoward had happened.

At about 1005, the steering gear broke down again. Navigating officer Gropius and a few men rushed aft to reach the hand-steering gear. Still the helm failed to answer, however, and the ship had then to be steered by the screws. As a result of the breakdown, *Emden* had slewed hard-a-starboard. Now the enemy could rake our port side. This was singularly unfortunate, as the British ship landed three decisive hits in quick succession. The first landed near the bridge, carrying away the range-finder and the range-takers. Leutnant z.S. Zimmermann immediately left the conning tower, striving to reach the port forecastle gun, where a shell must have killed him; he was found dead near the gun after the fight.

The second hit killed the remaining men at the guns forward of the conning tower, some of whom were already severely wounded. Several splinters entered the conning tower through the observation slits, wounding Kapitänleutnant Gaede, Oberleutnant z.S. Witthoeft and two seamen. Kapitän von Müller must also have received a couple of splinter wounds, though he did not discover them until later. The two wounded seamen left the conning tower, as the destruction of the instruments left them with nothing to do. Both were killed on the way to the dressing station.

The third hit did the most damage, as it caught the ready-use ammunition by the No.4 port gun. The ammunition exploded, the fearful flames incinerating all the men near it. Thus my friend von Levetzow fell at his post on the quarterdeck. Other flammable material ignited, until the whole after part of the ship was ablaze.

Navigating officer Gropius, who had been wounded, was unable to return forward. He and a few survivors from the after guns were completely cut off by the fire. Finally there had been nothing to do but jump overboard or be cremated. Gropius gave three cheers for the War Lord, and the heroes jumped. Three were rescued after the battle to tell us their tale.

Severe losses continued. One after another, the port guns fell silent. No longer were there men to man them. When Kapitän von Müller realized that the guns had been overcome, he tried to get near enough to the enemy to launch a torpedo – *Emden*'s last hope. This was when we had received 'Ready starboard tube!' in the torpedo flat. The time was 1025. It proved impossible to fire the

HMAS *Sydney* of the Chatham class, conqueror of *Emden*. Note that she is essentially similar to the ships of the Weymouth class (cf., *Yarmouth* above), but that the forecastle extends back virtually abreast of the mainmast – allowing the No.3 guns to be carried a deck higher than previously – and the ram bow has been superseded by a cruiser pattern. By courtesy of the Trustees of the Imperial War Museum, London; negative Q 21817.

1 An utter wreck, *Emden* lies ashore on North Keeling Island. This picture was taken from the deck of HMAS *Sydney* on 10th November 1914. By courtesy of the Trustees of the Imperial War Museum, London; Q 22718.

2 This view inside the wrecked bridge shows the extent of damage. During the battle, however, most of the key personnel – including von Müller and the helmsman – were below in the armoured conning tower or on deck in the lee of the bridge structure. By courtesy of the Australian War Memorial, Canberra; negative EN0240.

torpedo, as the enemy vessel, at times reaching 27 knots, was able to keep out of torpedo range. The distance was usually 7,000 metres; to put in an effectual torpedo strike, we should have to get within a thousand metres. Our speed – originally lower than our opponent's – had been reduced by the destruction of the forefunnel and a lack of steam. The rudder was not answering at all and manoeuvring with the screws took away a great deal of power. Speed continued to fall away.

While we had been striving to get into torpedo range, the enemy had reappeared to starboard. There was nothing more for the British gunners to overcome, for by now our guns were almost silent. Suddenly, our opponent turned to port and fired a torpedo at 1035hrs. The range was something more than three thousand metres. Though the British vessel had more modern equipment than we did, the distance was still excessive; we were not surprised when the shot failed.

What had once been a battle was now only a game for the enemy. The guns of *Emden* no longer threatened, and the British ship steered a zigzag course to frustrate our torpedoes. The cruiser turned to starboard and finally steamed off at speed back to a range where we could no longer threaten her.

Shortly afterwards, gunnery officer Gaede left the conning tower. As control of the broadside had become impossible, he tried to restore our fire by bringing all the survivors of the guns' crews together and directing fire personally from the forecastle. Two guns were brought back into action, but to little effect – the enemy simply kept at a safe distance and maintained a steady fire.

Continual hits caused great loss and more damage. The foremast was shot away to port at about 1045, flinging Leutnant z.S von Guérard and a signalman to their deaths. Another shot hit and wrecked the captain's bridge. By then our guns were silent, from which it was clear that Gaede must be incapacitated.

Before giving up the fight, Kapitän von Müller wanted to make a last attempt to get within torpedo range. This manoeuvre was complicated by the fact that communications between the conning tower and the starboard engine-room had failed, forcing the orders to be called down through the engine-room skylight by a gunnery rating. Despite the hail of shells, the orders were passed regularly and the seaman concerned was not even slightly wounded.

Our last attempt to destroy the enemy was a complete failure, as the British ship steered clear of every attempt to approach her and kept well out of torpedo range. As we were manoeuvring, our two remaining funnels were shot away and our speed – already meagre – was reduced to a minimum. This meant the end for *Emden*; with what could we now fight? The guns had been silenced and lack of speed rendered the torpedoes useless.

Kapitän von Müller decided to run *Emden* aground on the coral reefs of North Keeling Island. This had two great advantages. First, our ship would not fall into enemy hands; secondly, lives would be saved. If the ship were to sink, many men would certainly drown – especially those whose action stations were below the armoured deck, and the severely wounded.

To execute the manoeuvre properly, the starboard engines were stopped to turn the ship. Then we ran straight for the island at about nineteen knots. Our enemy soon recognized our intention, trying to sink us by increasing her rate of fire and then crossing our bows in the hope of cutting us off. This exposed our port side again, and *Emden* received a hail of hits. Amazingly, she remained seaworthy in spite of them. Yet many of our men lost their lives at this point.

The British captain wished to destroy us before we could run aground. He wanted to enjoy the triumph of *Emden* vanishing into the depths, but this was to be denied him. When he realized that we could not be prevented from running for the island, he had to give us room whether he wished to or not. If he came too close, we could launch a torpedo or even attempt to ram.

At 1115 *Emden*, with her engines stopped, ran on to the lee or south side of North Keeling. Once aground, the engines were put to full speed ahead so that the ship wedged firmly on the coral reef. The engines were then stopped, the fires drawn and the sea-cocks opened. Our gallant ship, which had achieved so much, was a wreck.

As this was done, *Buresk* appeared and made vain efforts to draw off the enemy ship. As we lay defenceless on the reef, however, the British vessel continued to fire for another five minutes. Only at 1120 did she cease fire.

The prolonged shooting at our wreck prompted the captain to give the ship's company permission to jump overboard and swim for the island, about a hundred metres distant. This was far from easy owing to the strong surf breaking over the reef.

Shortly after permission to make for the shore had been granted, I arrived on deck and was a witness to the subsequent events. I did not avail myself of the chance of a swim, as the wounded needed as much help as possible. The guns had to be immobilized, while the sights, range-finders, navigating instruments, and all secret codebooks had to be destroyed.

The breechblocks and firing mechanism of the guns were removed and thrown overboard, followed by the sights and the instruments. The secret papers and the war logbook were burned.

Many severely wounded men lay about the ship, so I and a few others tried to get aft from the waist between decks. We could not progress farther than the engine-room hatch; the heat aft was still too great, the metal glowing dully in a way that threatened severe burns if we tried to pass. Everything looked so very bad.

A hit had pierced the side of the upper coal bunker in the gangway, allowing coal to roll out and virtually block the passage. There was nothing to be done but creep over the coal. In the laundry we found two of our Chinese washermen, dead on the deck. They had been surprised by a shell as they worked, but would not have been thinking of such an end as *Emden* had always got well away from trouble. The Chinamen had the greatest confidence in our luck, for when we went to fight they would say 'Makee boom boom! Masky!', which meant 'Keep firing! Never mind!' Now the Chinamen lay dead where they had fallen in the execution of their duty, like so many of our gallant company.

From the laundry we tried to get farther aft, but were beaten back by unbearable heat and extensive flooding. We found a few wounded men, however, and brought them forward.

When we reached the transport hatch into the torpedo flat, I had the cover taken off. The flat was already full of water; had we stayed there after the second hit, we would all have drowned.

I returned to the deck. All the severely wounded men had been brought onto the forecastle, where bandages were being applied as best they could. When supplies ran out, we used bed linen and tablecloths. A few men had tried to reach the shore, but the swim looked easier than it was. The surf fell onto the reef with such colossal force that many men were killed on the jagged coral. This fate was shared by Assistenzarzt Dr Schwabe and my Torpedo-Maschinist Pyttlik in spite of their great physical strength. They were found on the island shore the next day, the machinist dead and the surgeon dying of head injuries.

By this time we had determined that our opponent was Australian, a cruiser of the Melbourne class.* She was making no attempt to send *Emden* lifeboats, but was instead going after *Buresk*. Consequently, we tried to establish communications with the island so that water could be obtained for our wounded. The water tanks above the armoured deck had been shot away and the drinking water compartments lay beneath the torpedo flat, which was full of seawater. We could not get to these compartments as the pumps no longer worked, partly because they had been damaged and partly because the fires had been drawn. The small amounts of drinking water remaining in the pipes were used to the last drop to moisten the fever-parched tongues of the most severely wounded.

* These ships were known as the Chatham Class.

We hoped to be able to find enough coconuts on the island to quench the men's thirst with their milk. Meanwhile, everyone on deck suffered greatly in the heat. The sailcloth and other material used to protect the crew from the sun had been stowed in compartments that were now under water. We could no longer reach them.

We had no boats to reach the island. Several had been taken by the landing party while the gig, which had remained aboard *Emden*, had been burned to cinders. However, a few men had managed to swim to the island and we were hopeful of establishing a link between ship and shore. We tried to float a thin line onto the beach on rafts of empty ammunition boxes and matting. The line was to be caught by the men on the shore, whereupon a hawser could be bent-on and hauled to the beach. The current strove to prevent our floats reaching the shore. Once the attempt did succeed, but the recipients were not quick enough and the line parted on the sharp edges of the coral. All other attempts failed, and we had as little luck with the thin line fired from the life-saving rifle.

Finally, our of two strongest swimmers tried to get a line to the island. They tied it round their waists and did their best to swim through the surf. But soon they had to return to the ship, completely exhausted. Careful observation showed that there was only one place where a swimmer could cross the reef safely, but it lay much too far from the ship.

Luck had deserted us. Our miseries aboard the shattered ship increased as the hours past. The severely

This picture of *Emden* from seaward, looking toward the reef from astern, was taken on 18th January 1915 by a seaman aboard HMS *Pioneer*. While the mainmast provides a handy perch for parakeets, the funnels loll drunkenly amidships and the charthouse is open to the sky. By courtesy of the Australian War memorial, Canberra; negative A02174.

wounded men were treated with the greatest care, morphine being administered in hopeless cases to ease the terrible pain. However, as soon as we had treated one patient and left him for the next, he was immediately assailed by gulls. These were of a family we knew as 'Döskoppe',† but now hovered over the helpless men and tried to peck out their eyes. We bludgeoned as many birds as we could, shooting others with our pistols.

About 1600hrs, the enemy cruiser returned after chasing our companion. We later learned that she had captured *Buresk*, but only after Kapitänleutnant Klöpper, seeing the cruiser approach, had opened the sea-cocks and thrown the valves overboard. *Buresk* had sunk.

I was standing on the shattered bridge of our poor *Emden* to observe the returning cruiser's moves. She stopped about four thousand yards dead astern of us with two of *Buresk*'s boats in tow. We anticipated that she would send boats over immediately. Instead, she hoisted an international signal. We could not read it, as the signal books had been burned. Kapitän von Müller ordered a signalman to morse a reply, in English, 'No signal book!'

What the British understood by the message I do not know, but suddenly, to our great astonishment, they opened fire again. I saw smoke puff out fore and aft, shouted a warning to the captain and rushed down from the bridge. I had no wish to be caught by a shell splinter.

I had scarcely got down when the first shell arrived. A stoker standing near me sunk down without a sound, killed instantly by a splinter that had struck him in the back of the head. Kapitän von Müller immediately announced 'those who can swim may jump overboard if they wish!'

Many men availed themselves of this opportunity; I leapt over the side to port, seized a floating plank and tried to get through the surf to land. Thank heaven there were no sharks about. Usually they abound in these waters, but they must have been frightened away by the shells that had exploded in the water during the fight.

As enemy shells exploded around us, the wrecked *Emden* received several hits. Fire broke out anew.

Several members of the ship's company who could not swim well had also jumped overboard. The better swimmers tried to supply these men with planks and baulks. Now several clung to my plank, reducing its buoyancy considerably. I left it and swam back to *Emden* after my attempt to swim through the surf had failed.

I had been in the water for a good half-hour, during which the enemy had ceased fire. *Emden*'s ensign had been hauled down and a white flag run up. English newspapers later stated that Kapitän von Müller had surrendered, but one can only do so if a ship's weapons work! As our ship was a total wreck and all our guns had been destroyed, there could be no talk of surrender. The flag was hauled down because a wreck no longer has the right to fly it, and also because additional bloodshed could not be justified. We had forgotten the ensign on running aground on the reef, as other work was more pressing. It did not occur to any of us that a flag at the maintop of a wreck would provide a reason to resume the bombardment.

These superfluous shells claimed several more victims. It was a wonder that no shell struck the forecastle, where the wounded were being succoured by most of the uninjured officers and men.

We later learned the story from our comrades on *Buresk*, which to our opponents' fury had scuttled as they approached her. Our colleagues, between the decks of the cruiser, said that their hearts had stopped when they realized that fire had been re-opened on the wreck that had once been *Emden*.

Once the cease-fire had sounded, the Australian cruiser, as we now knew her to be, sent one of *Buresk*'s boats over with Leutnant z.S. Fikentscher and some of our seamen. The cruiser steamed off towards Direction Island, no doubt intending to capture Kapitänleutnant von Mücke and the landing party.

It was Fikentscher who told us the name of our conqueror: HMAS *Sydney*. As we had guessed, she had gone to Direction Island and would be back to fetch us from *Emden* the next day.

We expected that the attempt to land a party on Direction Island would encounter stiff resistance from our colleagues. We knew only too well the spirit of von Mücke. Now we were not so certain that the Australian cruiser would return the next day to get us! So, as we had one of *Buresk*'s boats to help us, we redoubled our efforts to establish communication with North Keeling Island.

Darkness fell before an attempt could be made, and work had to be abandoned. Everyone needed a chance to recuperate.

Each man made himself as comfortable as he could aboard the wreck that night. The clear tropical sky was wonderful, with the Southern Cross – that so characterized the southern hemisphere – over us as we slept. But night did not pass easily. Fires kept breaking out aboard and had to be extinguished at once lest they spread. The work was undertaken under the supervision of Leutnant Fikentscher. Most of the rest of us were quite exhausted. We had had nothing to eat the whole day, and the frightful heat had been particularly debilitating.

We were on our feet again at dawn. Somewhat refreshed by our night's rest, but not in the best humour, the ship's company wondered what would happen next. The work of establishing communications with the island left little time for grumbling, however.

As we were genuinely in distress, the international signal 'Am in distress! Need help!' was hoisted. This was a prudent measure. If *Sydney* did not fetch us, we hoped that a passing merchantman would take pity on us.

During the morning I ventured aft onto the shattered quarterdeck. I did not wish to miss an opportunity of looking for my friend von Levetzow. I discovered his remains near the mainmast. Though there were only

† These 'boxheads' are believed to have been brown boobies, *Sula leucogaster*, which had large and angular bills.

bones – the rest had been burned to ash – I was certain that it was really von Levetzow from the shape of the head and an Oberleutnant's star. He must have been killed by the explosion of the ammunition in the after battery. His remains were duly committed to the deep in nautical custom.

I had missed my friend at the end of the fight, but then the frightful fire aft had made it impossible to look for him immediately. His loss saddened me greatly. He had not only been my comrade-in-arms, but also a true friend from whom I could always seek sound advice and selfless assistance.

Several of the most severely wounded men had died during the night, among them one unfortunate seaman whose whole skin had been burned. His pain had been terrible; now, mercifully, it was all over.

The attempts to link ship and shore failed, but the work was not abandoned. We still had *Buresk*'s boat, but this precious reserve was to be used as a last resort. We would wait to see whether *Sydney* returned; if not, we would chance the boat.

The steam pinnace and the ship's gig prepare to leave Direction Island for the barquentine *Ayesha* (seen in the middle background), watched by curious Islanders. One of *Emden*'s Maxims is visible on the stem-post of the gig, while the men carry a selection of Gewehre 98 and Pistolen 1904. Kapitänleutnant von Mücke is standing on the bow of the pinnace, reading; Leutnant z.S. Gyssling sits in the stern of the gig while Leutnant z.S. Schmidt, later killed in the Arabian Peninsula, is in the pinnace. By courtesy of the Trustees of the Imperial War Museum, negative Q 22706.

Sydney reappeared at 1300 on 10th November. We could tell she intended to take us off as her boats had been swung out. We were more assured of a future now, though the thought of captivity was depressing.

Two cutters came across under the command of a Royal Navy officer, who told Kapitän von Müller that the captain of HMAS *Sydney* was willing to take our ship's company aboard – plus the men on the island – if von Müller would guarantee our proper behavour aboard the Australian vessel. This our captain solemnly promised.

Soon the transhipment of *Emden*'s company began, starting with the most severely wounded. Owing to the heavy seas running towards the land, there was a constant danger that the lifeboats would be crushed against *Emden*. Some of the seas were washing over the stern and occasionally breaking over the side onto the deck. This greatly hindered the transfer of the wounded.

The boats made fast to the port side aft – or at least a stout line was passed, making fast properly being impossible. The crews of the enemy's cutters showed great skill in keeping the boats in such a position that they were not dashed against the ship's side. Thus the wounded could be manhandled into the boats with giving the poor fellows too much extra pain. The worst casualties were lashed into carrying hammocks and lowered with the greatest care.

The lightly injured men were more easily transferred, to be followed by the uninjured. Kapitän von Müller was

the last to leave, after unsuccessfully trying, with the assistance of Fikentscher, to start a fire that would ignite the magazine and blow the wreck to pieces.

Sydney's captain sent over his gig for Kapitän von Müller as a mark of respect. Von Müller had to accept this, though he had previously requested no preferential treatment.

When a final roll had been called, we found that of the men who had been aboard at the beginning of the fight – 317, including four civilians – six officers, a Marine-Oberzahlmeister, four warrant officers, 24 petty officers, 91 men, a civilian cook, the barber and three Chinese washermen (a total of 131 men) had died aboard *Emden* or in the surf around North Keeling Island. Marine-Ingenieur Stoffers, a petty officer and a sailor later succumbed to their wounds aboard *Sydney*, making the final toll 134.

A warrant officer had been seriously wounded, together with three petty officers and seventeen men. So, as two officers, two warrant officers, nine petty officers and 31 men had been slightly injured, only 117 of us had emerged unscathed: six officers, five warrant officers, 39 petty officers and 67 men.

The unforgettable exploits of *Emden* were at an end. I hoped that they would inspire our descendants, and that the example of *Emden* would once again awake in our people the spirit of loyal co-operation in times of joy or sorrow.

Looking forward from the deck to port of the mainmast, this view of utter devastation shows the damage wreaked by *Sydney*'s shells. It seems a wonder that anyone could survive such a holocaust, particularly when caught in the open serving the guns. By courtesy of the Australian War Memorial, Canberra; negative EN0399. **1**

This picture of the wardroom of *Dresden* II, taken in 1918, shows how the severity of a warship's interior was softened in peacetime. Padded upholstery, armchairs and even a piano allowed officers the comforts of home. It is easy to understand why Prinz Franz Joseph was so aggrieved when the fittings were thrown overboard! Bundesarchiv, Bild 134-C518. **2**

2

A TRIP TO MALTA

Tuesday 10th November – Sunday 6th December 1914

Before I relate how we became prisoners, I must give an idea of how the newspapers of the time saw our exploits, as they show what an impression *Emden* and her immortal Kapitän von Müller made even in 1914.

The following reports come from the *Deutsche Geschichtskalendar* and a collection entitled *Der Völkerkrieg*.

'1st November 1914. The German light cruiser *Emden* has, according to *The Times*, to date sunk fifteen British ships, and captured and set free another five. The British victims of *Emden* total 93,000 tons.'

'On the same date His Majesty the Kaiser sent to the mayor of the town of Emden the following telegram: "I congratulate the town of Emden on [the success of] its foster-child in the Indian Ocean, whose fine cruiser work fills all German hearts with pride and joy. – WILHELM I.R."

'On 4th November it was reported: "The Iron Cross, first and second class, is awarded to the captain of *Emden*, and the Iron Cross, second class, to all officers and warrant officers, and to fifty petty officers and men of the ship's company."

'9th November. The light cruiser *Emden* was attacked near the Cocos Islands in the Indian Ocean by the Australian cruiser *Sydney*, while a landing party was ashore destroying the British cable and wireless stations. Fires were started by the shells, and after a hard fight she was run aground by her own ship's company, where she burned out. The party landed for the destruction of the cable station, 3 officers and 46 men [sic], with four machine-guns, escaped in the little schooner *Ayesha*.'

'The captain of *Emden*, Fregattenkapitän v. Müller, sent the following report to the German admiralty: "The cruiser *Sydney* approached the Cocos Islands at full speed exactly as the landing party from *Emden* succeeded in destroying the cable. The fight between the two cruisers began at once. Our shooting was initially good, but after a short period the fire from the heavier British guns gained the upper hand and caused heavy losses among our guns' crews. The ammunition came to an end and the guns had to cease fire. In spite of the fact that the steering gear was damaged by enemy fire, an attempt was made to get within torpedo range of the cruiser *Sydney*. This attempt failed, as the [fore-]funnel was destroyed and the speed of *Emden* greatly reduced in consequence. The ship was therefore run at full speed onto the reef on the ...[south]... (lee) side of the Cocos Islands. Meanwhile, the landing party had succeeded in escaping in a schooner belonging to the island. The British cruiser gave chase, but returned in the afternoon and fired on the wreck of *Emden*. To avoid unnecessary bloodshed, I therefore surrendered with the rest of the ship's company. *Emden*'s losses were: 6 officers, 1 Marine-Oberzahlmeister, 4 warrant officers, 26 petty officers and 93 men killed, 1 petty officer and 7 men severely wounded." [Note: this does not include the officer and men who died of their wounds aboard *Sydney*, nor the three Chinese washermen.]

'Telegram from His Majesty Kaiser Wilhelm to the municipal representatives of the town of Emden: "Hearty thanks for your message of sympathy on the distressing and heroic end of my cruiser, the *Emden*. The gallant ship gained further laurels for the German ensign in her last fight. A new and stronger *Emden* shall be built, on whose bows the Iron Cross will be affixed in memory of the fame of the old *Emden*. – WILHELM I.R."

The announcement that *Emden*'s famous run had ended caused great grief throughout Germany, mingled with pride in the performance of the ship and her gallant company.

The *Norddeutsche Allgemeine Zeitung* wrote that 'For three full months, under the most difficult conditions, the *Emden*, with tenacious courage and exemplary seamanship, has harried the enemy and caused them [sic] heavy losses. Finally she had to succumb to the hunt organized for her by British, Russian, French and Japanese warships. The name *Emden* will, however, live in the memory of the German people for posterity. All honour to her officers and valiant men who continued to serve the Kaiser and the Empire faithfully to death!'

The Austrian Press also recognized our heroism, adventurous sprit and valour. For example, the Vienna *Fremdenblatt* noted: 'The *Emden* has shown the German people a magnificent example of German valour and initiative, and has covered the youthful German fleet with imperishable glory. Austria-Hungary sends her greetings to the heroic men who did their utmost, and is proud to call an ally the people that has produced such heroes. We are filled with admiration for the audacity of... Kapitän von Müller and congratulate him on way in which he combined initiative with humanity'.

Norwegian newspapers took a similar view. The Christiania* *Åftenposten* expressed its judgement thus: 'The performance of the *Emden* is without parallel in the history of the war. No-one would have believed that a single cruiser could do so much damage in a modern war,

* Now known as Oslo.

'S.M. Kleiner Geschützter Kreuzer "Emden". Tonnen: 3650. Länge: 118 m. Breite: 13,5 m. Besatzung: 361' – a good-quality postcard postcard published by NPG ('51'), though somewhat lacking detail aft.

while faced with overwhelming enemies, as *Emden* has done. Few names have, during the present conflict, been as often on the lips of the people as those of *Emden* and her gallant captain. How the *Emden* has succeeded in procuring the necessary supplies over so long a time is a question at which many guesses have been made, and which will now, perhaps, be solved. Whatever the answer, it speaks of great cleverness, foresight and administrative talent in her captain'.

In Britain, the news of our end was received with the greatest joy; at Lloyd's, premiums were immediately halved. Even the British Press could not avoid recognizing the outstanding performance of *Emden*'s ship's company. Thus the London *Daily Chronicle* could write: "The Captain proved himself to be not only a brave and capable officer, but to possess chivalry in his treatment of the crews and passengers of the captured ships. We can all take off our hats to the Captain".

The *Daily News* echoed: "The English nation has now only one regret, and that is that a great part of the *Emden*'s ship's company lost their [sic] lives. The Captain of the *Emden* is a gallant man, full or resource and chivalry. He treated his prisoners very well, and played his part to admiration. The *Emden*, like the *Alabama*,† will always live in naval history".

The Times added: "If all Germans had fought as well as the Captain of the *Emden*, the German people would not to-day be reviled by the world". Here one sees the spiritual ancestor of this paper: the chase before all.

† A famous raider and blockade-runner, built in Britain for the Confederacy during the American Civil War. She was sunk by the Federal sloop *Kearsarge* in June 1864, but not before she had taken nearly seventy prizes.

Italy's newspapers generally expressed their sympathy with our men, and pity for the fate of our ship. Even *Corriere della Sera* – which, heaven knows, was not pro-German – wrote on 12th November: "The only ship which despair made strong, and which embraced her inevitable fate, has won laurels for the German Navy which neither time nor fate can wither. And if the day ever comes when war shall be banished for ever, even then shall not the *Emden*'s fame diminish – even in the future,... the man who lays down his life for his duty will be the highest pattern of human virtue. This ship's company could, in Chinese waters subject to the German flag, have avoided fighting ships of equal strength... without damaging their honour. That was, however, not the wish of their Captain, Karl von Müller, a name that will live. He went out with his faithful men upon a hunt – the idea was his alone – by which he could do the greatest possible damage to the enemy. He did not seek to avoid his fate, but instead sought to postpone it with great power and audacity. Thus the *Emden* has become the wonderful adventurer of the Indian Ocean. Forty warships were searching for her, and one eventually succeeded in sinking her. But the ship herself crowned her fame when, mortally wounded, she sank beneath the sea [!]. The fame of the *Emden* lives in the depth of the sea, and in the thoughts of mankind".

On 2nd January 1915, the Wolff Telegraph Bureau announced that Captain Glossop of HMAS *Sydney* had made a report on the victory over us to the British Admiralty. The report apparently stated that "when on patrol duty we received a wireless message from the Cocos Islands, whereupon we at once laid a course for the islands, steaming at full speed. We soon reached a speed of twenty knots, sighted land at 9.15, and almost immediately afterwards saw the smoke of the *Emden*, which was approaching at great speed. She opened fire at 9.50. I kept at the greatest possible distance in order to take advantage of the longer range of my guns. At the beginning of the fight the fire of the *Emden* was very rapid and exact, but soon fell off. All the losses in *Sydney* occurred at the beginning of the fight. The foremost funnel of the *Emden* was first shot away, and then the foremast. A large fire broke out on board, and after the second, and finally third funnels had fallen, the ship made for the beach. We fired another two salvoes at the *Emden* and then gave chase to a merchant-ship which had approached during the fight. She was the captured British collier *Buresk*, manned by Germans and a few Chinese. The Germans bored a hole in the ship, which soon afterwards sank. The *Sydney* then returned to the *Emden* and rescued the men [three in all] who were in the water. The cruiser's flag was still flying at the masthead. We asked: 'Will you surrender?' and received no answer, so that against our will we were forced to open fire again at 4.30. Five minutes later, however, we ceased fire, and commenced to rescue the men in the water.

"The following day an officer had a conversation with the Captain of the *Emden*. It was decided to bring over to us the wounded and prisoners, which was difficult on account of heavy surf. The state of the *Emden* was indescribable. Eleven officers and 200 men were taken prisoners. Among the prisoners were 54 wounded.

"The officer of the *Sydney* who talked with Kapitän von Müller on the day after the fight made the following report: "At eleven in the morning we were at the place where the *Emden* was lying. I was sent over with one of our boats. It was not at all easy to get on board, but with help from the Germans, who were standing in a group on the after deck, I finally got on board and went up to Kapitän von Müller and greeted him. I greeted him from the Captain and said that if he would give his word to regard himself as a prisoner of war we would take him and his whole ship's company on board the *Sydney* and convey them straight to Colombo. He considered this, and finally fell in with it. Then came, however, the terrible task of taking the wounded across in our boats. There were, in all, 150 men, but luckily we had very practical gear with us, and finally succeeded in getting three of the most severely wounded men into each of our boats. The Germans were all suffering from terrible thirst, so we hoisted the water breakers from our boats

'Zu Ehren der Emden und ihrer Mannschaft': a green bordered commemorative photo-card by NPG ('5008') which combines a standard starboard-bow view of the ship with a retouched version of Greve's head-and-shoulders portrait of von Müller. The latter is set into a green-tinted wreath of oakleaves. The presence of the Pour le Mérite – dangling beneath the wreath – shows that this card dates from 1918 or later. By courtesy of The Lyon Press archives.

into the *Emden*. They rushed for them at once, but gave the wounded a drink first. As soon as I had an opportunity I went up to the German Captain and said: 'The *Emden* fought splendidly'. He started at the words and said shortly: 'No!' Immediately afterwards. however, he came up to me and said: 'It is very friendly of you to say that, but almost at the beginning you had the luck to shoot away my order transmitters'. Later I went round the ship, but have no great desire to describe what I saw. With the exception of the forward gunwhale, which was almost undisturbed, the whole ship was like a slaughter-house. The German doctor begged that the *Sydney* might be signalled to send over some morphia. I did not go below again. Among the officers, the Torpedo Officer W– [Witthoeft], was a very distinguished man. Lieutenant S– [Schall] was also very impressive, and he was half an Englishman. It made a great impression when I told them that our captain would take care that there was no cheering when we reached Colombo, and no celebrations. Naturally we did not wish for that when we had on board dead and dying enemies. Kapitän von Müller is a splendid man."

"More exact news was received of the gallant landing party which the *Emden* left at the Cocos Islands. According to this news, the *Emden* appeared at six in the morning in the entrance to the lagoon, and at once lowered a barge and two boats, which soon afterwards landed three officers and forty men [there were actually 47]. Besides their rifles, these men had four machine-guns with them. The little troop hurried to the telegraph station, where they removed the telegraphists, destroyed the instruments, and posted sentries in the building. All knives and guns were of course taken from the station staff. The telegraphists worked up to the moment the German seamen broke in. They succeeded in sending another cry for help before the wireless apparatus was destroyed. While the cable station was also put out of action a party of Germans got hold of the cable, to cut it, and at the same time the station magazine was blown up. The attempt to cut the cable was not successful. At nine o'clock the siren sounded from the *Emden* to recall the landing party who at once went back to the boats. They did not leave, however, as the *Emden* was already underway, and looking eastwards they could see a strange warship approaching. The *Emden* opened fire on her at 3,800 yards, at the same time manoeuvring to the northward. The more closely the two cruisers became engaged, the farther they went from the island, and they finally vanished from the gaze of the landing party, who could only see that the stern of the *Emden* was already in flames. The Germans thereupon landed again, spread out along the coast of the lagoon, and put themselves in a position for defence against a possible landing by the English. The cruisers lost themselves in the distance. The Germans thereupon possessed themselves of the schooner *Ayesha*, belonging to a Mr. Ross, provisioned her, and sailed away. This report was given by an inhabitant of Direction island."

I disagreed strongly with many details of the report, in regard to timing and the number of prisoners. But I feel

Taken shortly after the order had been given to cease fire, with *Emden* firmly aground on North Keeling Island, this photograph shows *Sydney* going after *Buresk* at full speed. Taken from the forecastle looking aft, it shows how little the Australian ship had suffered by comparison with *Emden*. Excepting splinter damage to the starboard wing of the bridge, nothing untoward is visible. By courtesy of the Australian War memorial, Canberra; negative EN0470.

that our opponent's view of the battle should also be shown.

We reached *Sydney* after a short journey in the boats. We were received at the boom by Fikentscher and Schall, and escorted to a position between decks. Our severely wounded men were immediately taken in hand by the doctors for immediate surgery. I can only say that a great deal was achieved in this respect, and that the first-aid team aboard *Sydney* took every conceivable trouble to help the wounded and ease their pain.

We washed in the officers' washroom, put on fresh underclothes and tropical uniforms placed at our disposal by the British, and then enjoyed a hearty supper. How good it tasted can be imagined; it had been 35 hours since we had eaten. Still better was the well-chilled beer.

The feeling that we were prisoners was repugnant, but the British officers took every trouble to help us forget our position. They brought us books, cigars and cigarettes. Our sleeping quarters were in the large flat of the wardroom, where we made ourselves as comfortable as possible on the settees and in the hammocks. Kapitän von Müller was given the run of the British captain's cabin. Our men slept on the forecastle, with the wounded in the waist supported by hammocks laid on deck. This was the best place in the warm tropical night, as there was always fresh air. The main and side awnings were erected during the day to provide some shelter.

Aboard *Sydney* we learned some interesting details of the approach of the cruiser to the island. We had had no idea how an Australian vessel came to be so near the Cocos. We now discovered that, on the morning of 9th November, the Australian ships *Melbourne* and *Sydney* – plus the Japanese armoured cruiser *Ibuki* – were only fifty nautical miles north-east of the islands. These three were on their way from Australia to Colombo, escorting a convoy of troopships, and were then to proceed westward to Egypt. For *Sydney*, which was a fast ship, it had been a trifle to reach Direction Island in two hours once the cry for help had been sent by the wireless station. Our assumption that the ship had been 250 nautical miles from the islands had been mistaken. We always transmitted on full power but *Sydney*, by using a reduced-strength signal, had deceived our operators about the true distance.

The captain of *Melbourne* had command of the convoy, and on receipt of the message ordered *Sydney* to seek us out and force a fight. The two captains had prudently agreed that should the constant wireless transmission from *Sydney* cease, her sister would rush to assist. We realized that had we sunk *Sydney*, unlucky *Emden* would have been engaged by another ship of similar power.

We heard that *Ibuki* had wished to engage us and pluck a few cheap laurels. She had apparently even set her mast-head flags before being ordered back to the convoy.

Sydney's meagre casualties relected her margin of superiority – four dead and seventeen wounded – even though we had hit her about sixteen times.

One shell of our third salvo had struck home, but failed to explode. However, it carried away the enemy's forward range-finding apparatus and wounded the attending personnel, including an officer. This explained why *Sydney*'s fire had begun so poorly. One shell of the next salvo exploded near No.2 starboard gun, putting the entire crew out of action. A second hit the upper shield of No.1 starboard gun, but had not done much damage. Cordite had been ignited in the waist by another of our hits; one exploded in the boys' mess. Three hits had been obtained on the side armour, but we could see how laughably ineffectual our shells had been at long range. I examined one of the strikes closely. It looked as though someone had taken nothing more than a giant sledgehammer to the side plating.

Hits had also been scored on the forecastle, in one of the starboard boats, and in the first officer's cabin. One shell cut the steampipes of the ice-making machine, which stood on the battery deck, while another pierced the ventilation shafts on the boat deck. A hit on the forward face of the foremast had achieved nothing more than a slight splintering.

Potentially the most dangerous of our shells had entered an ammunition hoist, throwing burning cordite towards a magazine. With great presence of mind, however, one of the seamen had thrown the stuff aside and extinguished it. Though he burned his arms severely, his decisive action saved his ship. Had the ammunition in the magazine exploded, that hour would have been *Sydney*'s last.

Our leisurely examination of the Australian cruiser gave us some idea of her strength. All her fittings were well armoured or of strong construction. She had modern long barrelled six-inch guns, beside which our 10.5cm guns looked like toys.

We also learned the fate of our landing party. After firing on *Emden* for a second time, *Sydney* had gone straight to Direction Island. Captain Glossop intended to summon the men of our shore party to surrender, and, if they refused, overcome them by force. A landing party was told-off under a British officer, taking with them one of our seamen from *Buresk* to act as interpreter after Leutnant z.S. Schall had refused his co-operation. Confident in the hope of a second victory, the party had been towed ashore. Astonished by the lack of resistance, the British landed unhindered and were greeted joyously by the inhabitants of Direction Island. The first question concerned our landing party. The answer was equally prompt: 'The Germans have left in our schooner, the *Ayesha*!'.

The rage of the British officer may be imagined. Waiting now would achieve nothing. Our men had finally got away.

Taking the station doctor with them, the British returned to *Sydney*. The news of the escape of *Emden*'s landing party was immediately reported to Captain Glossop. He cruised for a time in the vicinty of Direction Island, but could find no trace of the fugitives. On 10th

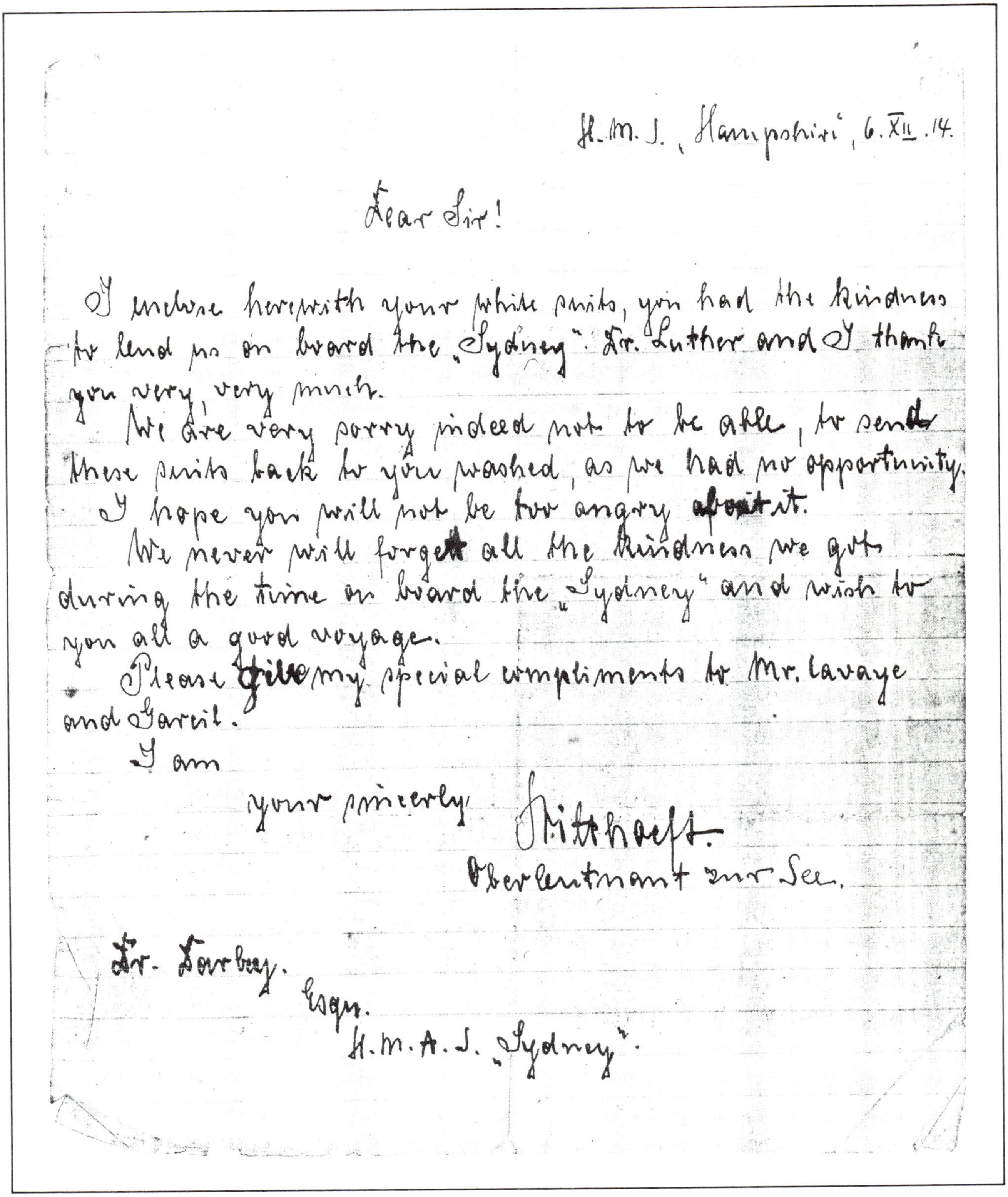

H.M.S. „Hampshire", 6.XII.14.

Dear Sir!

I enclose herewith your white suits, you had the kindness to lend us on board the „Sydney". Dr. Luther and I thank you very, very much.

We are very sorry indeed not to be able, to send these suits back to you washed, as we had no opportunity.

I hope you will not be too angry about it.

We never will forget all the kindness we got during the time on board the „Sydney" and wish to you all a good voyage.

Please give my special compliments to Mr. Cavaye and Garcil.

I am

your sincerely

Witthoeft.

Oberleutnant zur See.

Dr. Darby.

Esqr.

H.M.A.S. „Sydney".

November, therefore, *Sydney* returned to the wreck of *Emden* and took us off for Colombo.

We were delighted than von Mücke and his men had escaped so nicely. Even the British officers agreed that our Kapitänleutnant had handled the situation well.

Leutnant z.S. Schall was sent ashore in the evening of 10th November to collect the men who had reached North Keeling Island. Early next morning they were taken off in *Sydney*'s boats.

Written to Surgeon Darby of HMAS *Sydney* by Oberleutnant z.S. Robert Witthoeft, first torpedo officer aboard *Emden*, this letter reads: "I enclose herewith your white suits, you had the kindness to lend us on board the 'Sydney'. Dr. Luther and I thank you very, very much. We are very sorry indeed not to be able, to send these suits back to you washed, as we had no opportunity. I hope you will not be angry about it. We will never forget all the kindnesses we got during the time on board the 'Sydney' and wish to you all a good voyage. Please give my special compliments to Mr Cavaye and Garcil [Lieutenant C.R. Garcia RAN]. I am yours sincerely, [signed] Witthoeft, Oberleutnant zur See."

Naval Association of Australia, New South Wales Section, Sydney.

Although we could not forget the events of the two preceding days, the fatigue caused by severe strain forced us to sleep well throughout the night of 10/11th November. Our humour had improved somewhat by morning. Schall soon returned with the men from North Keeling Island, who looked almost mad. They were desperately hungry and had an unquenchable thirst, even though the British had had the foresight to take plenty of drinking water with them. Once aboard, our 'Islanders' were fed and received attention to their wounds.

From Schall we learned that Assistenzarzt Dr Schwabe, whom we knew had swum to the island, died during the night from his wounds. He was buried on the island with others who had been washed ashore. Our men told us that food had been very scarce on the island. There had been coconuts and a few gulls' eggs, but these had been generously given to the wounded.

When the last man was aboard, *Sydney* returned to Direction Island with the local doctor, who had done good work among our wounded, and then steamed off for Colombo.

Glad as we were of the rest after our strenuous, anxious days, we were still desperately worried about our seriously wounded colleagues. Two of the men died on 12th November: a technical petty officer and a seaman who had lost half his head to a splinter. Operations to save them had been impossible. Marine-Ingenieur Stoffers, whose recovery from a lengthy illness seemed certain before the fight, had received shell splinters in the head and chest. All attempts to save him now failed. He could take no food, and his breathing steadily deteriorated. He died fully conscious in the early morning of 13th November, served faithfully to the last by Stoker Dehorn.

The three men were committed to the sea on 14th November in an impressive ceremony corresponding entirely with our own customs. A day earlier, a British seaman who had also died of his wounds had been buried in exactly the same way.

Sydney was too small to deal with large numbers of wounded men, and the sick-bay staff was desperately overworked. The captain, therefore, appointed the armed merchant cruiser *Empress of Russia* as a hospital ship. Being a large passenger liner in peacetime, she had plenty of room.

Empress of Russia arrived on 14th November, taking off not only all the seriously wounded men but also many of the lightly injured, and then fell in line astern. She proved a boon to the wounded, owing to better accommodation and better medical treatment. The men made great progress; soon the danger of death had receded, and the succeeding days passed quietly.

We arrived in Colombo at about 1000hrs on 15th November. The harbour had an aura of strength owing to the number of warships gathered there – including the cruiser *Askold* and some Japanese vessels, together with many Europe-bound troopships.

As midday approached, those of us who had remained aboard *Sydney* were taken aboard the hospital ship. We had scarcely assembled on deck when the first officer of *Empress of Russia* came up and read an order from the War Office authorizing the return of swords to our officers and warrant officers. This was meaningless, as we

Prinz Franz Joseph had anticipated a comfortable trip into captivity aboard the Canadian Pacific Steam Ship Company's liner *Empress of Russia* (sister of *Empress of Asia* shown here), which was summoned to act as hospital ship for the *Emden* wounded. It was not to be, however, and the smaller *Orvieto* had to suffice. By courtesy of Laurence Dunn.

had no swords; but the order was doubtless intended as an honour for *Emden* and pleased us greatly.

We learned that we were to proceed to England aboard *Empress of Russia*. The news heartened us, as she was modern and well adapted for such a long journey. Most of us had a cabin to ourselves. I shared with Schall, who had also joined the navy in 1911; this was all the more pleasing, as Schall and I had shared during the whole time we had been aboard *Emden*.

The men were also well accommodated, the only disadvantage being that they were guarded by French marines. We officers, probably deliberately, were guarded by British sentries. The Frenchmen behaved very strictly to our men, which may explain why the British seamen took every opportunity to bring our lads cigarettes, chocolate and food. It was particularly noticeable that the French showed antipathy toward us, while the British, though we were enemies, had a certain empathy.

The wounded were landed in lighters at about midday and taken to two hospitals. This transportation was, however, not particularly efficient. The lighters had absolutely no protection against the sun; consequently, the wounded had to endure the terrible heat. We could change nothing; indeed, casualties from *Sydney* had to undergo the same treatment. But it still seemed poor organization.

Our stay in *Empress of Russia* unexpectedly ended during the afternoon, and we were transferred to lesser Australian and New Zealand transports. The *Empress* was not going to Britain after all, but was to remain in Colombo.

Kapitän von Müller, Leutnant z.S. Fikentscher, Stabsarzt Dr Luther and I were taken to the steamship *Orvieto* of the Orient Line, together with two warrant officers and thirty of our men. Each of the remaining transports took a couple of officers, some warrant officers and a corresponding number of men.

Oberleutnant z.S. Geerdes, on account of his wounds, was the only one of *Emden*'s officers to remain in Colombo. This pleased us, as it reassured us that our wounded men would be adequately supervised by an officer of the Kaiserliche Marine during their convalescence. Geerdes was lucky, returning home much sooner than we who were to be interned in Malta.

Our accommodation aboard *Orvieto* was very good. Each officer had an adjoining cabin on the upper deck, separated from the remainder of the ship by two screens. On either side stood sentries with sidearms. Twice daily we were allowed to walk on part of the large promenade deck on the starboard side, accompanied by a British officer. We ate in what had once been the nursery, again under supervision of a Briton. These officers were very pleasant, only one cutting a laughable figure. He said not a word at table, and this offspring of Mars sat with his hand permanently on his revolver. He wished to appear martial – but only elicited smiles of pity.

On 17th November, the convoy left Colombo for Aden. The Royal Navy cruiser *Hampshire* had the maritime command, but the central command, with the appropriate support, was aboard *Orvieto*. This comprised an Australian general, his staff and a Royal Navy captain in command of the transports. The Briton was accompanied by a staff of Royal Marine officers.

The voyage to Aden was generally pleasant, though we were often reminded that we were prisoners of war. When we wished to answer nature's call, for example, it was not easy to do so immediately. We had to call a sentry, who first planted his revolver under our noses. When we had communicated our necessity, the strong locks were released and we were let through. We could not go alone, however, but were dutifully accompanied by the sentry. Our companion waited outside the door as long as we were inside. Otherwise, one suspected, the danger to the ship would have been too great; or, perhaps, we 'ingenious Germans' may have escaped on the high seas!

The procedure was more degrading for the men, for the sentry stationed himself opposite the OPEN door and supervised the entire event.

No communication between officers and men was permitted. As far as I can remember, Kapitän von Müller was only allowed to see his men once during the entire voyage. The reasons are still obscure, but we may assume that the military authorities had a very strong respect for us. This impression was confirmed many times during my time as a prisoner of war.

We had the most splendid weather during the voyage. In the absence of work, the days were idled away. Sometimes I played cards or chess with Fikentscher. The rest of the time I ferreted in English or German books the British had loaned us. For part of the voyage, at the captain's request, I occupied my time writing my report of the final battle. Kapitän von Müller had already started to assemble all the news about *Emden*. This was necessary, as our war logbook had been burned immediately after the fight to prevent it falling into the enemy's hands. Of course, one could while away many an otherwise wearying hour with such 'official literature' and it was a pleasure to return, if only in thought, to *Emden*.

But the return from these memories to the reality of captivity in a British troop-transport was unfailingly bitter.

There was a welcome concert by an Australian regimental band each evening at the salute of the colours. These bandsmen played very well, but mostly only the latest English compositions in which there was more noise than harmony.

We arrived in Aden on 28th November. However, the transport only remained there long enough to take on coal and fresh water.

Then came the passage through the Red Sea, which was fine and warm owing to the hot south wind that had blown almost the whole passage long. Next we reached Suez and the entrance to the canal of the same name. Here variety was not lacking, as the Arabian and African coasts were in view continually.

As we neared the head of the Red Sea, we heard that we were to transfer to HMS *Hampshire* either at Suez or Port Said, as *Orvieto* and the remainder of our convoy were to remain in Egypt.

At this news the British cursed frightfully, as they would have been glad to spend some time back in the 'Old Country'. Their chagrin was understandable, as most of them had been in the colonies since their youth and were understandably anxious to get home. However, Turkey had thrown its lot in with Germany, and the plans had been changed. I considered that many of the colonials had enlisted in the hope of seeing home once again, for there was then no general military service in Britain.

When we arrived off Suez, *Emden*'s officers (excepting those of us aboard *Orvieto*) and many of our men were transferred to *Hampshire*. The passage through the canal was smooth, but we were locked up like criminals. We were not allowed on deck at all, and sentries – now armed to the teeth – were posted in front of our doors and portholes. The passage was very interesting: we could see many of the British fortifications. Many troops were already there, largely Sudanese or Indian. The whole length of the canal was like one giant fort. Trench followed trench, and battery followed battery. It seemed as though a successful attack on the canal could only be achieved by huge forces.

The greater part of the trip from Suez to Port Said was made at night, so that our imprisonment was not so obvious. We arrived in Port Said on 2nd December. *Hampshire* already lay at the buoy. The harbour looked crammed to capacity, among the warships being many acquaintances from out East. They included the French armoured cruisers *Dupleix* and *Montcalm*, plus troopships, torpedo-boats, minesweepers and patrol craft, hospital ships, and even a few German merchantmen that had been interned at the outbreak of war.

Once *Orvieto* had made fast, we were taken over to join our colleagues aboard *Hampshire*. All of *Orvieto*'s passengers now crammed the rail to stare at us. Naturally, there were many cameras recording our transfer for posterity.

Aboard *Hampshire* we were received with great cordiality by her commander, Captain Grant. It was immediately noticeable that we were back among members of our own profession as the whole atmosphere was far warmer. Indeed, that we were received so well aboard *Hampshire* was remarkable in itself: she had been the ship detailed to chase us. Captain Grant had carried out the search admirably, but our good luck and his ill fortune had brought *Emden* safely through.

Our accommodation aboard the armoured cruiser was excellent. Captain Grant had entirely abandoned his cabin to us. We could go on deck at any time, which was very pleasant at sea and in good weather. Our men, quartered in the forecastle, also enjoyed good treatment.

While in Port Said we were given the chance to replenish our wardrobes, by now less than scanty, with apparel suited to a voyage to cold and foggy Britain. We bought civilian clothes and a warm overcoat apiece, while the men were given sturdy Royal Marine uniforms.

Captain Grant presented us with a good selection of German- and English-language books he had bought especially some time previously. The gesture was greatly appreciated.

Hampshire put to sea the next morning, when good weather and a calm sea allowed us to forget our captivity for a time. Wireless messages, containing fascinating news of the war, were received daily. Thanks to the kindness and chivalry of Captain Grant, we were given these messages to read. Thus we learned of the victory of von Spee's squadron, the Kreuzergeschwader, over the Royal Navy at Coronel.

On 4th December, however, we had a disappointment. A message was received from the War Office ordering *Hampshire* to take us not to England but to Malta, where preparations were being made to receive us. At a stroke, our hopes of getting to Britain – and thus close to home – had been dashed.

On Sunday 6th December 1914, the worst day of my life, we reached Malta. As *Hampshire* entered the Grand Harbour, we were forced below so that we should not learn the position of the mine barrier and safe channel.

That afternoon we were taken ashore. The officers were taken in a cart to the Verdala Barracks, where we were to be incarcerated for the remainder of the war. The warrant officers and men were housed in Fort Salvatore.

At once, the difference between the British Army and the Royal Navy became all too clear. The hearty comradeship of our fellow professionals was missing. Instead, we faced the coldness noticeable in the tone of the army officers.

Shortly after 1800hrs on 6th December we arrived at Verdala Barracks, The huge, heavy gates slammed shut behind us. Our real captivity had begun.

FINIS

APPENDICES

I·The Roll of Honour

This section — which does not take into account changes of personnel prior to 31st July 1914 — owes a great debt to the pioneering work of the late R.K. Lochner, author of *Die Kaperfahrten des kleinen Kreuzers Emden*, whose premature death in 1984 robbed German naval history of one of its most distinguished students. The spelling of a few names remains doubtful, these being marked '(sic)'. The names of those who were killed in the last battle or subsequently died of their wounds are marked †.

THOSE WHO FOUGHT THE LAST BATTLE

Officers

MÜLLER, Karl von; Fregattenkapitän, captain.

ANDRESEN, Fritz; Marine-Ingenieur.
ELLERBROEK; Marine-Oberingenieur, chief engineer.
GAEDE†, Ernst; Kapitänleutnant, gunnery officer.
GEERDES, August; Oberleutnant z.S.
GROPIUS†, Hans; Kapitänleutnant, navigating officer.
GUÉRARD†, Albert von; Leutnant z.S., adjutant.
HAAS, Hugo; Marine-Ingenieur.
HOHENZOLLERN, Prinz Franz Joseph von; Leutnant z.S., second torpedo officer.
LEVETZOW†, Ernst von; Oberleutnant z.S.
LÜTHER, Dr Johannes; Marine-Stabsarzt, ship's doctor.
SCHWABE†, Dr. Ludwig; Assistenzarzt.
STOFFERS†, August; Marine-Ingenieur.
WITTHOEFT, Robert; Oberleutnant z.S., torpedo officer.
WOYTSCHEKOWSKY†, Arthur; Marine-Oberzahlmeister.
ZIMMERMANN†, Fritz Karl; Leutnant z.S.

Men

ADEN, Heyo; Maschinistenmaat.
ADLUNG, Adolf; Heizer.
ASTOR†; Oberheizer.
BACKMEYER; Obermatrose.
BARTOCHA†; Obermatrose.
BAUER†; Heizer.
BAUER, Johann; Heizer.
BAUKE†; Obersignalgast.
BAUM†; Oberheizer.
BEDNORS, Alfred; Matrose.
BEHREND, Paul; Oberheizer.
BENTHIN, August; Heizer.
BERGIEN; Obermaschinist.
BERGMANN†; Bootsmannsmaat.
BERGMANN†; Matrose.
BIEBER†; FT-Maat.
BLAUENBURG, Peter; Obermaschinistenmaat.
BLECHER, Otto; Heizer.
BLÜMEL, Karl; Heizer.
BOLT, Wilhelm; Dienst. Maschinisten-Oberanwärter.
BOOK†; Obermatrose.
BORSKI†; Matrose.
BÖTTJER† [I]; Matrose.
BÖTTJER† [II]; Matrose.
BRACKMANN†; Heizer.
BREDEBORN†; Dienst. Maschinisten-Oberanwärter.
BREDENKÖTTER†; Matrose.
BROCKMANN†; Obermaschinistenmaat.
BRÜNNING; Heizer.
BUCK, Johann; Matrose.
BÜLOW, Ernst; Matrose.
BUNKE, Robert; Maschinistenmaat.
BÜRGER, Georg; Heizer.
BÜSING†; Obermatrose.
BURMANN†; Schreibersmaat.
CZIBA†; Oberwachmeistersmaat.
DAAMS, Josef; Oberheizer.
DAMANN, Julius; Heizer.
DANSCHKE; Heizer.
DEBELIUS; Maschinistenmaat.
DEHORN; Heizer.
DIEKMANN; Heizer.
DIESEL, Fritz; Maschinistenmaat.
DIETZE†; Heizer.
DOPHEIDE†; Matrose.
DRESSLER†; Obermaschinist.
DREYER†; Heizer.
EHLERS†; FT-Gast.
ENGEL, Paul; Matrose.
ENGELS†; Bootsmannsmaat.
ERFURTH, Richard; Maschinistenmaat.
EWEGEN†, von; Maschinistenmaat.
FENKER, Kurt; Obersignalgast (Dienst.).
FERBER; Oberbotteliersmaat.
FENSKE†; Oberbootsmannsmaat.
FIEDLER†; Matrose.
FISCHER†; Heizer.
FLINT; Heizer.
FORMBERG†; Heizer.
FORNACON, Ernst; Obermaschinistenanwärter.
FORST, Hans; Heizer.
FRANZ†; Bäckersgast.
FREYE, Heinrich; Zimmermannsmaat.
FRIEDRICH, Arthur; Heizer.
FRIESE†; Maschinistenmaat.
GARBE, Friedrich; Obermaschinistenmaat.
GEIBEL, Jacob; Heizer.
GIERLOFF, Richard; Maschinist.
GOLDBAUM; Heizer.
GOLLATZ, Paul; Maschinistenmaat.
GONSCHEROWSKY; Heizer.
GOTTSCHALK, Herman; Heizer.
GRAEWE†; Signalgast.
GRENZ†; Obermatrose.
GRUMBACH; FT-Gast.
GRÜN, Karl; Oberverwaltersmaat.
GRZYBOWSKI; Matrose.
GURAK, Otto; Heizer.
GUTMANN†; Obermatrose.
HAAS†; Heizer.
HAASE†; Segelmachersmaat.
HABBEN, Martin; Malersgast.
HÄCKEMESSER†; Sanitätsmaat.
HANDEL, August; Obermaschinistenmaat.
HANDTKE†; Heizer.
HARMS; Maschinistenmaat.
HARTMANN†; Artillerie-Obermechanikersgast.
HARTUNG, Fritz; Artillerie-Obermechanikersmaat.
HEERING, Heinrich; Obermaschinistenmaat.
HELLWEGE, Harry; Maschinistenmaat.
HELLWIG†; Matrose.
HENKES†; Bäckersgast.
HENNINGER†; Matrose.
HENSELER; Dienst. Maschinisten-Oberanwärter.
HENZELMANN, Friedrich; Bootsmannsmaat.
HERWARTZ; Heizer.
HILBIG†; Matrose.
HILLBOLD†; Oberheizer.
HILGENSTOCK, Fritz; Torpedoheizer.
HOEF, Peter; Maschinistenmaat.
HOFFMANN, Johann; Schuhmachersgast.
HOLTHAUSEN†; Heizer.
HOLZE; Heizer.
HUCH, Otto; Heizer.
HUHN†; Schuhmachersgast.
HÜLSBUSCH, Heinrich; Heizer.
HÜLSMANN, Bernhard; Obermaschinistenanwärter.
HUSTER†; FT-Gast.
HUTSCH, Peter; Torpedo-Oberheizer.
ISSLEIB†; Heizer.
JAGUTTIS, Michael; Obermaschinistenmaat.
JUNG†; Heizer.
JUNK, Hans; Heizer.
JUNKER†; Heizer.
JÜRGENS, Karl; Maschinistenmaat.
KAISER; Kriegsfreiwillige Heizer.
KALBE†; Matrose.
KAMMER; Oberheizer.
KAMPF; Maschinist.
KAPUSZINSKY†; Matrose.
KAUFNER†; Zimmermannsgast.
KEIL, Hermann; Obermaschinistenmaat.
KEIL†, Wilhelm; Matrose.
KELLER, Georg; Obermaschinist.
KIENAPFEL, Wilhelm; Heizer.
KIRCHHOFF†; Heizer.
KLAGES, Alfred; Maschinistenmaat.

KLAWITTER, Paul; Bootsmannsmaat.
KLEE†; Matrose.
KLEIN; Oberheizer.
KLEINECKE†; Matrose.
KLÖPPEL, Johann; Heizer.
KLUGE, Gustav; Maschinistenmaat.
KLUTH; Heizer.
KNABE; Heizer.
KNASIAK; Matrose.
KNITTEL, August; Heizer.
KOPLIN, Friedrich; Matrose.
KÖPPEN†; Obermaschinistenmaat.
KÖRBER, Georg; Maschinist.
KÖRVER; Heizer.
KÖSTER; Heizer.
KÖSTER; Torpedo-Maschinistenmaat d.R.
KOTZWARA; Kriegsfw. Heizer.
KRÖHLING†; Matrose.
KRUGGEL, Adolf; Feuerwerksmaat.
KUGELMAIER†; Matrose.
KÜHL; Matrose.
KUHLMANN, Richard; Torpedoheizer.
KÜHNEL†; Matrose.
KUNKEL, Adolf; Matrose.
KUTZMUTZ, Paul; Heizer.
LAABS; Heizer.
LADEWIG†; Matrose.
LANGE, Karl; Heizer.
LEICHT, Georg; Obermaschinist.
LEUK, Matthias; Oberheizer.
LEVEN†; Obermatrose.
LEVEQUE, Fritz; Heizer.
LEVY†; Matrose.
LIEBE, Albert; Artillerie-Obermechanikersgast.
LINDNER, Hans; Signalgast.
LINNEMANN, Wilhelm; Heizer.
LINNIG†; Signalmaat.
LOCHAU; Matrose.
LÖFFLER†; Schneidersgast.
MAASS, Robert; Torpedo-Oberheizer.
MARTH†; Heizer.
MACHELETT, Karl; Heizer.
MARTINI, Alois; Heizer.
MARX†; Matrose.
MAYER, Karl; Zimmermannsgast.
METZING†; Signalgast.
MEYBOHM; Heizer.
MEYER†; Bootsmannsmaat.
MEYER†, August; Obermatrose.
MEYER, Nikolaus; Matrose.
MICHEL, Fritz; Torpedo-Oberheizer.
MÖLLER†; Heizer.
MÖLLER†; Signalgast.
MÖNKEDIEK, Otto; Steuermann.
MÜLLER; Heizer.
MÜLLER; Torpedomatrose.
MÜLLER†, Leo; Obermatrose.
MÜLLER, Walter; Heizer.
MÜLLER, Walter; Oberheizer.
NAGELS, Kornel; Heizer.
NIEBUHR; Matrose.
NOHKE†; Signalgast.
ODENTHAL†; Heizer.
OFFERMANN, Otto; Matrose.
OLM, Wilhelm; Maschinistenmaat.
PALLIDA, Paul; Heizer.
PARK†; Matrose.
PETERS†; Bootsmannsmaat.
PEYRONNIE; Oberheizer.
PFEIFFER†; Feuerwerker.
PFEIL†; Heizer.
PIEPER, Wilhelm; Maschinistenmaat.
PIERITZ; Heizer.
PLOTHA, Johann; Oberheizer.
PLÖTZ, Hugo; Steuermannsmaat.
POHLMANN†; Heizer.
PÖRRER; Torpedoheizer.
POSSEHL; Torpedo-Obermatrose.
PRIES†; Barbier.
PULS, Karl; Heizer.
PÜSCHEL, Ernst; Torpedo-Maschinistenmaat.
PYTTLIK†; Torpedo-Maschinist.
QUADFLIEG, Josef; Heizer.
RECHE; Oberheizer.
REICH†; Matrose.
REICHELT; Oberzimmermannsgast.
RIEGELMEIER, Otto; Maschinistenmaat.
RIEGER†; Signalmaat.
RIEHL†; Heizer.
ROHR†; Heizer.
RÖHRER; Heizer.
ROMBACH; Matrose.
ROSS†; Heizer.
RÖTTGEN, Jakob; Matrose.
RUHMER; Heizer.
RUSINSKY; Bootsmannsmaat.
RÜTZ, Carl; Maschinistenmaat.
RYSSE†, van; Feuerwerksmaat.
SABLOWSKI†; Bootsmannsmaat.
SANDERS†; Heizer.
SCHALLER, Paul; Heizer.
SCHAU†; Matrose.
SCHELLER†; Heizer.
SCHEMBER; Heizer.
SCHEPPUTAT, Georg; Dienst. Maschinisten-Oberanwärter.
SCHERER†; Matrose.
SCHLAUSS; Heizer.
SCHLECHTWEG†; Matrose.
SCHMIDT, Josef [I]; Heizer.
SCHMIDT, Josef [II]; Heizer.
SCHMIEDTKE†; Dienst. Maschinisten-Oberanwärter.
SCHNEIDER†; Maschinistenmaat.
SCHNELLE†; Matrose.
SCHOOLMANN†; Dienst. Maschinisten-Oberanwärter.
SCHUHMACHER; Heizer.
SCHULTZE†; Maschinist.
SCHULZ†; Offizierskoch.
SCHÜTZ; Heizer.
SCHWARZ; Signalmaat.
SCHWARZ, Wilhelm; Maschinistenmaat.
SELLMEYER†; Matrose.
SIEMENS†; Oberheizer.
SPIELMANN, Albert; Bootsmannsmaat.
STAUCH†; Bootsmannsmaat.
STECHMEYER, Konrad; Oberheizer.
STEIDEL, Theodor; Heizer.
STEINFURTH; Feuerwerksmaat.
STRAKA, August; Heizer.
TANNERT†; Matrose.
TESCHNER; Matrose.
THOMAS†; Oberheizer.
TIETZ†; Matrose.
TREPPENS†; Matrose.
TULL; Maschinist.
UEBE, Hermann; Dienst. Maschinisten-Oberanwärter.
UHDE, Karl; Heizer.
UNGER; Heizer.
USTER†; Heizer.
VEITH†; Heizer.
VELTEN, Wilhelm; Oberfeuerwerksmaat.
VOGT, Wilhelm; Dienst. Maschinisten-Oberanwärter.
VORWERK†; Heizer.
VIEREGG, Fritz; Maschinistenmaat.
WACHTEL, Ferdinand; Heizer.
WAGNER; Matrose.
WECKE, Otto; Oberhoboistenmaat.
WEHLER; Heizer.
WEHLING; Heizer.
WEISE, Alfred; Matrose.
WERKMEISTER, Adam; Maschinstenmaat.
WERNER, Arthur; Matrose.
WESEMANN, Diedrich; Maschinistenmaat.
WETZEL†; Heizer.
WEX†; Heizer.
WIELAND†; Heizer.
WILLE†; FT-Gast.
WILKING†; Schreibersmaat.
WILLMS; Matrose.
WILZEPOLSKY†; Heizer.
WINTER; Heizer.
WIRTH, Johann; Heizer.
WITT† [I]; Matrose.
WITTENBERG†; Maschinistenmaat.
WITTENBROCK†; Matrose.
WITTICH; Heizer.
WOLFF, Rudolf; Oberheizer.
WOLLBURG; Matrose.
WOYTAKOWSKY, Franz; Zimmermannsmaat.
ZEIDLER†; Matrose.
ZIEHR†; Matrose.
ZIMMER†; Heizer.
ZIMMER, Georg; Wachtmeistersmaat.

THOSE WHO MISSED THE LAST BATTLE

Officers

FIKENTSCHER, Erich; Leutnant z.S. Left with *Buresk*, 8th November 1914.
GYSSLING, Eugen; Leutnant z.S. Detached with the Landing Party, Direction Island, 9th November 1914.
KLÖPPER; Kapitänleutnant d.R. Left with *Buresk*, 8th November 1914.
LAUTERBACH, Julius; Oberleutnant z.S.d.R. Left with *Exford*, 8th November 1914.
METZENTHIEN; Kapitänleutnant d.R. Left with *Gneisenau*, 13th August 1914.
MÜCKE, Hellmuth von; Kapitänleutnant, first officer of *Emden*. Detached with the Landing Party, Direction Island, 9th November 1914.
SCHALL, Robin; Leutnant z.S. Left with *Buresk*, 8th November 1914.
SCHMIDT†, Roderich; Leutnant z.S. Detached with the Landing Party, Direction Island, 9th November 1914.

Men

BARTHOLOMÄUS; Torpedomatrose. Detached with the Landing Party, Direction Island, 9th November 1914.
BECKER, Hans [I]; Heizer. Left with *Pontoporos*, 16th September 1914.
BECKER, Hans [II]; Heizer. Detached with the Landing Party, Direction Island, 9th November 1914.
BENIGK (sic), Richard; Maschinistenmaat. Left with *Pontoporos*, 16th September 1914.

BERG; Matrose. Detached with the Landing Party, Direction Island, 9th November 1914.
BOOCH; Torpedo-Maschinistenmaat. Detached with the Landing Party, Direction Island, 9th November 1914.
BORDEAUX, Franz; Marinezahlmeisters-Applikant. Left with *Markomannia*, 30th September 1914.
BRODBECK; Heizer. Hospitalized in Tsingtau, 6th August 1914.
BURGWEDEL; Bootsmannsmaat. Detached with the Landing Party, Direction Island, 9th November 1914.
DOLLERZICH; Matrose. Left with *Pontoporos*, 16th September 1914.
DORL, Albert; Matrose. Detached with the Landing Party, Direction Island, 9th November 1914.
ECKSTEIN; Heizer. Left with *Exford*, 8th November 1914.
ELLERMANN, Heinrich; Obermaschinistenmaat. Left with *Buresk*, 8th November 1914.
ENGEL, Wilhelm; Matrose. Left with *Pontoporos*, 16th September.
FISCHER; Maschinist. Left with *Exford*, 8th November 1914.
FREUND, Gerhard; Maschinist. Left with *Pontoporos*, 16th September
FÜRCHTENICHT, Richard; Matrose. Left with *Pontoporos*, 16th September 1914.
GIERSCH, Richard; Oberheizer d.R. Left with *Buresk*, 8th November.
GOLDMANN; Signalgast. Detached with the Landing Party, Direction Island, 9th November 1914.
GOLTZ, Hermann; Bootsmannsmaat d.R. Left with *Buresk*, 8th November 1914.
GRANZOW; Obermatrose. Left with *Buresk*, 8th November 1914.
GRONAU; Obermatrose. Left with *Buresk*, 8th November 1914.
GRUBE; Obermatrose. Detached with the Landing Party, Direction Island, 9th November 1914.
HÄRTTRICH, Adolf; Maschinistenmaat. Detached with the Landing Party, Direction Island, 9th November 1914.
HEGEL; Obermatrose. Detached with the Landing Party, Direction Island, 9th November 1914.
HEIMANN; Heizer. Detached with the Landing Party, Direction Island, 9th November 1914.
HEINRICH, Otto; Kriegsfreiwillige Heizer. Left with *Exford*, 8th November 1914.
HILBERS; FT-Oberanwärter. Detached with the Landing Party, Direction Island, 9th November 1914.
HOFF, Walter; Obersignalgast. Detached with the Landing Party, Direction Island, 9th November 1914.
HOLEN; Maschinistenmaat. Detached with the Landing Party, Direction Island, 9th November 1914.
HUBER; Torpedomatrose. Left with *Exford*, 8th November 1914.
JAHNKE, Franz; Maschinistenmaat. Left with *Exford*, 8th November.
KEIL†; Matrose. Detached with the Landing Party, Direction Island, 9th November 1914.
KELLE; Obersignalgast. Left with *Buresk*, 8th November 1914.
KERN, Eugen; Kriegsfreiwillige Heizer. Left with *Exford*, 8th November.
KIRBACH; Matrose. Detached with the Landing Party, Direction Island, 9th November 1914.
KLEIN, Paul; FT-Maat. Left with *Exford*, 8th November 1914.
KLIEMT (sic); Kriegsfreiwillige Heizer. Left with *Exford*, 8th November.
KNOPP; Obermatrose. Detached with the Landing Party, Direction Island, 9th November 1914.
KÖHLER; Matrose. Left with *Exford*, 8th November 1914.
KOSCHINSKY, Heinrich; Obermatrose. Detached with the Landing Party, Direction Island, 9th November 1914.
KRAUSE; Obermatrose. Detached with the Landing Party, Direction Island, 9th November 1914.
KREUTZ, Jakob; Heizer. Detached with the Landing Party, Direction Island, 9th November 1914.
LAKAY; Kriegsfreiwillige Heizer. Left with *Buresk*, 8th November 1914.
LANIG†; Heizer. Detached with the Landing Party, Direction Island, 9th November 1914.
LAPP, Heinrich; Obermaschinistenmaat. Left with *Buresk*, 8th November 1914.
LEUCHT; Obermaschinistenmaat der Seewehr. Left with *Buresk*, 8th November 1914.
LINEL; Heizer. Hospitalized in Tsingtau, 6th August 1914.
LÖHMANN, Walter; Obermatrose. Detached with the Landing Party, Direction Island, 9th November 1914.
LOOK, Hermann; Heizer. Left with *Pontoporos*, 16th September 1914.
LUTHER, Gustav; Heizer. Detached with the Landing Party, Direction Island, 9th November 1914.
MAURITZ; Matrose. Detached with the Landing Party, Direction Island, 9th November 1914.
MEYER; Vizesteuermann d.R. Left with *Pontoporos*, 16th September 1914.
MEYER, Karl; Matrose d.R. Left with *Buresk*, 8th November 1914.
MICHAELIS; Bootsmannsmaat. Detached with the Landing Party, Direction Island, 9th November 1914.
MICHULETZ; Torpedo-Maschinistenmaat. Left with *Pontoporos*, 16th September 1914.
MÜLLER; Bootsmann. Left with *Exford*, 8th November 1914.
MÜNCH; Heizer. Detached with the Landing Party, Direction Island, 9th November 1914.
OETTIGER, Hermann; Bootsmannsmaat. Left with *Exford*, 8th November 1914.
OLSCHEWSKY, Emil; Maschinistenmaat. Left with *Exford*, 8th November 1914.
OSTERMANN, Karl; Heizer. Detached with the Landing Party, Direction Island, 9th November 1914.
PASCHKEWITZ; Matrose. Left with *Pontoporos*, 16th September 1914.
PATZIG, Friedrich; Matrose. Left with *Pontoporos*, 16th September.
PETERSEN; Torpedomatrose. Detached with the Landing Party, Direction Island, 9th November 1914.
PIDUCH; Matrose. Left with *Exford*, 8th November 1914.
PINKERT; Matrose. Detached with the Landing Party, Direction Island, 9th November 1914.
POHLMÜLLER; Heizer. Hospitalized in Tsingtau, 6th August 1914.
RADEMACHER†, Josef; Matrose. Detached with the Landing Party, Direction Island, 9th November 1914.
RE(E)DLICH; Steuermannsmaat. Left with *Exford*, 8th November 1914.
REICH; Obermatrose. Detached with the Landing Party, Direction Island, 9th November 1914.
ROHDE; Matrose. Left with *Pontoporos*, 16th September 1914.
RÖLLE; FT-Gast. Left with *Buresk*, 8th November 1914.
ROSSBACH; Maschinistenmaat. Detached with the Landing Party, Direction Island, 9th November 1914.
SAAKE, Ernst; Heizer. Left with *Pontoporos*, 16th September 1914.
SANGEN; Matrose. Detached with the Landing Party, Direction Island, 9th November 1914.
SCHMIDTBERGER; Matrose. Detached with the Landing Party, Direction Island, 9th November 1914.
SCHWALBE; Heizer. Detached with the Landing Party, Direction Island, 9th November 1914.
SCHWENTEIDT (sic); Matrose. Detached with the Landing Party, Direction Island, 9th November 1914.
SIAT, Ludwig; Maschinistenmaat. Left with *Exford*, 8th November 1914.
SIEBERT; Matrose. Detached with the Landing Party, Direction Island, 9th November 1914.
STEPHAN; Heizer. Detached with the Landing Party, Direction Island, 9th November 1914.
STEEGE; Matrose. Detached with the Landing Party, Direction Island, 9th November 1914.
STOLLE; Heizer. Hospitalized in Tsingtau, 6th August 1914.
STOVES, Walter; Heizer. Detached with the Landing Party, Direction Island, 9th November 1914.
SÜSS; Obermatrose. Detached with the Landing Party, Direction Island, 9th November 1914.
TIEDEMANN; Obermatrose. Detached with the Landing Party, Direction Island, 9th November 1914.
WADEPHUL, Alfred; Matrose. Detached with the Landing Party, Direction Island, 9th November 1914.
WAHLMANN; Matrose. Left with *Exford*, 8th November 1914.
WALUSCHEWSKY; Heizer. Hospitalized in Tsingtau, 6th August 1914.
WARNECKE; Oberheizer d.R. Left with *Buresk*, 8th November 1914.
WICHERT; FT-Gast. Detached with the Landing Party, Direction Island, 9th November 1914.
WINTERLING; Heizer. Detached with the Landing Party, Direction Island, 9th November 1914.
WITT [II]; Matrose. Detached with the Landing Party, Direction Island, 9th November 1914.
WITTKOPF; Torpedomaschinist. Left with *Buresk*, 8th November 1914.
WÖHNER, Erich; Maschinistenmaat. Left with *Pontoporos*, 16th September 1914.
WOLFF, Rudolf; Matrose. Detached with the Landing Party, Direction Island, 9th November 1914.

2·The Kreuzergeschwader

The sister-ships *Scharnhorst* (flag) and *Gneisenau*, displacing 11,616 tonnes, were the most powerful German 'schwere Kreuzer' excepting the hybrid *Blücher*. Authorized under the 1903/4 budget, they were laid down by Blohm & Voss and AG 'Weser' (yard numbers 175 and 144) respectively. *Scharnhorst* was commissioned on 24th October 1907; her sister followed on 6th March 1908. Measuring 144 metres on the waterline, each ship carried eight 21cm, six 15cm and eighteen 8.8cm guns, plus a handful of 8mm machine-guns and four 45cm torpedo-tubes. Their triple expansion machinery, driving three shafts, could propel them at a little over 23 knots. Victorious at the Battle of Coronel, virtually contemporaneously with *Emden*'s demise, both were vanquished a month later at the Battle of the Falkland Islands with a loss of 1,458 crewmen.

A Bremen-class kleiner Kreuzer, displacing 3,278 tonnes and measuring about 111 metres on the waterline, *Leipzig* was laid down in the AG 'Weser' shipyard in 1904 (yard no.143) and commissioned on 20th April 1906. Armed with ten 10.5cm L/40 guns, ten 3.7cm machine-cannon and two 45cm torpedo-tubes, she had twin-shaft triple-expansion machinery and could exceed 22 knots when new. Successful at the Battle of Coronel, *Leipzig* was overwhelmed and sunk at the Battle of the Falkland Islands on 8th December 1914 with the loss of 315 of her crew.

Nürnberg, built in the Kaiserliche Werft, Kiel (yard no.32), and commissioned on 10th April 1908, was similar to *Leipzig* excepting that ten 5.2cm L/55 guns replaced the 3.7cm cannon. Displacing 3,469 tonnes and measuring 117 metres on the waterline, she could be distinguished from the earlier cruiser by the prominent gap between the second and third funnels. When new, she could raise 23½ knots from her twin-shaft triple-expansion engines; however, *Nürnberg* was long overdue for a refit by 1914 and her boilers were in particularly poor state. Two burst as she attempted to flee from the Battle of the Falkland Islands, materially contributing to her destruction and the loss of 327 men.

Dresden was *Emden*'s sister-ship, differing primarily in being driven by turbines rather than triple-expansion engines. Built by Blohm & Voss of Hamburg (yard no.195) and commissioned on 14th November 1908, she attained 25.2 knots on trial – but could be worked up to at least 27 in favourable conditions, as her successful flight from the carnage of the Battle of the Falkland Islands proved when she outran HMS *Glasgow*. The only survivor of Coronel and the Falkland Islands other than *Glasgow*, SMS *Dresden* was finally cornered in supposedly neutral waters off Mas à Tierra, Chile, scuttling on 14th March 1915 after an inconsequential skirmish with the blockading Royal Navy which cost the lives of seven German seamen.

Iltis, *Jaguar*, *Tiger* and *Luchs* were all Iltis-class gunboats. The earlier pair were built by Schichau of Danzig (yard numbers 630 and 631), being commissioned on 1st December 1898 and 4th April 1899 respectively. Each displaced 894 tonnes, measured about 64m on the waterline and could attain about 14½ knots. Armament comprised four 8.8cm L/30 guns and six 3.7cm revolver cannon. *Tiger* and *Luchs* were essentially similar, but built by the Kaiserliche Werft, Danzig, and commissioned on 3rd April and 15th May 1900 respectively. Two 10.5cm L/40 replaced the four 8.8cm guns. They proved to be a good half-knot slower than their sisters on trials. All four were scuttled at Tsingtau: *Iltis* and *Luchs* on 28th September, *Tiger* on 29th October, and finally *Jaguar* – credited with sinking the small Japanese destroyer *Shirotaye* – on 7th November 1914. The crews and 10.5cm guns of *Luchs* and *Tiger* had already been transferred to the armed merchant cruiser *Prinz Eitel Friedrich* (q.v.).

There were also three river gunboats. The 223-tonne *Tsingtau* and *Vaterland*, built by Schichau of Elbing (yard numbers 710 and 711) and commissioned on 3rd February and 28th May 1904 respectively, measured about 48m on the waterline and could attain thirteen knots. Each mounted a single 8.8cm SK L/30, a 5cm SK L/40 and several 8mm Maxim machine-guns. *Tsingtau* was laid up at Canton in August 1914, scuttling on 21st March 1917 to avoid falling into Chinese hands; *Vaterland*, interned at Nanking, was seized by the Chinese on 20th March 1917 and served as *Li-Sui* until 1932. She was then transferred to the Manchukuo authorities, serving for at least another decade as *Risui*.

SMS *Nürnberg*, pictured after the battle of Coronel, allegedly on 2nd November 1914. In the background is the fleet flagship, SMS *Scharnhorst*. Built by the Kaiserliche Werft, Kiel, and commissioned in April 1908, *Nürnberg* displaced 3,469 tonnes and could make 23 knots. Main armament remained ten 10.5cm guns. Note the distinctive gap between the second and third funnels, characteristic only of *Nürnberg*, *Stettin* and *Stuttgart*. *Nürnberg* was sunk by HMS *Kent* at the Battle of the Falkland Islands, 8th December 1914, with the loss of 327 men. By courtesy of the Trustees of the Imperial War Museum, London; negative Q 80704.

The newest and largest of this trio of Flusskanonenboote, the 266-tonne *Otter*, had been launched from the Tecklenborg yard in Geestemünde (yard no. 232) on 15th July 1909. Commissioned on 1st April 1910, she carried two 5.2cm SK L/55 and three 8mm machine-guns. A little over fifteen knots could be attained from triple-expansion machinery. Interned at Nanking in August 1914, *Otter* was taken over by the Chinese navy on 20th March 1917 as *Li-Tsieh* and eventually went to the breakers in 1929.

Torpedo-boat *S90* — officially known as 'T90' by August 1914 — was built by Schichau (no.644) and commissioned on 24th October 1899. The first of the perfected German sea-going designs, she displaced a mere 310 tonnes and measured about 63 metres on the waterline. Armed with three 5.2cm guns and three 45cm torpedo-tubes, she could make about 26½ knots from triple-expansion engines driving twin propellor shafts. *S90* torpedoed and sank the Japanese protected cruiser *Takachiho* off Tsingtau on 17th October 1914, but was then deliberately run aground on the Chinese shore.

The 8,797grt auxiliary cruiser *Prinz Eitel Friedrich* briefly joined the Kreuzergeschwader, before being detached shortly after von Spee left for Coronel and the Falkland Islands. Built by AG 'Vulcan' of Stettin-Bredow (yard no. 254) for Norddeutscher Lloyd, *Prinz Eitel Friedrich* was launched in June 1904 and had served on the Far East route before the war. Her home port was Bremen; her call sign, QHVN. Measuring 149 metres on the waterline and capable of about fifteen knots from her quadruple-expansion machinery and twin propellors when new, she received the crews and guns of *Luchs* and *Tiger* at Tsingtau — four 10.5cm SK L/40, six 8.8cm SK L/40 and twelve 3.7cm cannon. She was eventually interned in Newport News, Virginia, USA (9th April 1915) after sinking eleven Allied ships. Impressed as the troopship *De Kalb* in April 1917, she was sold to the United America Line (as *Mount Clay*), laid up in 1924, and eventually dispatched to the breakers in 1935.

The 1,920grt auxiliary *Titania* served as a tender to the Kreuzergeschwader. Built by Armstrong, Mitchell & Co. Ltd, of Newcastle upon Tyne (yard no.645), she was sold on completion in May 1896 to Finska Ångfartygs AB of Helsingfors and initially sailed under the Russian flag.* Sold to the Diedrichsen company of Kiel in the Spring of 1901 and then impressed as a naval auxiliary, *Titania* was sent to Tsingtau in 1910 and eventually scuttled off Mas à Fuera (Juan Fernandez) on 19th November 1914. Measuring about 86m on the waterline and capable of about eleven knots, she carried a single 6cm L/18 gun.

Completed in Blohm & Voss's Hamburg yard in March 1901 (yard no.142), Hamburg-Amerika-Linie merchantman *C. Ferd. Laeisz* — home port Hamburg, call-sign RMBG — served as a guardship at Tsingtau when war was declared. Displacing about 12,000 tonnes (4,931grt) and measuring 122m on the waterline, she was capable of about eleven knots. Taken as a prize by the French armoured cruiser *Dupleix* off Tsingtau on 21st August 1914, when commanded by Otto Geissel, she subsequently served as the auxiliary *Aisne* before being sold to Italy (as *Andreino*, then *Elio*) and finally went to the breakers in 1932.

The old Austro-Hungarian cruiser *Kaiserin Elisabeth* also berthed in Tsingtau. Laid down in the Pola navy yard in July 1888 and completed in January 1892, one of two protected cruisers of the Kaiser Franz Joseph I class, she displaced 3,967 tonnes, was a hundred metres long and had been able to reach nineteen knots in her prime. By 1914, her original guns had been replaced by eight 15cm and fourteen 4.7cm quick-firers, plus two 7cm short-barrel landing guns and four torpedo tubes. As *Kaiserin Elisabeth* was incapable of much more than fourteen knots by 1914, and as even her replacement guns were obsolescent, she was disarmed and scuttled on 2nd November. The guns were sent ashore to equip 'Elisabeth' battery.

* Finland was then part of the Russian Empire, remaining so until seizing the chance to regain independence after the the October Revolution.

† However, the Landing Party had already been detached to join the Schutztruppe Deutsch-Ostafrika, fighting under Paul von Lettow-Vorbeck. Most of the remaining crewmen also joined the land forces after the cruiser had been destroyed, but only a handful survived the war — fighting and disease killing the others.

Other colonial-service warships, 1914

ON THE AUSTRALIAN STATION

The ageing gunboat *Cormoran* had been built by the Kaiserliche Werft, Danzig, and commissioned in July 1893. However, despite an extensive rebuild in 1907-8, she was all but useless by 1914. Displacing 1,612 tonnes, *Cormoran* had been docked in Tsingtau for extensive repairs when the First World War began. Her eight 10.5cm guns were removed to *Emden*'s prize *Ryazan* (which subsequently became *Cormoran* II), and the gunboat hulk was scuttled off the Chinese coast on 28th September 1914.

Geier, built by the Kaiserliche Werft, Wilhelmshaven, and commissioned in October 1895, had also been extensively rebuilt in pre-war days. Designated 'Kreuzer IV.Klasse', and armed with eight 10.5cm SK L/35 and five 3.7cm cannon (plus two torpedo tubes), she displaced 1,608 tonnes. Her effectiveness as a fighting unit was greatly compromised by her lack of protection and low speed — 15½ knots when new, but no more than twelve by 1914. Accompanied by the collier *Bochum*, *Geier* steamed across the Pacific after encountering *Emden* and was interned in Honolulu. Impressed by the US Navy in April 1917, becoming USS *Carl Schurz*, she collided with the tanker *Fluida* in June 1918 and sank off the North Carolina coast.

ON THE EAST AFRICAN STATION

The small cruiser *Königsberg* had an eventful career. Built by the Kaiserliche Werft, Kiel (yard no.31), she displaced 3,390 tonnes, measured 115 metres on the waterline and could attain 24 knots when new. Armed with ten 10.5cm SK L/40 and ten 3.7cm cannon, *Königsberg* had been extensively rebuilt at Danzig in 1911-13 before being sent to Dar-es-Salaam. After sinking HMS *Pegasus* off Zanzibar in September 1914, *Königsberg* was blockaded in the Rufiji Delta and finally sunk by bombardment on 11th July 1915 (nineteen dead†).

ON THE SOUTH AMERICAN STATION

The small cruiser *Karlsruhe* was a product of Krupp Germaniawerft, Kiel (no.187), commissioned on 15th January 1914. She displaced 4,900 tonnes and measured 139 metres on the waterline. Armed with twelve 10.5cm SK L/40 and two 50cm torpedo-tubes, *Karlsruhe* enjoyed a successful commerce-raiding career in the Caribbean and off the South American coast before succumbing on 4th November 1914 to an internal explosion that killed her captain, Otto Köhler, and 262 of his crew.

ON THE WEST AFRICAN STATION

The gunboats *Panther* and *Eber* belonged to the Iltis class (see above). Each displaced 977 tonnes, measured 64.1 metres on the waterline and could attain about fourteen knots. Armament comprised two 10.5cm SK L/40 and six 3.7cm cannon. Under repair when war was declared, *Panther* had been built by the Kaiserliche Werft, Danzig, and commissioned on 15th March 1902. Modified for survey duty after the First World War, she served the Reichsmarine until sold for breaking in 1931. *Eber*, built by AG 'Vulcan' of Stettin (yard no. 257), was commissioned on 15th September 1903; late in August 1914 she disarmed, her guns passing to the mercantile cruiser *Cap Trafalgar*. *Eber* was interned at Bahia in September under the German merchant flag, and eventually gutted by fire on 26th October 1917.

One of the principal achievements of *Emden*'s cruise was to draw off many Allied ships that would have been better used elsewhere, instead of escorting troopships and supply convoys across the Indian and Pacific Oceans.

Compared with the limited strength of the Kreuzergeschwader in April 1914, Anglo-French naval forces were impressive. Excluding destroyers and torpedo-boats, the Royal Navy mustered the battleship *Triumph*; heavy armoured cruisers *Minotaur* and *Hampshire*; protected cruisers *Encounter, Pioneer, Philomel* (on loan to New Zealand), Pyramus and *Psyche*; light cruiser *Yarmouth* and sloops *Cadmus, Clio* and *Vernon*. The Royal Australian Navy had the powerful battle-cruiser HMAS *Australia* plus light cruiser sister-ships *Melbourne* and *Sydney*. French vessels included the armoured cruisers *Dupleix* and *Montcalm*, sloop *Kersaint* and gunboat *Zêlée*, plus a handful of destroyers and torpedo-boats. The Imperial Russian Navy had the armoured cruisers *Askold* and *Zhemchug*, while the Japanese, if war was to be declared against Germany, could make an entire fleet available.

Though some of the most powerful units — including *Australia* and *Triumph* — soon withdrew to more pressing engagements, no fewer than eight vessels were still actively pursuing *Emden* by 1st October 1914 (at least according to Winston Churchill in *The World Crisis*); in addition, thirty were being employed against the Kreuzergeschwader, forty to protect the Indian and Pacific Oceans, and eight more on Indian Ocean convoy escort duty. *The World Crisis* names the eight major ships on 'Emden Hunt' as the cruisers *Hampshire, Yarmouth, Psyche, Pyramus* and *Philomel*; HM Australian Ships *Melbourne* and *Sydney*; the Russian cruisers *Askold* and *Zhemchug*; and the Japanese cruiser *Chikuma*. In addition, the Armed Merchant Cruisers *Empress of Asia, Empress of Russia* and *Himalaya* were also directly involved.

Though *Sydney* was to provide the Royal Australian Navy with its first ever battle honour, she did so largely as a result of chance: when *Emden* had raided Direction Island, a large ANZAC troop convoy was a mere sixty nautical miles distant.

The prize for doggedness was surely *Hampshire*'s, as Captain Grant had shadowed *Emden* for many thousands of nautical miles. On one occasion he had missed his quarry by a matter of hours. On another, *Hampshire* had been called away from an interception course to answer a false alarm. However, owing to the close relationship of the quarry's crew — the British ship had been a regular visitor to Tsingtau before the war — many men aboard *Hampshire* were later to express relief privately that they had not been forced to fire on *Emden*.

BRITISH, AUSTRALIAN AND NEW ZEALAND SHIPS

Hampshire. One of six Devonshire-class first-class armoured cruisers, built by Armstrong at Elswick and laid down on 1st September 1902, *Hampshire* was completed on 15th July 1905. Displacing 10,850 tons at load draught, 473½ feet between perpendiculars and capable of 22 knots, she served on the China Station in 1912-14 before being recalled to join the Northern Patrol. *Hampshire* was mined in the North Sea on 5th June 1916, sinking with a heavy loss of life that included Lord Kitchener. Armed with four 7.5-inch and six 6-inch QF guns, plus two 12-pdrs and eighteen 3-pdrs QF, she would have been more than a match for *Emden* had dogged pursuit brought the confrontation it deserved. Though the German ship was nominally somewhat faster, *Hampshire*, despite a reputation for steaming poorly at full speed, would have maintained way better than *Emden* in a heavy sea.

Melbourne and ***Sydney***, both ships of the Royal Australian Navy, were members of the six-strong Chatham class of light cruisers. Like their immediate predecessors, the Weymouths (*Yarmouth*, q.v.), they had 'all big gun' armament. However, the forecastle extended much farther aft and a new raked stem made them even more seaworthy. Better armoured and appreciably larger than *Emden*, displacing 5,400 tons at load draught anc measuring 458 feet overall, the Australian ships were credited with a maximum service speed of 25½ knots — but could usually maintain 26 knots even in a heavy swell. Eight 6-inch QF L/45 and four 3-pdr QF guns, plus two 21-inch torpedo-tubes, proved more than a match for *Emden* once *Sydney* had withdrawn out of range of the 10.5cm German guns. *Melbourne* was a product of Cammell Laird of Birkenhead, laid down in April 1911 and completed in January 1913. After serving in the Pacific in 1913-14 and then in the

HMS *Dartmouth*, pictured here shortly before being paid-off for the last time in 1929, was a light cruiser of the Weymouth class, essentially similar to *Yarmouth* (q.v.). By courtesy of Wright & Logan, Portsmouth.

West Indies, *Melbourne* joined the 2nd Light Cruiser Squadron of the Grand Fleet in 1916. She was ultimately sold for breaking in December 1928.

Built by the London & Glasgow Shipbuilding Co. of Glasgow, *Sydney* was laid down in February 1911 and completed in June 1913. After similar service to *Melbourne*, she paid off in May 1928 and was dismantled in 1929/30. Her foremast still stands in her home town as a memorial to the deaths not only of five men in the fight against *Emden*, but also to the entire crew of the later *Sydney* — lost in a fatal encounter with the German raider *Kormoran* (HSK 8, 'Raider G') in November 1941.

Minotaur. Name-ship of a class of three first-class armoured cruisers, this powerful vessel served on the China station in 1914 before being recalled to the 2nd Cruiser Squadron in the North Sea (1915). A near-contemporary of *Emden*, laid down in the Royal Dockyard, Devonport, in January 1905 and completed in April 1908, *Minotaur* displaced 14,600 tons at load draught, measured 519 feet overall and could attain about 23 knots. Though very seaworthy, *Minotaur* and her sisters were weakly protected in relation to their impressive offensive strength: four 9.2-inch and ten 7.5-inch guns, plus sixteen 12-pdr QF and five 18-inch torpedo tubes. Though no match for a German battle-cruiser, however, she would have blown *Emden* out of the water in a confrontation. After serving at Jutland, and then as flagship of the 2nd Cruiser Squadron, *Minotaur* went to the breakers in 1920.

Newcastle represented the five-ship Bristol class, the first light cruisers of their type in the Royal Navy. Laid down in Armstong's Elswick yard in April 1909 and completed in September 1910, *Newcastle* displaced 4,800 tons at load draught, measured 453 feet overall, and could reach 25 knots. She was sent to the China Station on completion, searching from August 1914 for *Prinz Eitel Friedrich*. She left the Pacific area in November 1916, for the East Indies and then the Adriatic, before returning to the South American Station in 1918. *Newcastle* was sold for breaking in May 1921.

Emden's crew initially believed *Sydney* to be a member of the Bristol class, particularly when she appeared to be using only fore and aft guns for ranging: *Newcastle* had only two 6-inch QF L/50 guns, ten additional 4-inch QF L/50 being disposed five-a-beam. There were also four 3-pdrs QF and two 18-inch torpedo tubes. Though the bigger British ship was more seaworthy (despite a low freeboard aft) and had an edge on speed, the German 10.5cm guns outranged the British 4-inch pattern and an encounter on approximately equal terms could have been possible.

Philomel was the sole surviving Pearl-class third-class cruiser, laid down in the Royal Dockyard, Devonport, in May 1889 and completed in November 1891. Displacing 2,575 tons at load draught, measuring 278 feet overall and capable of nineteen knots with forced draught — when new — *Philomel* was transferred to the Royal New Zealand Navy in 1914. By this time, however, her machinery had deteriorated significantly and maximum speed had dropped to fifteen knots. Her armament comprised eight 4.7-inch QF and eight 3-pdr QF guns, plus several 0.303-inch machine-guns and two 14-inch torpedo-tubes. After fruitlessly participating in the search for *Emden* and service in the Dardanelles, she was stricken in 1919. After serving as a depot ship, she was sold in 1947 and scuttled in deep water in 1949.

Psyche and ***Pyramus*** belonged to the Pelorus class of third class cruisers, once ten ships strong. Displacing merely 2,135 tons at load draught, 300 feet long between perpendiculars and capable of twenty knots under forced draught, they each carried eight 4-inch QF and eight 3-pdr QF guns, plus three 0.303-inch machine-guns and two 18-inch torpedo tubes. *Psyche*, a product of the Royal Dockyard at Devonport, was laid down in November 1897; *Pyramus*, built by Palmer of Jarrow, was begun in May 1897. Both were completed in 1900. By August 1914, however, neither was in particularly good shape, speed having dropped to no more than sixteen knots. In addition, they rolled badly and were widely regarded as poor

'EMDEN, v. Müller'. An illegibly-signed coloured souvenir postcard by 'AVB' ('1520/2'), depicting a questionably proportioned *Emden* — with a wrongly coloured bow-shield — accompanied by an equally suspect picture of von Müller (adapted from the Greve Portrait) within a convenient lifebelt. The patriotic verse reads "Du fegtest den Indischen Ocean,/Der Feind wurd'genarrt u. gehetzt,/Du machtest da hinten rasch reine Bahn,/Und kämpftest als Held bis zuletzt.": "You roamed the Indian Ocean,/lauded and hunted by the enemy./You made the final decision steadfastly/And, as a hero, fought to the end". By courtesy of The Lyon Press archives.

seaboats. *Psyche* was transferred to the Royal Australian Navy in 1915 and went for breaking in 1922. *Pyramus*, after serving in the Indian Ocean, became a depot ship in Mudros harbour. She was sold in 1920. Neither vessel would have been a match for *Emden* in a confrontation; a sister-ship, *Pegasus*, was overwhelmed and sunk by *Königsberg* – comparable to *Emden*, if older – off Zanzibar in September 1914. Like *Zhemchug* in Penang, however, *Pegasus* had been caught by surprise and speed of her demise was misleading.

Yarmouth, the second of four Weymouth-class light cruisers (but the last to be completed), derived from the earlier Bristol type exemplified by *Newcastle* (q.v.). She displaced 5,250 tons at load draught, measured 453 feet overall and could attain 25 knots. Laid down by the London & Glasgow Shipbuilding Co. of Glasgow in January 1910 and completed in April 1912, *Yarmouth* had an 'all big gun' armament – eight 6-inch QF L/50 and four 3-pdr QF guns – plus two 21-inch torpedo tubes. Regarded as robust and well armed, though somewhat wet owing to the comparatively low freeboard abaft the extended forecastle, she would have proved too much for *Emden* in a fair fight. Attached to the 4th Battle Squadron in the Mediterranean on completion, *Yarmouth* served on the China Station from August 1913 until the end of 1914. After fruitlessly chasing *Emden*, she had to be satisfied with recapturing *Pontoporos* and precipitating the scuttling of *Markomannia*. After service with the 2nd and 3rd Light Cruiser Squadrons, and an appearance at the Battle of Jutland, *Yarmouth* was scrapped in 1929.

FRENCH SHIPS

Dupleix, the name-ship of a class of armoured cruisers, was laid down in the Rochefort yard in February 1898 and completed in 1903. Smaller and marginally slower than *Montcalm* – 7,550 tonnes, 130 metres overall, 20½ knots – she carried eight 16.3cm QF L/45, four 10cm QF, ten 5cm QF and four 3.7cm QF guns, plus two 45cm torpedo tubes. Despite nearly twice the displacement of *Emden*, the weakly armed *Dupleix* may have proved too slow and clumsy in an encounter had *Emden* got in the first shots.

Montcalm was a Gueydon-class armoured cruiser, displacing 9,323 tonnes, 138 metres overall and capable of about 21 knots when new. Laid down in the La Seyne shipyard in April 1898 and completed in 1902, she was hulked in 1933. Despite an impressive-sounding heavy armament of two 19.3cm L/40, eight 16.3cm QF L/45 guns, four 10cm QF, sixteen 5cm QF and four 3.7cm QF guns, plus two 45cm torpedo tubes, *Montcalm* was clumsy, obsolescent and unhandy by 1914 standards. Many of *Emden*'s officers believed that she could be overwhelmed in a fight provided the French could be caught by surprise, and were willing to take on both *Montcalm* and *Dupleix* if they proved to be at Penang.

JAPANESE SHIPS

Chikuma. Somewhat similar to HMS *Yarmouth*, with a battery of eight 6-inch QF and four 3.1-inch QF guns, *Chikuma* was laid down in the Sasebo navy yard and completed in May 1912. Displacing 5,000 tons at normal load, 440 feet between perpendiculars and capable of 26 knots, she would have been more than a match for *Emden* had her commander elected to fight at long range. Stricken in 1931, she is believed to have gone to the breakers a year later.

Ibuki. Had not the commander of the ANZAC troop convoy been Australian, this Japanese battle-cruiser would have gone to Direction Island instead of *Sydney*. However, despite the overwhelming superiority of 14,636-ton *Ibuki*'s four 12-inch L/45, eight 8-inch L/45, fourteen 4.7-inch QF L/40 and four 3.1-inch QF L/40 guns, her comparatively low speed of 21½ knots may have given *Emden* a chance to escape by delaying arrival at Direction Island by at least a half-hour. Laid down in Kure naval dockyard in May 1907, *Ibuki* was completed in September 1909 and scrapped in 1924.

Tone. An elegant clipper-bow light cruiser laid down in Sasebo naval dockyard in November 1905 and completed in May 1910, *Tone* was a near-contemporary of *Emden* and *Newcastle*. Displacing 4,113 tons at normal load, measuring about 373 feet overall and capable of about 23 knots, she would have made an interesting match for *Emden*; though her armament of two 6-inch QF L/45, eight 4.7-inch QF and four 3.1-inch QF guns (by 1914) was not unlike *Newcastle*'s, she was slower than either the British or German ship and the performance of her crew would have been an unknown quantity. *Tone* was stricken in 1931 and sunk as a target in April 1933.

RUSSIAN SHIPS

Askold, a protected cruiser, was a product of Krupp Germaniawerft, Kiel, being laid down in August 1898 and completed in 1901. Displacing 5,905 tons at load draught, 437 feet overall and capable of nearly 24 knots when new, she carried twelve 15.2cm guns, twelve 7.5cm and eight 5cm QF, two 3.7cm saluting guns and six 38cm torpedo tubes. Known to British seamen as 'Packet of Fags' owing to her five spindly funnels, *Askold* was scrapped in 1921. With a good crew, she could have caused *Emden* serious problems, though the old Russian 15.2cm guns were outranged by the German 10.5cm SK L/40.

Zhemchug of the two-ship Izumrud class of protected cruisers was originally distinguished by her unique combination of three funnels and three masts. A product of the Nevski shipyard in St Petersburg (Leningrad), she was laid down in 1901, completed in 1904 and essentially similar to *Emden* – 3,103 tons at load draught, 364 feet overall and capable of 24 knots when new – *Zhemchug* carried eight 12.2cm, six 5cm and two 3.7cm QF guns by 1914, plus three 45cm torpedo tubes. Surprised by *Emden* in Penang Harbour on 28th October 1914, she was blown apart by gunfire and two torpedo hits without landing so much as a single shell on her opponent.

DUTCH SHIP (NEUTRAL)

Marten Harpertzoon Tromp. This coast-defence battleship was built by Royal Netherlands navy dockyard, Amsterdam, and launched in 1904. Displacing 5,216 tonnes and about 101 metres long, she could attain 16½ knots when new. Despite an armament of two 24cm, four 15cm, eight 8cm and four 3.7cm guns – plus three 45cm torpedo-tubes – she would not have been much of a match for *Emden* in a fight. Stricken in 1927, *Tromp* was broken up in 1932.

Auxiliaries

ARMED MERCHANT CRUISERS

The 570-foot quadruple-screw turbine steamships *Empress of Asia* (16,909grt, Board of Trade Registry 135226, home port London, call-sign JCKF) and *Empress of Russia* (16,810grt, 135197, JBSQ) both belonged to Canadian Pacific Steamships Ltd. The sister-ships were completed by Fairfield Co. Ltd in 1913. Owing to their speed – and the inclusion of gun mountings in the structure – they were immediately commissioned as armed merchant cruisers when the First World War began, their peacetime colours – buff funnels, white topsides over red boot-topping – immediately giving way to warship grey. Both were fast, capable of twenty knots even in heavy seas, and might have given *Emden* a fright.

In the quest for *Emden* the Royal Navy also employed the P. & O. Steam Navigation Company's single-screw passenger ship *Himalaya* (Board of Trade registry 99776), built by Caird & Co. Ltd of Greenock in 1892. Registered in Greenock with the call-sign MQDN, distinguished by four masts and two funnels, this 6,929grt 466-foot single-screw vessel was neither fast nor powerful enough to have been anything more than cannon-fodder for *Emden*. Her participation in the story was limited to recapturing *Exford* (q.v.) in December 1914.

Operated in peacetime by the Peninsula & Oriental Steam Navigation Company (P&O), the 1892-vintage steamship *Himalaya* was impressed as an armed merchant cruiser when the First World War began. Her part in the *Emden* story, apart from taking part in the fruitless searching, was to recapture the collier *Exford* in December 1914. By courtesy of the Trustees of the National Maritime Museum, Greenwich.

4 • German merchantmen

Bochum. A product of Schiffswerft u. Maschinen-Fabrik 'Neptun' of Rostock (no.321), this 6,161grt or 11,400-tonne displacement single-screw steamship was delivered to Deutsch-Australische Dampfschiffs-Gesellschaft of Hamburg in July 1912. Measuring about 140 metres on the waterline, the twelve-knot *Bochum* (call-sign RSJD) was interned in Manila on 23rd August 1914 and impressed into the US Navy on 6th April 1917 as the transport *Montpellier*. Renamed *Nevadan* after the First World War, she was briefly loaned to the Russians in 1943-4 (as *Jan Tromp*) and eventually went to the breakers in 1956.

Choising. Built by Rickmers AG of Geestemünde, yard no.120, this 1,657grt 77.4m-long single-screw steamship was completed in 1901 as *Madeleine Rickmers*. Sold to Norddeutscher Lloyd of Bremen in January 1906, she has achieved lasting fame as the ship on which *Emden*'s Landing Party sailed westward across the Indian Ocean. *Choising* was then commanded by NDL-Kapitän Minkwitz and had the call-sign QHKB. Interned in Massawa Harbour (Italian Somaliland) in January 1915, she was impressed into Italian service as *Carraccio* in June 1916. On 15th March 1917, she was sunk in the Adriatic Sea by the Austro-Hungarian destroyers *Balaton* and *Csepel*.

Elsbeth. Completed in October 1905 by Schiffswerft H. Koch of Lübeck (no.162), as *Wilhelm Oelssner* for Gerhard & Heye, this steamship was sold to Rhederei M. Jebsens AG of Apenrade in 1913 and renamed *Elsbeth* (call-sign RNTP). She displaced about 3,000 tonnes (1,651grt) and measured 75 metres on the waterline. Speed was about 9½ knots. *Elsbeth* was sunk by HMS *Hampshire* off Yap on 11th August 1914.

Frisia. Ordered in Britain by Hamburg-Amerika-Linie, this 4,997grt (13,600 tonne) eleven-knot steamship – call-sign apparently RVDT – was completed by the Northumberland Shipbuilding Co. Ltd of Newcastle upon Tyne on 18th April 1914. *Frisia* was taken as a prize by HMS *Triumph* off Tsingtau on 22nd August 1914. Renamed *Huntress*, she was sold to Greece in 1930 (as *Andromeda*) but went to the breakers a year later.

Gouverneur Jaeschke. Built by Howaldtswerke AG, Kiel, as yard no.373, and delivered to Hamburg-Amerika-Linie in 1900, this 1,738grt (3,200 tonnes displacement) steamship survived the First World War only to be torpedoed in the Caribbean by *U156* in May 1942. She measured about 73 metres on the waterline and could make about eleven knots.

Holsatia. Built by A. MacMillan & Son Ltd of Dumbarton (yard no.452) for Hamburg-Amerika-Linie, this eleven-knot steamship displaced about 11,000 tonnes (5,644grt) and had a waterline measuring about 127 metres. Her home port was Hamburg; her call-sign, RVFS. Delivered in May 1914, she was interned at Honolulu on 12th October 1914 when commanded by HAL-Kapitän Deinat. Impressed into the US merchant marine in April 1917, as *Tippecanoe*, she was torpedoed by *U91* in the North Atlantic on 23rd July 1918.

Linden. Built by Flensburger Schiffbau Gesellschaft (yard no.256) for Deutsch-Australische Dampfschiffs-Gesellschaft, this twelve-knot single-screw steamship was delivered in April 1906. Her home port was Hamburg, her call-sign being RPCV. Displacing about 7,800 tonnes (4,188grt) and measuring 115 metres on the waterline, *Linden* was taken by the Dutch warship *Tromp* on 10th September 1914 while under the command of DADG-Kapitän Hauth. After the First World War she served the Dutch merchant marine as *Eemland*, until sold to Turkey (as *Van*) in 1956. The longest-lived of all these ships, with an active life of sixty years, she finally went to the breakers in 1966.

Loongmoon. Built by Wigham, Richardson & Co. of Newcastle upon Tyne (yard no.317) for the Hamburg-Amerika-Linie, this 1,971grt steamship was delivered in May 1896. Her call sign was RKLG. Measuring nearly 87 metres on the waterline and capable of 11½ knots when new, she was interned in Honolulu on 17th September 1914 when commanded by HAL-Kapitän Hellhof. Subsequently impressed into the US merchant marine on 6th April 1917 (as *Coosa*), she went to the breakers in 1924.

Mark. Another of the comparatively large German merchantmen, displacing about 13,500 tonnes (6,579grt), the three-deck single-screw *Mark* measured 143 metres on the waterline and could attain 12½ knots. Built by Bremer Vulcan of Vegesack for Norddeutscher Lloyd (call-sign QKJF) and delivered in November 1913, she was interned in Manila two days before *Emden*'s demise while under the command of NDL-Kapitän Ernst Löwe. Passing into the US merchant marine on 6th April 1917, she had a long career as *Suwanee*, *Poznan* and *Paul Luckenbach* before being torpedoed in the Pacific in September 1942.

Markomannia. Built by Irvine's Shipbuilding & Dry Dock Co. Ltd of West Hartlepool (yard no.505) and completed in May 1911 as *Nigaristan*, for F.C. Strick, this 114m-long single-screw steamship displaced about 11,600 tonnes (4,505grt) and could attain 12½ knots. Purchased by Hamburg-Amerika-Linie in March 1913 and re-registered in Hamburg with call-sign RSQF, she was *Emden*'s principal collier throughout most of the cruise under the command of HAL-Kapitän W. Faass.‡ Detached on 30th September 1914, when her duties were taken over by *Buresk*, she was scuttled near the Simaloer Island when challenged by HMS *Yarmouth* on 12th October 1914.

Offenbach. Wigham, Richardson & Co. of Newcastle upon Tyne was responsible for this 7,700 tonne (4,336grt) steamship, ordered by Deutsch-Australische Dampfschiffs-Gesellschaft and delivered in December 1900. Registered in Hamburg, with the call-sign RLVM, *Offenbach* measured 119 metres on the waterline and could attain about twelve knots. She was interned by the Dutch on 27th August 1914. After passing briefly into British hands in 1919-21, she returned to Germany; renamed *Anna Kayser* and then *Nordsee*, she went to the breakers in 1933.

Princess Alice. Built by Stettiner Maschinenbau AG 'Vulcan' in 1900 (yard no.246), as Hamburg-Amerika-Linie *Kiautschou*, she was sold to Norddeutscher Lloyd of Bremen in February 1904 and re-registered with the call-sign RLVN. The 10,981grt twin-screw steamship measured about 160 metres overall. Interned at Cebu on 20th August 1914 when commanded by NDL-Kapitän Johann Bortfeldt, having achieved nothing of note in the opening weeks of the war, *Princess Alice* was seized by the US Government in March 1917 to serve as the troopship *Princess Matoika*. Subsequently renamed *Prince Arthur* and then *City of Honolulu*, she went to the breakers in 1933.

Prinz Waldemar. A product of G. Seebeck AG of Geestemünde (no.191), delivered to Norddeutscher Lloyd in July 1903, this 3,227grt twelve-knot twin-screw steamship measured about a hundred metres on the waterline. Her call sign was QHPF. Interned in Honolulu in September 1914, she was impressed into the US merchant marine in April 1917 to serve as *Wacouta*. Renamed *Yucatan* after the First World War, she went to the breakers in 1925.

Professor Woermann. Built by Reiherstieg Schiffswerke, Hamburg, as yard no.445, and completed in September 1912 for Woermann Linie KG of Hamburg, this ship — call-sign RSLC — displaced about 9,300 tonnes (6,061grt), measured 120 metres on the waterline and could attain about 12½ knots. She was commissioned as an auxiliary transport for the Kreuzergeschwader and the armed merchant cruisers on 2nd August 1914, when apparently being commanded by Kapitän Ludwig Ihrke, but was captured three weeks later by HMS *Carnarvon* and became the British troopship *Professor*. After returning to Germany, she became Stinnes' *Edmund Wagenknecht* and was sold to Brazil in 1922. Renamed *General San Martin* and then *Almirante Jaceguay*, she was scrapped in 1958.

Staatsekretär Kraetke. An enlargement of *Gouveneur Jaeschke* from the same builder (yard no.425, completed in 1905), *Staatsekretär Kraetke* had been the command of Julius Lauterbach since the summer of 1908. Displacing about 3,350 tonnes (2,009grt), eighty metres long and capable of about eleven knots, she was destroyed by fire in 1924. Her call-sign had been RNSV, the port of registry being Hamburg.

Tannenfels — registered in Bremen, call-sign QGMJ — was built by Wigham, Richardson & Co. of Newcastle upon Tyne. Delivered to Deutsche-Dampfschiffs-Gesellschaft 'Hansa' of Bremen in March 1898, she displaced about 7,400 tonnes (5,341grt) and measured 123 metres on the waterline. Capable of only about ten knots, even when new, *Tannenfels* was captured by the British destroyer *Chelmer* in the Straits of Basilan on 14th September 1914. After serving the Merchant Navy, appropriately as *Basilan* (later *Hunslet*), she was returned to Germany in 1921. Renamed *Waganda* by the Woermann line, she went to the breakers in 1932.

Ulm. A product of the Neptun yard, Rostock (yard no.337), this 4,706grt twelve-knot steamer was accepted by Deutsch-Australische Dampfschiffs-Gesellschaft, Hamburg, on 22nd April 1914. Her call sign was RVDL. Measuring about 122

‡ Sometimes rendered as 'Fahss'.

Kapitänleutnant Hellmuth von Mücke (talking to the boy) with his officers — Leutnants z.S. Gyssling, Geerts and Willmann — and men being feted after their return to Constantinople in 1915. By courtesy of the Trustees of the Imperial War Museum, London; negative Q 64246.

metres on the waterline, *Ulm* was taken by the Dutch warship *Tromp* on 12th September 1914, when commanded by DADG-Kapitän Carl Saegert, and interned in Batavia harbour for the duration of the First World War. After August 1919 she served the British merchant marine as *Tapti* (later *Leana*) before being sunk by *U198* in the Strait of Mozambique in July 1943.

Yorck. A product of Schichau's Danzig shipyard (no.722), the 8,909grt 14½-knot four-deck twin-screw *Yorck* — a passenger ship delivered to Norddeutscher Lloyd in April 1906 — was registered in Bremen, had the call-sign QJFP, and measured 141 metres on the waterline. Commanded by NDL-Kapitän Loeser in August 1914, she was interned in Valparaiso, Chile, at the end of October 1914. Returning to NDL in September 1921, *Yorck* was renamed *Columbus* and eventually went to the breakers in 1933.

5 • Bibliography

Note: a more exhaustive coverage of the hundreds of relevant books and articles will be found in Lochner's *Die Kaperfahrten des Kleinen Kreuzers Emden*, pp.466-80 (or pp.309-21 of the English-language translation).

Anon.: *Die Taten der Emden und andere Kreuzer*. Hesse & Becker, Leipzig, *c*.1915.

— *Das Emden-Spiel im Indischen und Grossen Ozean*. Frankh'sche Kriegsbilderbogen, Stuttgart, 1915.

— *Illustrieter Deutscher Flotten Kalender für 1915*. Wilhelm Köhler, Minden, 1915.

Bartz, Karl: *Der Kommandant der Emden* ('Das Leben des Kapitäns von Müller'). Deutscher Verlag, Berlin, 1939. A dramatized and largely apocryphal life of *Emden*'s commander.

Bennett, Geoffrey: *Coronel and Falklands*. B.T. Batsford Ltd, London, 1962.

Bermbach, J.: *Zittere England: Unsere 'Emden' ging nicht unter*. Dietrich & Brückner, two parts, 1914 and 1915.

Bess, Fregattenkapitän a.D.: 'S.M.S. Emden während des zweiten chinesischen Bürgerkriegs vor Nanking und den Tung-Lean-Chan-Forts im Jahre 1913', in *Marine-Rundschau*, XXX.Jahrgang, 1925.

Brechsenmacher, J.K.: *Die Heldenfahrten des Kapitänleutnants v. Mücke — Schilderungen aus dem Weltkrieg*. Berlin (?), 1916.

— *Heldenfahrten und Untergang der Emden — Schilderungen aus dem Weltkrieg*. Berlin (?), 1915.

Bredt, Alexander: *Die deutsche Kriegsflotte 1914 bis 1918 und ihr Verbleib*. J.F. Lehmanns Verlag, Berlin and München; fifth edition, 1939.

Busch, Korvettenkapitän Fritz Otto: *Die Emden jagt*. Franz Schneider, Leipzig and Wien, 1935.

Cardwell, Robert: 'The History of the Raiding of the Cocos and the Capture and Sinking of the "Emden"...', in *The Zodiac — The Submarine Cable Service Paper*, vol.XIII, no.148 (November 1920).

Chatterton, [Commander] E. Keble: 'The cruise of the Emden' in *Daring Deeds of Sea Rovers*. Seeley Service & Co., London, 1930.

— *The Sea Raiders*. Hurst & Backett, London, 1931. An accurate and entertaining guide to the exploits of surface raiders other than *Emden*.

Cheret, G.K.: *Der Emden letztes Gefecht — Heldenkampf des deutschen Kreuzers im Indischen Ozean*. Berlin, 1941.

Churchill, [Sir] Winston L.S.: *The World Crisis*. Various editions.

Corbett, Sir Julian: *History of the Great War — Naval Operations*. Longmans, Green & Co. Ltd, London, five volumes, 1920-31.

Cranwell, J.P.: *Spoilers of the Sea. Wartime Raiders in the Age of Steam*. London, 1941.

Darby, Surgeon-Commander Leonard, RAN: 'The Official Report of the Sydney-Emden Engagement on November 9, 1914' in *Journal of the Royal Naval Medical Society*, London, 1915.

Dettmers, Kapitän z.S. Theodor (Jochen Brenneke, ed.): *Kormoran* ('Der Hilfs Kreuzer, der die "Sydney" versenkte'). Koehlers-Verlag, Biberach an der Riss, 1959.

Eckman, P.O.: *S.M.S. Emden*. Axel Abrahamsons, Karlskrona, 1964.

Erdmann, Gustav Adolf: *SMS Emden und sein Kommandant*. Fock, Leipzig, 1916.

Farrère, Claude, and **Chack**, Paul: *La Mort de l'Emden*. Velhagen & Klasing, undated (*c*.1935).

Fayle, C. Ernest: *Seaborne Trade*. Longmans, Green & Co. Ltd, London, three volumes, 1920-4.

Feuga, Jean: *S.M.S. Emden* ('Ein deutscher Heldenkampf im Indischen Ozean'). Eugen Salzer, Heilbronn, 1935. A translation, by Friedrich Gudehus, of an original French-language work — *L'Emden, Croiseur Corsaire* (Librarire Alphonse Lemerre, Paris, 1931) — based on the diary of Prinz Franz Joseph von Hohenzollern-Emden.

Fikentscher-Emden, Fregattenkapitän Erich: *Aus Malta in die Freiheit*. Steiniger, Berlin, undated.

— *Erinnerung an unsere 'Emden'-Zeit*. Privately published, 1964.

— *Ostasien und die Süasee* ('1912-1914 an Bord des Kreuzers S.M.S. Emden'). Privately published, München, 1976.

Floericke, Dr Kurt: *Der Schiffsjunge der Emden* ('Erzählung aus dem grossen Weltkrieg für die reifere Jugend'). Frankh'sche Verlagshandlung, Stuttgart, 1915.

Friedag, B.: *Führer durch Heer und Flotte*. E.S. Mittler & Sohn, Berlin; eleventh edition, 1914. Reprinted by Jürgen Olmes, Heere der Vergangenheit, Krefeld, *c*.1981.

Funke, Dr Alfred (ed.): *Ayesha-Fahrten und Abenteuer der Emden-Mannschaft von der Kokoinseln bis Konstantinopel*. Volkskraft-Verlag, Berlin, 1915.

— *Unsere Seehelden: Ayesha* ('Fahrten und Abenteuer der Emden-Mannschaft von den Kokoinseln bis Konstantinopel'). Marinedank-Verlag, Berlin, undated.

Garcia, Lieutenant C.R., RAN: 'An Account of the Sydney-Emden Action' in *The Times*, London, 15th December 1914.

Gardiner, Robert (ed.): *Conway's All the World's Fighting Ships 1860-1905*. Conway Maritime Press, Greenwich, London, 1979.

— *Conway's All the World's Fighting Ships 1906-1921*. Conway Maritime Press, London, 1985.

Gellert, Georg: *Heldenfahrten der 'Emden' und 'Ayesha'* ('Abenteuer und Kämpfe der "Emden"-Mannschaft während des Weltkrieges'). Meidingers Jugendschriften, Globus-Verlag, Berlin, undated (*c*.1915-17).

Gottschalk-Emden, G. (W. Alberty, ed.): *Ich war dabei* ('Meine Erlebnisse im Weltkrige 1914-18 auf der "Emden"...'). Friedrich Brandstetter, Leipzig, 1935.

Gröner, Erich: *Die deutschen Kriegsschiffe 1815-1945*. Bernard & Graefe Verlag, München, 1982-9. A six-volume revision of a classic work (Lehmanns, München, 1966/8), by Dieter Jung and Martin Maass, containing a tremendous amount of information about warships and impressed merchantmen alike.

Hansen, Hans Jürgen: *Die Schiffe der deutschen Flotten 1848-1945*. Urbes-Verlag Hans Jürgen Hansen, Gräfelfing vor München, 1973.

Haws, Duncan: *Merchant Fleets: Blue Funnel Line*. TCL Publications, East Grinstead, West Sussex; revised edition, 1988.

— *Merchant Fleets: British India S.N. Co.* TCL Publications, East Grinstead, West Sussex; 1987.

— *Merchant Fleets: Ellerman Lines*. TCL Publications, East Grinstead, West Sussex; 1989.

– *Merchant Fleets: Thos. & Jas. Harrison.* TCL Publications, East Grinstead, West Sussex; 1988.
Heaton, Paul M.: *Tatems of Cardiff.* Privately published, Pontypool, Gwent; 1987.
Heichen, Walter: *Unsere Emden.* Hillgers Verlaghaus, Berlin, *c.1916.*
– *Helden zur See – Heldentaten unsere Marine 1914/1918.* A. Weichert-Verlag, Berlin, 1918.
Heuler, Felix: *Mit Volldampf ran an der Feind. Ein Heldenbuch der Deutschen Marine aus den Kriegsjahren 1914/15.* Würzburg, 1916.
Hildebrand, Hans H., **Rohr**, Albert, and **Steinmetz**, Hans-Otto: *Die deutschen Kriegsschiffe. Biographien. Ein Spiegel der Marinegeschichte von 1815 bis zur Gegenwart.* Koehlers Verlagsgesellschaft, Herford; six volumes, 1979-89.
Hofe, Konteradmiral Eugen Kalau von: *Kampf und Untergang des Kreuzergeschwaders.* Verlag Kameradschaft Wohlfahrtgesellschaft, Berlin, 1915.
– *Kriegszug des Kreuzers Emden und seiner Helden weitere Fuhrt.* Verlag Kameradschaft Wohlfahrtgesellschaft, Berlin, 1916.
– *Unsere Flotte im Weltkrieg.* Verlag E.S. Mittler & Sohn, Berlin, 1915.
Hoehling, A.A.: *Lonely Command; The Epic Story of the Emden.* Cassell & Co. Ltd, London, 1959.
Hohenzollern-Emden, Oberleutnant z.S. a.D. Prinz Franz Joseph von: *Emden – Meine Erlebnisse auf SM Schiff Emden.* Richard Eckstein Nachfolger, Leipzig, 1925. Translations included an English version, *'Emden'. The Story of the Famous Raiding Cruiser* (oddly, on the title page, '*Emden.* My Experiences in S.M.S. Emden') by Herbert Jenkins Ltd, London, 1928; and the French *L'Emden* (by 'François-Joseph de Hohenzollern') by Librarie Payot, Paris, 1929.
Hoyt, Edwin Palmer: *Defeat at the Falklands* ('Germany's East Asia Squadron 1914'). Robert Hale Ltd, London, 1981.
– *The Fall of Tsingtao.* Arthur Barker Ltd, London, 1975.
– *The Last Cruise of the Emden.* André Deutsch, London, 1966.
Hurd, Archibald S.: *From Heligoland to Keeling Island.* H.C. Bywater, London, 1915.
– *The German Fleet.* Hodder & Stoughton Ltd, London, 1915.
– *The Merchant Navy.* Longmans, Green & Co. Ltd, London, three volumes, 1921-9.
Irving, J.: *Coronel and the Falklands.* A.M. Philpot Ltd, London, 1927.
Jose, A.W.: *Official History of Australia in the War of 1914-1918* ('Vol. IX, The Royal Australian Navy').
Köhler, Wilhelm (ed.): *Deutsches Heldentum zur See.* Wilhelm Köhler, Vaterländischer Verlag, Minden, *c.*1915.
Koop, Gerhard: *Emden. Ein Name – fünf Schiffe.* Bernard & Graefe, München, 1983.
Kroschel, Günter, and **Evers**, August-Ludwig: *Die deutsche Flotte 1848-1945.* Verlag Lohse-Eissing, Wilhelmshaven, 1962.
Lauterbach, Schiffskapitän Julius: *1000 Pf Sterling Kopfpreis – tot oder lebendig* ('Fluchtabenteuer des ehemaligen Prisenoffiziers SMS Emden'). August Scherl, Berlin, 1917.
– *Mis Aventuras de Guerra en el Mar 1914-1918.* Joaquín Gil, Madrid, 1936.
Lehfels, G. [Gustav Lehmann-Falskowski]: *Der Herr des Meeres* ('Fahrten und Abenteuer der Emden in Weltkrieg'). Velhagen & Klasing, Bielefeld, 1915.
Lochner, R.K.: *Die Kaperfahrten des Kleinen Kreuzers Emden.* Wilhelm Heyne Verlag, München, 1979. Undoubtedly the finest of all the 'Emden' books published to date.
– *The Last Gentleman of War* ('The Raider Exploits of the Cruiser *Emden*'). Naval Institute Press, Annapolis, Maryland, 1988. An edited translation of the previous book, by Thea and Harry Lindauer, omitting some of the original material.
Lohmann, Walter, and **Mielke**, Otto: *Bravo, Kleiner Kreuzer* ('S.M. Kleiner Kreuzer "Emden"...'). Arthur Moewig, München, 1955.
Luckner, Graf Felix von (ed.), and **Lauterbach**, Julius: *Mein Freund Juli-Bumm* ('Die Abenteuer des Kapitän Lauterbach von der Emden'). Koehler & Amelang, Leipzig, *c.1934.* A revised version of Lowell Thomas's *Lauterbach of the China Sea* (q.v.).
Ludwig, Emil: *Die Fahrten der Emden und Ayesha* ('Nach Erzählungen des Kapitänleutnants von Mücke, seiner Offiziere und Mannschaften'). S. Fischer, Berlin, 1915-16.
Marder, Arthur J.: *From Dreadnought to Scapa Flow – The Royal Navy in the Fisher Era.* Oxford University Press; five volumes, 1961-70.
Middlemas, Keith: *Command the Far Seas.* Hutchinson & Co. Ltd, London, 1961.
Middlemiss, Norman L.: *Gathering of the Clans* ('History of The Clan Line Steamers Ltd'). Shield Publications Ltd, Newcastle upon Tyne; 1988.
– *Travels of the Tramps. Twenty tramp fleets.* Shield Publications Ltd, Newcastle upon Tyne; 1989.
Mücke, Kapitänleutnant Hellmuth von: *Ayesha.* August Scherl, Berlin, 1915, and Langerkuysen, Amsterdam, the Netherlands, 1917. Revised edition: Scherl, 1926.
– *Die Abenteuer der Emden-Mannschaft.* Verlag Ensslin, Reutlingen, 1921.
– *Die Taten der Emden und anderer Kreuzer* ('mit einer Einf. v. Hermann Kirchhoff'). Hessisches Volksbucherei, Leipzig, 1915.
– *Emden.* August Scherl, Berlin, 1915; Ritter & Co., London, 1917; and Langenkuysen, Amsterdam, the Netherlands, 1917.
– *The Ayesha. A Great Adventure* ('The Escape of the Landing Squad of the *Emden*'). Phillip Allan & Co. Ltd, London, 1930. An English-language version of *Ayesha* (Scherl, Berlin) edited by J.G. Lockhart.
Nagel, Alfred Georg: *Drei Kreuzer Emden* ('Ein Gedenkbuch deutschen Heldentums zur See'). Georg Bröker Verlag, Berlin-Lichterfelde, 1934.
– *Emden: Eine Gedenkbuch deutschen Heldentums zur See.* Mühlau, Kiel, 1927.
Nauheimer, A.M.: *S.M.S. Emden* ('Zum Besten der Invaliden des [sic] Emden'). Xenien-Verlag, Leipzig, 1915.
Oesterwitz, Heinrich (ed.): *Auf der Emden und Ayesha. Erlebnisse eines Teilnehmers.* Wallmanns-Verlag, Berlin, 1916. Based on the recollections of Matrose Alfred Wadephul.
Ottiger-Emden, Hermann: *Das Buch von der Emden.* K. Thienemanns Verlag, Stuttgart, 1936.
Pitt, Barrie: *Coronel and Falklands.* Cassell & Co., London, 1960.
Plötz-Emden, Hugo: 'Todeskampf des Kreuzers Emden' in *Rhein-Ems-Zeitung*, Emden, November 1954.
Roehle, Reinhard: *Emden-Ayesha* ('Heldenfahrten und Abenteuer deutscher Seeleute im Weltkrieg'). Union-Verlag, Stuttgart, 1915.
Selow-Seman, K.E.: *Kapitänleutnant v. Müllers letzte Fahrt.* August Scherl Berlin, 1917.
Spencer-Cooper, Commander Henry E.H., MVO RN: *The Battle of the Falkland Islands. Before and After.* Cassell & Company Ltd London, 1919.
Steinberg, J.: *Yesterday's Deterrent: Tirpitz and the Birth of the German Battle Fleet.* Macdonald & Company, London; 1965.
Sternau, Theodor von [W. Heuer, pseud.]: *Die Siegesfahrt der Emden* ('Nach Schilderungen des Kapitänleutnants v. Mücke'). Graphische-Werke, Leipzig, 1916.
Thomas, Lowell: *Lauterbach of the China Sea.* Hutchinson & Company, London, undated (c.1930).
Toeche-Mittler, Siegfried: *Unsere Auslandskreuzer im Weltkrieg 1914-1915.* Verlag E.S. Mittler & Sohn, Berlin, 1915.
Tuchmann, Barbara: *The Guns of August.* Macmillan & Company, New York, 1962.
Urban, Woldemar: *Die Kriegsfahrten der Emden* ('Erzählung

für die Jugend'). Union-Deutsche Verlagsgesellschaft, Stuttgart, Berlin and Leipzig; undated.
Vat, Dan van der: *The Last Corsair* ('The Story of the Emden'). Hodder & Stoughton, Dunton Green, Sevenoaks, 1983.
Vollerthun, Fregattenkapitän Waldemar: *Der Kampf um Tsingtau*. Herzel-Verlag, Leipzig, 1920.
Waldeyer-Hartz, Hugo von: *Der Kreuzerkrieg 1914-1918*. Gerhard Stalling Verlag, Oldenburg, 1930.
— *Ran an der Feind*. Verlag Jugendhort Walter Bloch Nachf., Berlin, 1915.
— *Von Tsingtau zu den Falklandinseln* ('Eine Erzählung von den Heldenkämpfen um Tsingtau und der ruhmreichen Fahrt des deutschen Kreuzergeschwaders in Weltkrieg 1914'). Verlag E.S. Mittler & Sohn, Berlin, 1917.
Walker, Fred M.: *Song of the Clyde* ('A history of Clyde shipbuilding'). W.W. Norton & Company, London, 1985.
Witthoeft, Korvettenkapitän Robert: *Unsere Emden* ('Erlebnisse auf den Kaperfahrten im Jahre 1914'). Reimar Hobbing, Berlin, 1926.
— [Heinz Oskar Wuttig, ed.] *Unsere Emden* ('Kaperfahrten im Indischen Ozean'). Ernst Steiniger, Berlin, 1938.
Wolff-Emden, Rudolf: *Von der Kokoinseln nach Deutschland* ('Meine Erlebnisse beim Landungszug der "Emden-Ayesha", 1914/15'). A. Ziemsen, Wittenberg, undated.

Index

The suffix 'p' refers to an illustration, 'n' to a footnote and 'ff' to 'subsequent pages'. Officers' ranks are those held in November 1914. For the names of *Emden* I's crew, see pp.116-18.